THREE PLAYS

THREE PLAYS

Dark River,
Arthur Aronymus and His Ancestors,
and *I and I*

ELSE LASKER-SCHÜLER

Edited and with an introduction by INCA MOLINA RUMOLD
Translated from the German by JANE CURTIS

NORTHWESTERN UNIVERSITY PRESS | EVANSTON, ILLINOIS

Northwestern University Press
Evanston, Illinois 60208-4170

This English translation follows the Reclam edition of 1977 for *Dark River*, the Kösel Verlag edition of 1962 for *Arthur Aronymus*, and the Kösel Verlag edition of 1980 for *I and I*.

Printed in the United States of America

10 9 8 7 6 5 4 3 2 1

ISBN 0-8101-2197-2 (cloth)
ISBN 0-8101-2189-0 (paper)

Library of Congress Cataloging-in-Publication Data

Lasker-Schüler, Else, 1869–1945.
[Plays. English. Selections]
Three plays : Dark river, Arthur Aronymus and his ancestors, and I and I / Else Lasker-Schüler ; translated from the German by Jane Curtis ; with introduction by Inca Molina Rumold.
p. cm. — (European drama classics)
Includes bibliographical references.
ISBN 0-8101-2197-2 (cloth : alk. paper) — ISBN 0-8101-2198-0 (pbk : alk. paper)
1. Lasker-Schüler, Else, 1869–1945—Translations into English. I. Title: Dark river. II. Title: Arthur Aronymus and his ancestors. III. Title: I and I. IV. Lasker-Schüler, Else, 1869–1945. Wupper. English. V. Lasker-Schüler, Else, 1869–1945. Arthur Aronymus und seine Väter. English. VI. Lasker-Schüler, Else, 1869–1945. Ichundich. English. VII. Curtis, Jane, 1927– VIII. Title. IX. Series.
PT2623.A76A234 2005
832'.912—dc22 2005010144

⊗The paper used in this publication meets the minimum requirements of the American National Standard for Information Sciences—Permanence of Paper for Printed Library Materials, ANSI Z39.48-1992.

CONTENTS

EDITOR'S INTRODUCTION

INCA MOLINA RUMOLD

In the last two decades, the Expressionist poet and playwright Else Lasker-Schüler (1869–1945)—a contemporary of Bertolt Brecht and one of the most eccentric authors in the coffeehouse scene in the Berlin of the teens and twenties—has become an icon among scholars in Jewish-German and gender studies. Her birthplace in the industrial town of Elberfeld, where the hills and valleys of the wider Ruhr area begin to stretch westward toward the Rhineland, has been converted into a museum and archive, and there now is an ambitious international Lasker-Schüler Society. A steady flow of new critical writing is being published every year, and conferences, whether in Germany, Jerusalem (2002), or even Philadelphia (1998), are dedicated exclusively to analyzing her oeuvre. Yet apart from translations of a few poems dispersed in various anthologies and a few passages from *Das Hebräerland* (1937) [*The Land of the Hebrews*], her work remains relatively unknown to the English-speaking world. And only now is there a focus specifically on her contributions to the theater. With this anthology, the provocative plays of this German-Jewish poet will for the first time be available to a diverse English readership, whether interested in theater, women's studies, Jewish-German studies, or modernism at large.

Both famous for her poetry and infamous for her bohemian lifestyle, as well as her association with political radicals, Else Lasker-

Schüler is one of the few women writers in the Expressionist movement in the teens and twenties of the last century. She now begins to occupy her place among the most advanced and accomplished of twentieth-century European poets, male or female. The younger poet Gottfried Benn (the somber "Giselher, the Barbarian" of her prose and correspondence), who certainly took a wrong turn in the early years of the Third Reich before being banned by the Nazis, did show proper judgment (rather than guilt) when he addressed her in a postwar eulogy as the "greatest poetess Germany ever had." Along with Expressionism, banned by the Nazis as "un-German" art, Lasker-Schüler, who died in Palestinian exile, was rediscovered in the 1950s.

Before that, her fame had rested exclusively on her poetry. Her anthologies, from *Styx* (1902) to the *Hebräische Balladen* (1913) [*Hebrew Ballads*, English translation published 1980] to *Mein blaues Klavier* (1943) [*My Blue Piano*, no published English translation], were typically read for their romantic soul and beauty, conceived of as essentially feminine. By the same token, literary criticism had long tended to ignore, if not dismiss, her complicated, multilayered prose as well as her iconoclastic dramatic works. This trend is presently being reversed.[1]

Lasker-Schüler's plays have been reevaluated as highly avant-garde and politically subversive, both in form and content.[2] Her three plays are *Die Wupper* (1909) [*Dark River*, no previous English translation]; *Arthur Aronymus und seine Väter* (1932) [*Arthur Aronymus and His Ancestors*, no previous English translation]; and *Ichundich* (1980) [*I and I*, English translation published 1992]. While small in quantity, her dramatic work, spanning the first half of the century, critically engages and—in a lively, spirited, unconventional manner unique to her—illuminates Germany's sociopolitical and cultural climate from the Wilhelminian Empire to the Weimar Republic and through the Second World War.

By breaking away from the traditional aesthetic canon, the plays show a unique formal development from Naturalistic Expressionist episodes in the lyrical *Dark River* to a historicizing politicization of the theater in *Arthur Aronymus* to the forms of montage and "epic" presentations in *I and I*. Furthermore, the representation of topics taboo in patriarchal societies, such as the interrelatedness of class, gender, and sexuality in *Dark River*, of religious and racist anti-Semitism in *Arthur Aronymus*, and her coping with the utterly painful split and loss of identity as a German-speaking Jew forced into exile by the National Socialists in *I and I*, places her plays squarely at the focus of present-day women's studies as well as Holocaust debates. Their introduction to an English readership will dispel the long-held notion that there were no German women playwrights in the early part of the twentieth century.

From the beginning, though older by a generation than the typical Expressionist poet, Lasker-Schüler was an artistic and social rebel. This is reflected in her life and work, for instance, in her play *Dark River* and her prose work *Der Malik* (1919) [*The Emperor*, no published English translation], which I have discussed elsewhere as a "political novel."[3] Written during the Wilhelminian Empire, the former play had to wait ten years for its Berlin premiere in 1919, when Germany had undergone a crucial political change from an absolute monarchy to the first significant German experiment and experience in democracy, the Weimar Republic. But even then, in spite of her fame as a lyrical poet, it was shown only on a secondary stage behind the main theater. Its performance has always been controversial, causing a great scandal then as well as at its 1958 revival in arch-Catholic Cologne for its alleged obscenity and amorality.[4]

The author's liberal leanings were reflected in her friendships with contemporary artists and writers such as the coal miner poet Paul Zech from her hometown, the radical workers' leader and intellectual Erich Mühsam, the painter of social satire George Grosz (addressed as "Leatherstocking" in her idiosyncratic live universe of poems, letters, and personal relations), and the poet Wieland Herzfelde, all members of the Spartacus League of the Communist Party.[5] Early on she had become keenly aware of society's double moral standard when her brothers, among others, ostracized her when she became a single mother in 1899.[6] By taking into account the author's autobiography, the play can be understood—this is her own perception of it—as "a city ballad and mean workers' tale" based on the interrelatedness of class, gender, and sexuality, tangibly experienced in her social laboratory of greater Wuppertal-Elberfeld during an era of rapid industrialization and modernization.

Criticism has overlooked this interrelatedness of class, gender, and sexuality in *Dark River*. It is generally interpreted as a Naturalistic play in the vein of Germany's celebrated playwright Gerhart Hauptmann's *Die Weber* (1892) [*The Weavers*, first English translation published in 1899].[7] Though Lasker-Schüler intended to focus on the sociopolitical milieu of the city as she defines the Wupper of her hometown as "the workers' artery," the play's issue is not purely one of class struggle—the main theme in *The Weavers*—but a class conflict that cannot be isolated from the conflicts that come with gender and sexuality. The central impulse in her play, as she says, was "life" itself (*Hauptakzent, also das Leben*). By no means an ideological feminist, the author nevertheless presented a woman's point of view sensitive to the issues that she herself had confronted. From today's vantage point, it becomes clear that Lasker-Schüler's difficulty in having her drama performed or favorably reviewed was caused by the fact that it subverted the taboos on gender and sexuality of her day in a manner and style strikingly different from dramatic (male) conventions.[8] It is therefore uniquely illuminating to encounter an early favorable appreciation that is singular in the play's obstructed literary reception.

The occasion of the second performance of *Dark River* in Berlin in October 1927, and a parallel showing of Hauptmann's *Dorothea Angermann* (1925)—in which sexuality, seduction, and the crossing of class barriers are also the main issue—becomes a test case of differing aesthetics and judgment. Here the woman playwright's avant-garde experimentation with the aesthetic form of the drama, valorizing the "visual" over concepts, stands against traditionally action-driven rhetorics.

It is fascinating to compare the reception of the two plays by two of Berlin's most prominent theater critics during the Weimar period, Herbert Ihering and Alfred Kerr. Kerr, a long-time friend of Hauptmann's, considered the "master playwright" of the Republic, had to grudgingly admit: "four fifths of (Hauptmann's) drama should be sawed away," while Ihering called it a "stuffy museum-evening"; Kerr praises Lasker-Schüler's *Dark River* as "a visionary document of the Wilhelminian era."[9] Also, Harry Kahn's astonishing review in the Berlin newspaper *Weltbühne* sheds light on the all-too-effective discrimination against the woman author. The critic finds the world-renowned playwright's *Dorothea Angermann* "clumsy" and without "inner necessity, therefore without ultimate truth, reality, effectiveness," leaving the audience utterly "untouched." By contrast, he praises Lasker-Schüler's *Dark River,* the "almost forgotten" drama of the poet, a "lyrical" text that disregards the canon's stage rules, as possessing such a "deep urgency from beginning to end that even days later its spell cannot be broken."[10] Had *Dark River* received more such reviews, sensitive to its unique status between poetry and drama, public reception might have been as favorable to this avant-garde work, albeit written by a woman, as it had been in the case of Strindberg's lyrical dramatic works such as *Dream Play* [first English translation published 1912] or Frank Wedekind's *Frühlingserwachen* (1891) [*Spring Awakening*], and thereafter, Brecht's provocative early plays *Baal* (1918) and *Trommeln in der Nacht* (1919) [*Drums in the Night*]. Yet, instead of assessing the evocative uniqueness of this image-laden text, canonical criticism overshadowed a genuine reception. It focused on the drama's "stylistic confusion" and whether it should be classified as Naturalistic, Symbolist, Neoromantic, Expressionist, or Surrealist, implying, on the one hand, that a play is worthwhile only if it adheres to a particular movement or trend, although conceding, on the other hand, that this "very unusual and poetically unified" play is open to all the possibilities of the modern drama.[11]

The possibilities for women playwrights in the early twentieth century were frustrating, to say the least. Yet Lasker-Schüler was one of the very few women dramatists in the Weimar Republic who managed—albeit with great difficulties—to be staged during their lifetime. Others, such as Marieluise Fleisser (1901–1974) and Elsa Bernstein (1866–1949), were also lucky.[12] How did they do it? It is indeed interesting to see the strategies that led to their successful—even if brief—incursion into the woman-hostile territory of drama.[13] On the one hand, neither playwright challenged the canon structurally but rather, followed it—in itself a step in an acceptable direction. On the other hand, young Fleisser was sponsored by Brecht, the leading Berlin dramatist of his day, while Elsa Bernstein used the male pseudonym Ernst Rosmer. It was under the pseudonym that Bernstein was able to have her *Maria Arndt* staged in 1908, the year Else Lasker-Schüler wrote her subversive *Die Wupper*. Incidentally, *Maria Arndt* experienced a fabulous revival in Chicago, where it was staged by the Steppenwolf Theater to a full house during several weeks in March 2002, ninety-four years after its premiere in Berlin. This revival under her own name certainly attests to the enduring interest and value of the play itself. Fleisser's career also merits our interest. The two plays *Fegefeuer in Ingolstadt* (1926) [*Purgatory in Ingolstadt*, first English translation published 1991] and *Pioniere in Ingolstadt* (1929) [*Pioneers in Ingolstadt*, first English translation published 1991] by the twenty-five-year-old Fleisser, from the provincial town of Ingolstadt in Bavaria, had briefly conquered Berlin by storm, garnering rave reviews. *Pioneers* was performed forty-three times.[14] Unfortunately, the young playwright undid her early and brilliant success as further "unwritten dramas" were acted out in her private life.

As a woman, as a Jewish German, and as a bohemian, Lasker-Schüler faced multiple marginalizations. Not surprisingly, then, *Dark River* is written from the poet's view as an outsider not only from bourgeois society but also from the mainstream literary scene. The play problematizes social norms, class, gender, religion, and implicitly aesthetic norms. The subversion of patriarchy becomes most obvious through the archetypal and multifaceted Mother Pius. Also a card-reader and faith healer, this witchlike character freely crosses social borders, pulling the sexual strings between the classes. The centrality of this figure portrays sexuality as an instinctual, animal force—shared by all humanity—that subverts any hierarchies, be they social, economic, or religious. This view is reinforced by the three vagabonds, the poetic Amadeus, the transvestite Long Anna, and the exhibitionist Dangling Frederick. Voices of life-forces outside of social norms, the vagabonds observe and comment from the distance, without moralizing, on the sexual entanglements across social boundaries. The tightly knit dialogue in the carnival act and the melancholy tune of the folksong "O, du lieber Augustin," heard at crucial moments as a leitmotif, underscore the inevitable tragedy occurring behind the scenes: most notably Heinrich's seduction of the minor Liesken, who is sent to a reformatory, and his subsequent suicide. As part of the aura of this play's evocative nature imagery centered on the river, it is undoubtedly the playwright's technique of suggesting, yet withholding, the origin of disaster in terms of distinctly articulated social causes that casts the spell that Harry Kahn mentions. Throughout, the viewer is left to ponder the ambivalent connections suggested by the tip-of-the-iceberg dialogue and a pattern of images that never quite become fully developed symbols. As in the early plays of Brecht, there is no space for a facile jump to ready-made melioristic, charitable conclusions or a falling into ideological comfort; instead, lived- and worked-through experience receives its voice and vision.

Lasker-Schüler was born in 1869 in Elberfeld, since 1929 a component of the city of Wuppertal, on the Wupper River. She was the youngest of six children of a well-to-do, assimilated Jewish family that had lived in the area for generations. Jewish religion and customs were not overly cultivated in her family, where the Day of Atonement, Yom Kippur, the most somber Jewish holiday, was more like a family celebration.[15] As educated people, her family—especially her mother—shared with others an admiration for German literature, particularly Goethe, and her enlightened view of the world was shaped by classical and romantic authors.[16]

In 1894, Else Schüler married the dermatologist Jonathan Berthold Lasker, brother of the well-known chess master Emmauel Lasker. The couple moved to Berlin, where the young woman painted, drew, experimented with photography in a rented studio, and began her professional writing career. The marriage lasted four years. In 1899, Lasker-Schüler published her first verses and gave birth to her only son, Paul, as a single mother. She never disclosed the name of the father. In early 1903 she divorced Lasker and later that year married Georg Levin (Herwarth Walden), editor of the literary Expressionist journal *Der Sturm*. After her second marriage ended in 1912, Lasker-Schüler continued her bohemian existence in Berlin, writing and discussing in the cafés that served as her literary salon, where she impressed many a male poet also with her looks: "boyishly slender, pitch-black hair, cut short, rare in those days, big raven-black eyes with an evasive, enigmatic gaze."[17] Yet, without a regular income, nomadic from one rented room to another, she and her "Paulchen" faced many hardships. In 1919, she started enjoying some success with the premiere of her drama *Dark River* at the Deutsches Theater and the publication of a ten-volume edition of her works by Paul Cassirer. Bitter irony would have it that the very year she finally received Germany's highest literary distinction, the Kleist Prize, in November 1932, her career and life in Germany ended. After being beaten in the street by uniformed Nazis, she fled to Switzerland in April 1933. During the reign of Nazi terror, her books were burned and her name fell into oblivion. In 1939 she went on a trip to Palestine. This became her final destination against her will, as the Swiss authorities did not permit her re-entry. She died in Palestine in 1945.

Lasker-Schüler's relationship to Judaism is not, at the very beginning, an integral part of her career, but it soon intrudes on her life and work. In the 1870s, just after her birth, a wave of anti-Semitism had swept over Germany that led to the foundation of several important centers, such as the Central Verein deutscher Staatsbürger jüdischen Glaubens (Central Association of German Citizens of the Jewish Faith) and the non-Jewish Verein zur Bekämpfung des Antisemitismus (Association for the Repulse of Anti-Semitism). Both these groups were in opposition to the Zionistische Union Deutschlands (Zionist Union for Germany) that fought against assimilation and instead aimed at the settlement of Palestine.[18] Yet, in spite of the many controversies not only between Christians and Jews but also within the Jewish community, Lasker-Schüler never actively participated in any of these circles. Thus, in her early work— the collection of poems *Styx* (1902), *Der siebte Tag* (1905) [*The Seventh Day*, not translated], *Das Peter Hille Buch* (1906) [*The Peter Hille Book*, no published English translation]—there is a surprising absence of any specifically Jewish theme. Instead, a fabulous Oriental world—en vogue in European literature and the arts since the mid-nineteenth century—appears in *Die Nächte Tinos von Bagdad* (1907) [*The Nights of Tino of Bagdad*, no published English translation]. Here she develops the fairy-tale motifs, figures, and images that later on, according to her friend and critic Werner Kraft, will be "suffused with a Jewish substance" as in her *Hebrew Ballads*.[19] And, of course, there are the two later plays from the thirties and forties, *Arthur Aronymus* and *I and I*, in which Jewish-German relations are centrally problematized from a pre-Holocaust perspective to one in which the Holocaust is in horrifying progress.

Lasker-Schüler's love for Judaism was cosmopolitan, yet split. Her basic ignorance of Jewish traditions and customs led her to romanticize notions of Jewish spirituality, which she linked to the old Hebrew language and heroic Bible figures such as Joseph and Abraham.[20] Yet she totally rejected the Yiddish of the Eastern European Jews pouring into Berlin from the Russian Revolution, connecting them to the cliché images of petty merchants and money-lenders. After 1910, however, Lasker-Schüler defiantly and proudly admits her Jewish heritage. Thus, in her *Hebrew Ballads* and *Der Malik* she sings the praises of the "wild Jews," the great warrior figures from the Bible as witnesses of Jewish culture across the centuries. It seems likely that she may have been inspired by Martin Buber's call for "a Jewish . . . poetry that would not accidentally be made by Jews . . . but an art that would shape the fate of our tribe in content and form."[21]

In her second drama, *Arthur Aronymus and His Ancestors*,

Lasker-Schüler turns to nineteenth-century religious anti-Semitism in Germany, reflecting on the racist anti-Semitism that became ever more pronounced during the later years of the Weimar Republic. Rather than giving in to the threatening aspect of that phenomenon, however, the poet's vision is one of reconciliation between religions.

Arthur Aronymus premiered in Zürich, the first city of Lasker-Schüler's exile, in 1936. The playwright was delighted with the cast and their performance. However, to her great dismay, the play was cancelled after only two performances because of German political pressure.[22] The play foregrounds the religious conflicts between Jews and Christians, quite pronounced in the Wuppertal region during the nineteenth century. Though this struggle is suggested in *Dark River,* the author had apparently not yet been willing to openly tackle that charged topic. The drama of the early thirties—finished a year before Hitler's coming to power—centrally addresses the age-old issue of anti-Semitism and attempts to offer an aesthetic resolution. The children's pogrom play-within-the-play simulates the burning of a Jewish child as a witch. Little Arthur plays the part of his epileptic sister, Dora, whom the villagers accuse of being a witch. The children's play shows to both the audience in front of the stage and the Bishop on the stage that difference is a social construct. Differences of ethnicity, religion, and even gender are deconstructed by the children, as, for example, Arthur wears his sister's skirts, jettisoning them provocatively upon his exit. And in the wake of this powerful performance in the spirit of children's innocence and spontaneous wisdom, there is a symbolic reconciliation between Jews and Catholics when the Bishop of Paderborn, who came to halt the impending pogrom, shares the seder dinner at the house of Arthur's parents, the Schülers. That the protagonist bears the author's family name underscores the importance of a "transfigured" autobiographical aspect of her work (the subtitle of the play is "From My Beloved Father's Childhood Years").

The third and last play, *I and I,* was written during Lasker-Schüler's Palestinian exile (1939–45). It remained unpublished until 1980 because it had been misinterpreted (possibly a pretext) as senile babbling that would harm the poet's reputation.[23] It is now recognized as a work ahead of its time. Heinrich Böll, the later Nobel laureate, had recommended it to the publishing house Kiepenheuer and Witsch at the end of the sixties precisely as such, emphasizing "that this time is coming: that a work grows into a future time—and that seems to be the case with *I and I*."[24]

The fusion of I and I, rather than a mere yearning for finding the self, is a strategy by which the author becomes her own text. By presenting the subject—herself—as object, she confronts its multiple sociohistorical components on the "stage of her heart" (*Herzensbühne*). The "Hell play" (*Höllenspiel*), as Lasker-Schüler calls it, is staged as the poet's complex and conflicting identity at the possibly fictional Jerusalem location "Hell ground" (*Höllengrund*) against the invasive backdrop of German history. Its main characters are Faust; Mephisto; Hitler and his cohorts; the Hebrew god Baal from the Old Testament as well as Kings Saul, David, and Solomon; then-famous Berlin and Hollywood theater director Max Reinhardt; the audience; and the poet herself. In the course of the performance, it becomes less surprising that the hell to which the Nazi generals are invited by Mephisto, and in whose lava masses Hitler and his soldiers ultimately perish, is located at the site of the poet's exile, Jerusalem. It is, after all, a metaphor for the poet's own internal turmoil as she tries to understand and cope with the indescribable. By confronting the historical events that affected her life and the diverse cultural communities that shaped her, the play performs and analyzes the various social components of her identity.

The multiple ways of constructing and deconstructing identity—instead of a traditional portrayal of it—make the play a parable with an open perspective in which the main protagonists cannot be clearly separated from the secondary characters or from the author's staged persona. In the prologue and epilogue, the poet thematizes her split. The Faust-Mephisto action continues this split within the play-within-the-play structure, on the metaphorical level, on the stage of her heart (acts one and six). In acts two and five, the participating audience experiences the rise and fall of German National Socialism, while in the central acts three and four, the chess game between Faust and Mephisto constitutes a pondering over how the world keeps turning, with the same monarch of hell winning throughout time. Only in an abrupt turn at the end of the epilogue does the persona of the poet invoke the authority of God, revealed at the moment of apocalypse.

The play's title captures the fusion of the poet's multiple selves as a German Jew. Moreover, by involving the audience in the play, that is, by erasing the traditional separation between the action on stage and the audience, the author succeeds in shocking the audience into recognizing and understanding the involvement of their own multiple personae in the historical events taking place in Europe at the time.

The play is highly experimental avant-garde theater that blends the heterogeneous features of a theater of the absurd with Brechtian techniques of addressing the absurd and also with elements of an ancient *Mysterienspiel*. The interwoven layers of time and place—the biblical past (the three Kings), the classical literary Faust-Mephisto theme, the historical period of the 1940s, the author's stage role as "poet," and the erasure of borders between stage and audience—interact to create a metatheater that deserves our attention today, when an awareness of the heterogeneity of experience is the mark of a postmodern condition.

As an expression of the anguished identity conflict of the German-Jewish poet, the play rejects the distortion of the German linguistic and cultural heritage by the political extremists of the Hitler era, and at the same time it achieves salvation by blending that heritage with Expressionistic idealism and the messianism of her ancestral Jewish culture. Thematically and structurally, *I and I* is political theater as literary resistance in the 1940s, and it is theater of the German-Jewish memory for today.

Notes

1. While today Else Lasker-Schüler is still known mainly for her poetry, the focus of literary criticism has widened since the 1980s to encompass her neglected prose and dramatic oeuvre, most likely inspired by Sigrid Bauschinger's landmark book that for the first time analyzed the entire work of the poet within the historical context of her times: *Else Lasker-Schüler: Ihr Werk und ihre Zeit* (Heidelberg: Stiehm, 1980).

2. See Markus Hallensleben, *Else Lasker-Schüler: Avantgardismus und Kunstinszenierung* (Tübingen: Francke, 2000). Hallensleben's extraordinary contribution to Lasker-Schüler research is that he analyzes her work not from the usual biographical aspect but in the context of European avant-garde movements, convincingly demonstrating how the poet uses avant-gardist techniques that have characterized the literary modernity of the twentieth century, placing her in the company of such figures as Apollinaire, Breton, and others.

3. Inca Molina Rumold, "Class, Gender, and Sexuality in Imperial Germany: A Reading of Else Lasker-Schüler's Drama *Die Wupper,*" in *Society for the Interdisciplinary Study of Social Imagery* (Pueblo: University of Southern Colorado, 1998), 113–19; "*Der Malik:* Else Lasker-Schüler's Anti-War Novel," in *Women in German, Feminist Studies in German Literature and Culture* (Lincoln: University of Nebraska Press, 1999), 143–62.

4. The author's friend Theo Otto commented on the first performance of *Dark River* after the Second World War in 1958: In traditionally Catholic Cologne, the audience booed and slammed doors upon leaving the theater, outraged at the "obscenities" and "amoralities" of the play. See Theo Otto, "Ein bergischer Kräher berichtet," in *Lasker-Schüler: Ein Buch zum 100. Geburtstag der Dichterin*, ed. Michael Schmid (Wuppertal: Hammer, 1969), 41–49.

5. In 1983, three editors of *linkskurve* (*Left Curve*) founded a new publishing house in Kiel that, on the suggestion of the eighty-seven-year-old poet Wieland Herzfelde, received the name Neuer Malik Verlag (New Malik Press). One of its first publications was the reissue of *Der Malik* (*The Emperor*), which Michael Bauer (in the *Stuttgarter*

Nachrichten, 27 May 1984, p. 14) called "more than an homage, a committed program" (my trans.). Even the French newspapers *Le Monde* (10 March 1995, p. 3) and *Le Figaro* (25 March 1995, p. 4) feature reviews of *Le Malik*, published by Geneviève Capgras and Hilke Hass.

6. Erika Klüsener documents through photographs and letters the biography of this author, who kept her private life hermetically closed to the world. See her *Lasker-Schüler in Selbstzeugnissen und Bilddokumenten* (Reinbeck bei Hamburg: Rowohlt, 1980), 56–57.

7. Peter Tyson draws a parallel between the plots of Hauptmann's *Die Weber* (1892) [*The Weavers*] and *Die Wupper* (1909) without reassessing the latter from a new perspective, as Markus Hallensleben does in *Else Lasker-Schüler* by rejecting the notion of an imitation of Hauptmann's play, emphasizing instead its genre reactivation. Using intertextual strategies, Lasker-Schüler inserts motifs and sociocritical positions from the "model" into her text, which starts where *The Weavers* ends. See Peter Tyson, "Else Lasker-Schüler's Drama Die Wupper: From Naturalism to Expressionism," AUMLA 64 (1985): 144–53.

8. Helga Kraft's 1996 book *Ein Haus aus Sprache: Dramatikerinnen und das andere* Theater (Stuttgart: Metzler) demonstrates the pervasive gender discrimination women dramatists were subjected to by the canon in the German-speaking countries. This benchmark study is a historical recovery of women dramatists through the centuries, with incisive insights on individual dramatists of the twentieth century and before. Also, Michaela Giesing expands on the topic of gender discrimination against women dramatists around the turn of the century, from which even a prominent author like Else Lasker-Schüler was not exempt. As a lyrical poet she was readily accepted, even praised, but drama was considered an exclusively "male" realm; hence her difficulties in having *Die Wupper* staged. See Michaela Giesing, "Theater als verweigerter Raum," in *Schreibende Frauen*, ed. Hiltrud Gnüg and Renate Möhrmann (Stuttgart: Metzler, 1985), 240–59.

9. Alfred Kerr, *Hauptmann: Dorothea Angermann*, Deutsches Theater *Berliner Tageblatt*, Abend-Ausgabe (Berlin), 19 October 1927; Herbert Ihering, *Berliner Börsen Courier*, 19 October 1927.

10. Harry Kahn, "Gerhart Hauptmann und Else Lasker-Schüler," *Weltbühne* (Berlin), 19 October 1927.

11. Fritz Martini comments in his epilogue to the 1977 Reclam reprint of *Die Wupper:* "The confusion begins as soon as its style is to be determined, since Naturalism, Symbolism, Expressionism, and . . . Surrealism—none of these terms quite covers this unusual play. Nonetheless, it has all the possibilities of the modern drama" (my trans.). See E. N. Mennemeier, *Modernes Deutsches Drama* (München: Fink, 1979), 111.

12. In *Ein Haus aus Sprache: Dramatikerinnen und das andere Theater* (Stuttgart: Metzler), her 1996 book on women dramatists, Helga Kraft "rediscovered" many more playwrights from the Weimar Republic, such as Ilse Langner, Elisabeth Hauptmann, Anna Gmeyner-Wiesner, Alice Stein-Landsmann, and Elsa Bernstein, to name just a few who had long been forgotten (76ff.). Yet, quite interestingly, and to show how much they were in the public eye then, on February 14, 1930—just three years after radio had become the new technological medium of public communication—they all participated in "Funkstunde," a radio talk show by women dramatists (*Marbacher Magazin* 96, 2001, p. 22).

13. In "Theater als verweigerter Raum" ("Theater as Denied Space"), Michaela Giesing points out that women playwrights around the turn of the century and in the early twentieth century were relegated to the genre of fairy tales for children's theater, in which they had achieved great success. Not only did the psychomedical discourse of the time consider the female mentality closer to that of children, but the authors did not have to fear competition from other women since most of the time the authorship of children's plays was not stated on the theater posters, unless they had been penned by such male authors as the Brothers Grimm, Hans Christian Andersen, and so on (248).

14. *Marbacher Magazin*, Sonderheft 96, 2001, p. 30.

15. Bauschinger, *Else Lasker-Schüler*, 84

16. Jakob Hessing, *Else Lasker-Schüler: Biographie einer deutsch-jüdischen Dichterin* (Karlsruhe: von Loeper, 1985), 28.

17. Gottfried Benn's 1952 "Rede auf Else Lasker-Schüler," in *Gesammelte Werke* (Wiesbaden: Limes Verlag, 1968), 1101.

18. See Peter M. Baldwin, "Zionist and Non-Zionist Jews in the Last Years before the Nazi Regime," *Yearbook of the Leo Baeck Institute* 27 (1982): 87–108.

19. Werner Kraft, "Nachwort," in *Else Lasker-Schüler: Verse und Prosa aus dem Nachlass, Gesammelte Werke* (München: Kösel Verlag, 1961), 151.

20. Dagmar Lorenz's research shows that "Jewish educational practices of which earlier women like Rahel Levin and Fanny Lewald had complained in the nineteenth century, were the reason why women remained ignorant of religious matters. Barred from the study of the Scriptures, they attended Christian schools and engaged in secular pursuits—religious erudition could not possibly become the cornerstone of their identity." See her "1939: Else Lasker-Schüler Becomes Permanently Exiled in Jerusalem when Swiss Immigration Authorities Deny Her Reentry to Switzerland," in *The Yale Companion to Jewish Writing and Thought in German Culture, 1096–1996*, ed. Sander L. Gilman and Jack Zipes (New Haven: Yale University Press, 1997), 563–70.

21. Martin Buber, "Ost und West," *Illustrierte Monatsschrift für modernes Judentum Berlin* 1 (1901), 1.

22. Theo Otto, in "Ein bergischer Kräher berichtet," comments on the enthusiastic reception of the play by both the audience and the press on December 19, 1936. Yet the German consulate in Zürich forced the theater administration to cancel it after the second performance.

23. Ernst Ginsberg opined, "O, what noble spirit was destroyed here. Because this drama is the mirror of the most pitiful destruction and desintegration. One feels the poet's onset of senility" in *Else Lasker-Schüler: Verse und Prosa aus dem Nachlass*, 3 vol., ed. Werner Kraft (München: Kösel, 1961), 171. It reflects the reaction to *Ichundich* by Ginsberg and other conservative friends who wanted to protect her reputation.

24. See Heinrich Böll's letter of January 4 (no year), cited in Hallensleben, *Else Lasker-Schüler*, 289.

A NOTE FROM THE TRANSLATOR

Translating plays is different from translating other prose. Plays are written to be performed aloud: to be interpreted by a director and brought to life by a cast. The translator of a play not only interprets between a text and a reader but also between a text and all the theater personnel who may in turn interpret the text to an audience.

Unless a production is openly an adaptation, the translator's task is to reproduce the text with an effect as much like the original as possible. This cannot mean a completely literal translation or a totally free rendition but rather a combination of methods tailored to the task at hand. Creative writing itself has often been regarded as translation of the universe; Else Lasker-Schüler referred to her own writing as translation, sometimes from a mythical language she had created herself. Her plays withstand translation well because their universal elements offer a basis for understanding in any language, and her linguistic uniqueness can be conveyed from German to English in a manner reasonably comparable to the original. My principles for literary translating are: to become thoroughly familiar with everything written by the author, to translate literally to the greatest extent possible, to preserve effect at the expense of literalness when necessary, and to give priority to making the translated work of art read like a work of art in the second language as well.

There is a great deal of the author in these plays: personality, life history, other works. This does not necessarily need to be known to readers and audiences in order to appreciate the plays, but it does need to be understood by the translator in order to produce as full and just a translation as possible. Lasker-Schüler's beautiful and innovative lyric poetry is reflected throughout her three plays, and lyric passages are translated as lyric passages. Several of her essays and novellas supplement the background and even the action of the plays, especially *Arthur Aronymus*. Some of her allusions, such as the references to the animal hedges of Gaesecke, do not make full sense unless we know that hedges in some parts of Germany were and still are trimmed in the shape of animals and other figures.

Titles are always of great importance and need to be translated with at least as much care as the rest of the text. The title *Arthur Aronymus*, being the name of the central character, can simply be kept, with the subtitle translated. Lasker-Schüler chose a brilliant and striking title for her third play, *IchundIch*, a humor-filled lyric drama of reintegrating the good and evil in human beings and their world. The literal translation of the title, *I and I*, has the same unconventional effect as the original and, like it, encapsulates the action of the play. Lasker-Schüler's first play does present something of a translation problem. Her title was as usual very well chosen: *Die Wupper*. The Wupper is a small river flowing into the Rhine between Düsseldorf and Cologne. For German readers and audiences it conjures a nineteenth-century area of industrial blight and social contrasts. The title is not suitable in translation, however, not only because the river and its connotations are unknown in the world at large, but especially because the name sounds comical to English speakers, whether it is pronounced in German or as it looks in English. The title *Dark River* is phonetically similar to the original and preserves some of its connotations through the adjective "dark."

Parts of the Lasker-Schüler texts are written in dialect. This applies mainly to *Dark River*, in which some characters speak only dialect and others (significantly) speak dialect only part of the time. The dialect she writes is one she created, a realistic, consistent idiolect constructed from the various dialects spoken in the Wupper Valley in the 1870s and 1880s. Although dialect may be of great importance for characterization, contrast, tone, and sometimes humor, as used in the Lasker-Schüler plays, it is usually best not to write the translation in dialect. It can be very tedious for readers, can destroy a stage production if poorly done, and can damage comprehensibility for both readers and audiences. For maximum clarity and effect, the language used in each production or reading should be the dialect of the area where the play is being read or staged, but this is of course not possible in publishing or translating. The best solution is to translate the original phraseology into standard speech but to indicate which characters speak only dialect and which other parts of the text are in dialect. In this way readers and actors can understand the text without hindering the flow of the action and can convert it into some form of local dialect meaningful to them.

In most languages, many words have several different meanings, each with different shades of meaning and different connotations. Rich languages, most notably English, have many "synonyms"—which are not always identical, however, because of these different shades of meaning and connotation. The range of meanings of any given word seldom coincides exactly with the range of meanings of its equivalent in another language. While some words and phrases may translate literally, their actual usage and connotations may not. If a single word in one language is defined as "terrify, horrify, frighten" in English, which of them should be used in translating it? Each one has a different shade of meaning. The English expression "for the birds" is "for the cat" in German; the title *Die Wupper,* discussed above, would require something like "nineteenth-century Pittsburgh" in order to convey the same image. In translating it is essential to recognize these subtle distinctions in language and handle them so as to convey the author's message.

Meaningless refrains are a small but interesting problem. The only one in the three Lasker-Schüler plays is Granddaddy Wallbrecker's "C'm tingalingaling" in *Dark River.* He uses it constantly, in much the way one might say "By golly" in English. There is no reason to change it in translation, as it is a colorful touch and has no meaning anyway. In the original it is "Tum tingalingaling," the "tum" probably used for the word "zum" as a child or old person might slur it ("zum," meaning "to the," is pronounced "tsoom," with the "oo" as in "book"). The English "C'm" ("Come") is phonetically similar to "Tum" and also a meaningless part of the expression.

The Lasker-Schüler plays show a few of the usual errors, inconsistencies, and non sequiturs found in most texts. Obvious typographical errors and inconsistencies that are clearly slips of the pen are corrected without comment. Any other inconsistencies and all non sequiturs are examined very closely to make sure that some unexpected intent of the author is not being misunderstood; they are usually left as they stand, without comment.

Enjoy the plays.

THREE PLAYS

DARK RIVER

A Drama in Five Acts

CHARACTERS

Granddaddy Wallbrecker
Carl Pius, *his grandson*
August Puderbach, *a dyer*
Liesken Puderbach, *August's little sister*
Amanda Pius, *Granddaddy Wallbrecker's daughter*
Mother Pius, *Carl's paternal grandmother*
Three Vagrants: Dangling Frederick, Long Anna, *and* Amadeus
Two Accomplices
Bertha *and* Augusta, *maids in the Sonntag house*
Mrs. Charlotte Sonntag, *a factory owner*
Henry and Edward, *her sons*
Martha, *her daughter*
Business Friend *of Henry's*
Two Girlfriends
Several Gentlemen in Gray Top Hats
Girlfriends of the Gentlemen
Dr. Bruno von Simon, *a lawyer*
Rosa the Fat Lady
Willem, *a pimp, formerly a weaver*
Gretchen Stomms, *Liesken's friend*
Additional characters include workers of both sexes (factory workers, dyers, weavers, carnival workers), lower-class women, Croatian youths, Social Democrats, loiterers, various children

(street urchins, two little girls, group of boys), the crowd at the fair (townspeople, clerks, shop girls, serving maids, schoolboys, coarse men and women), priest, and so on.

The first and fourth acts take place in the workers' section of a small industrial city in Germany (in about 1880); the second act takes place in the garden of a villa, the third at the carnival, and the fifth in a room in the villa with windows and double doors giving out onto the same garden. The final scene of the fifth act takes place in the workers' section.

TRANSLATOR'S NOTE: The Sonntag family and Dr. Bruno von Simon speak the language of educated upper-class people, while the servants, vagrants, and working-class people speak the dialect of the lower classes. Crossing the line are Henry, who uses dialect in a friendly way with his social inferiors; Bertha, who has risen to the status of maid but expresses her scorn for Carl Pius in dialect; and Carl, who scorns the lower class from which he comes but falls back into dialect in moments of anger, cruelty, and despair.

ACT 1

[*Workers' section of an industrial city on a river in a narrow valley. In the background, wooded hills. To the left in the valley flows a narrow arm of the river, bending away in the distance. A bridge leads over the river to a path on which the Piuses' dilapidated little one-story house is located. Upstage to the right is a narrow street with dirty old tenements rented to workers. The Puderbachs live on the top floor of the first building, which is only half visible. To the left of the river is a meadow, beyond which can be seen smoking factory chimneys, other buildings, etc. In front of the Piuses' little house is a bench and next to it a spreading bush. By a path leading into the woods, in the background, burns an old streetlight, which fades slowly during the first act.*]

GRANDDADDY WALLBRECKER: Listen at your old granddaddy, Carl. Fire the booklearning junk out with the trash. You're just made to be a boss; you ought to have workers under your command.

CARL: Once I'm a pastor, Granddaddy, the bosses will be my workers.

GRANDDADDY WALLBRECKER: And you got to put in your bid for Liesken over there, too.

CARL [*deliberately, as to a child*]: She'll be all the more willing to marry me.

GRANDDADDY WALLBRECKER: For twenty-five years I sat at the loom with Liesken's granddaddy and the winding sheet was still too small for the both of us.

[*Pause.*]

She'll take a pastor for sure, but an educated man ought to have a fine woman and a pastor a Mrs. Pastor—and old Granddaddy don't belong in the fancy hothouse, neether!

CARL: I'll buy you a comfortable easy chair, Granddaddy, you'll sit on a soft cushion and do nothing all day long but sleep and go out walking and smoke. What do you say to that, Daddy Wallbrecker?

GRANDDADDY WALLBRECKER: I'll get into collision with the priests, for Daddy Wallbrecker's grandson to be a pastor; they already pestered me on account of your father being Lutheran.

CARL: The things you think about!

GRANDDADDY WALLBRECKER: Come tingalingaling, Carl, the old turkey kept giving your father an earful too. He was a hard-working dyer [*pointing to the river*]—there's his blood running. One day he suddenly gets the idea work ain't for him no more, and he gets sore at the owner and the owner's wife. She was all puffed up with her silk skirt, but she had a right to be snooty with so much money. In broad daylight in the middle of town he thrashed her noble bare behind.

CARL: That really must have worried you, Granddaddy, since you can't forget it.

GRANDDADDY WALLBRECKER: Come tingalingaling, they stuck him in the pokey for a year for his crime.

[CARL *shows sympathy*.]

Otherwise he was an honest worker.

[CARL *nods*.]

And the old turkey went to see him right away. She and her quackery, she smeared a fine lady a burning sore on the leg. See, Carl, and now Amanda thinks they're going to salt you away too, like your father when he got fed up and your grandmother with her putting on.

CARL: Times have changed, Granddaddy.

GRANDDADDY WALLBRECKER [*with childish slyness*]: See there, that's it. Next thing you won't remember your old granddaddy's tobacco no more, neether.

CARL: Oh, forget about it.

GRANDDADDY WALLBRECKER: Look how old you are now, boy! Puderbachs' August is already bringing home ten dollars. There he goes with his sister, like she was his sweetheart.

[AUGUST *and* LIESKEN *are seen coming home from the woods.*]

CARL: And I'll earn three times as much. Just give me time. When I'm a pastor you're going to chomp your favorite dish every day.

GRANDDADDY WALLBRECKER [*doubtfully*]: If the old turkey don't gobble it up on me.

CARL: She'll be staying right here, living by the river in her house.

GRANDDADDY WALLBRECKER: And you wanna go away and preach off there in the capital city? Come tingalingaling, you ought to stay in the Lutheran church right here and roar down from the pulpit on all the two-faced folks.

[*Short pause.*]

And I'll turn into a heretic in my old age too, if it's got to be—for your sake, Carl. I've unlearned this anyways [*crossing himself, then in a weepy tone*] even if the habit do hang on.

CARL: It's late, Granddaddy; I'll put you into the sack.

GRANDDADDY WALLBRECKER: Boy, boy, boy, if I live to see the day.

[*They proceed to their little house; as they are entering,* GRANDDADDY WALLBRECKER *is embraced from behind by* LIESKEN PUDERBACH, *who has run ahead of her brother.* WORKERS *are seen in the distance, and their rough voices are heard.*]

GRANDDADDY WALLBRECKER: What you want from Granddaddy, you dainty little critter? Looky, Carl, she likes the old granddaddy.

LIESKEN [*enjoying herself*]: Tomorrow for your birthday you're going to get a new pipe from me. I snitched August's little one in the blue velvet case and took it to Mr. Stomms today. In exchange I can pick out a long one like yours for you, a brand new one, Granddaddy, [*her voice rising to a high pitch*] with a deer's head on it.

GRANDDADDY WALLBRECKER [*with childish delight*]: She likes the old granddaddy, Carl.

[*He tickles* LIESKEN *on her bare neck.*]

I always knock for her when young Mr. Edward comes around, eh Liesken?

[*She looks embarrassed.* GRANDDADDY WALLBRECKER *winks at her confidentially.*]

He always asks me about her.

LIESKEN [*to* CARL, *acting grown-up*]: Mr. Edward says I'm his royal bride.

CARL [*speaking just to say something*]: And me—so you don't want to marry me.

GRANDDADDY WALLBRECKER: Come tingalingaling, but he's a rich gentleman, eh Liesken?

LIESKEN: Two big pictures, that's what he said he's bringing me from England—Looky! Looky! I think he's coming to visit you right now, Carl.

CARL [*pushing the child impatiently aside*]: Your brother's looking for you now, Liesken.

GRANDDADDY WALLBRECKER: The scallywag's got a blue bazoo from wolfing berries.

LIESKEN: Look at his nose, Granddaddy!

GRANDDADDY WALLBRECKER: It's painted up like a monkey.

LIESKEN: August, August, what you look like!

AUGUST [*looking at* CARL *with envy*]: I'm just an ordinary dyer; I ain't ashamed to feed on what grows in God's woods. You, Granddaddy Wallbrecker?

GRANDDADDY WALLBRECKER [*shaking his head*]: Nope.

AUGUST: You, Liesken?

[CARL *leans against one of the side beams of the little house, his arms crossed.*]

LIESKEN: August, if you'll ask Mother, can I help Auntie a little with the washing again, I'll tell you where your little pipe in the blue velvet case is at.

AUGUST: Tell!

[GRANDDADDY WALLBRECKER *shakes his head hard at* LIESKEN. *She laughs.*]

Come on and tell, you dumb female!

LIESKEN: Go on! How can I tell you when I don't know?

[GRANDDADDY WALLBRECKER *and* LIESKEN *make fun of* AUGUST, *who, with comical twistings and turnings, is trying to turn around but is prevented by* LIESKEN *from doing so.*]

August, dear August, ask Mother, huh? I'll give you a big fat kiss.

AUGUST: Stick your smack in your hope chest for when you get married.

LIESKEN: You can take my candies and the licorice stick out of Mother's bureau, August.

AMANDA [*coming to the open window after hearing* LIESKEN'*s last words*]: Have you got such a sweet tooth, August? How come you never go over to see Carl anymore?

[MOTHER PIUS *comes to the window behind* AMANDA.]

AUGUST: With such a fine gentleman—naw, Mrs. Pius!

MOTHER PIUS: What *should* our Carl have to do with a common cotton dyer like him?

[AUGUST *withdraws, with a profound and hilariously comic reverence.* MOTHER PIUS *to* LIESKEN.]

And now it's time for you to be off to the sack.

LIESKEN [*looking at* AMANDA *bashfully*]: I want to help Auntie with the washing so she can cook Granddaddy his favorite dish tomorrow.

MOTHER PIUS: And him without a tooth in his head.

LIESKEN: I can't sleep when the moon's like that anyways. It's looking down as red as Dangling Frederick's bloody eye.

AMANDA [*enigmatically*]: Have you ever seen it, Liesken?

LIESKEN: Me and Gretchen Stomms, he showed it to us one time.

MOTHER PIUS [*cynical*]: And you didn't see nothing else in his cellar, Liesken?

LIESKEN: All I did the whole time was look into his round red moon.

MOTHER PIUS: But you've turned into a strapping girl. Just look, Amanda, she's already got her a bosom like two little heads of spring lettuce.

[CARL *comes out of his corner and goes toward* GRANDDADDY WALLBRECKER.]

GRANDDADDY WALLBRECKER: Carl, I'm coming now.

[MOTHER PIUS *goes back inside.* LIESKEN *climbs in the window, helped by* AMANDA, *who then closes it.* GRANDDADDY WALLBRECKER *and* CARL *stroll slowly into the house.*]

Nah, how the whole business gets me a-going . . .

CARL: What?

GRANDDADDY WALLBRECKER: With your career, Carl.

CARL: You can sleep in peace, Granddaddy.

[*They enter the little house.* AUGUST *slips out of his narrow street, observes the Piuses' house closely, and hides carefully between the bush and the bench. Meanwhile the little attic room is illuminated by a dim oil lamp; the small window is half open. Drunken* WORKERS *come along the path, swear, laugh, etc.* AUGUST, *believing the noise will keep him from hearing, behaves like a furious clown. The* WORKERS *turn right into the narrow street.* AMANDA'*s voice is heard from above.*]

AMANDA: Daddy . . .

GRANDDADDY WALLBRECKER: Yeah . . .

AMANDA: You're usually not in such a hurry. Wake up!

GRANDDADDY WALLBRECKER: What *should* I do at midnight, Daughter?

AMANDA: What'd Carl say?

GRANDDADDY WALLBRECKER: What?

AMANDA: What he said. You did talk with him.

GRANDDADDY WALLBRECKER: Yeah, I just let it slip out what a good job August has.

AMANDA: And what does he say to that?

GRANDDADDY WALLBRECKER: Naw, he ain't having any; he's got pastor on the brain.

[THREE VAGRANTS *come slowly over the bridge, not speaking. One keeps up a sinister muttering; it is* DANGLING FREDERICK, *his left eye socket covered by a black patch. The second is* LONG ANNA, *who wears a concertina on a faded shoulder strap. The third is* AMADEUS *with the glass heart, who sits down cautiously on the step leading from the bridge to the path. The other two sit down on the bridge railing.* AUGUST *ducks farther behind the bush. While this is taking place, the conversation continues upstairs.*]

AMANDA: *You* don't know how to carry on a conversation! And I'm sick and tired of feeding the whole barnful, too.

GRANDDADDY WALLBRECKER: I did too carry on a conversation. You women think you're the only ones with a bazoo, don't you?

[AMANDA *bursts into tears.*]

Quit your bawling.

[*She sobs.*]

At that, I kind of like the idea of Carl in vestryments. [*Speaking with childish slyness*] Just a couple more little years, Amanda, my dear daughter, and then comes the reward. Believe your old daddy.

[*He crows once more and starts to doze off.*]

AMANDA: It's all Old Lady Pius's fault. She had her finger on my husband, but she ought to leave my boy alone.

GRANDDADDY WALLBRECKER [*triumphant, half asleep*]: And he won't invite her to his fine house by the emperor's court church, neether.

AMANDA: You must be dreaming.

GRANDDADDY WALLBRECKER: It's all the pree-cise truth, Amanda; this time Old Lady Pius has made a good bet.

AMANDA [*after a short pause*]: Ever since you quit praying to the Savior, everything's turned out like this.

[*She bursts into tears again.*]

GRANDDADDY WALLBRECKER: I pray every evening, my dear daughter; I'd rather lie than not say thanks for his great kindness.

[*The door squeaks softly*.]

AMANDA: Come on in! Liesken wants to say goodnight, Daddy, and then you can sleep as far as I'm concerned.

[*The door is heard slamming shut*.]

LIESKEN: Granddaddy, I'm sure looking forward to your new pipe.

[*Her voice rises to a high pitch*.]

It's got a deer's head!

[GRANDDADDY WALLBRECKER *laughs like a child*.]

Will you knock and whistle when he comes to see you?

[GRANDDADDY WALLBRECKER *whistles with great success*.]

Your big toe's peeking out of the feathers, Granddaddy! Just a second, I'll cover you up like a tiny baby.

GRANDDADDY WALLBRECKER: Open the window wider, too. I feel bum from the air in here.

LIESKEN [*opening the window wide*]: August, here I am.

[AUGUST *jumps, startled, and makes warning motions*.]

I'm going downstairs now. Good night, Granddaddy Wallbrecker!

GRANDDADDY WALLBRECKER [*half asleep*]: Come tingalingaling, if I could still have a young female like that in bed.

[LIESKEN *is downstairs in a second.* AUGUST *comes out of his hiding place. She hurries to him.*]

AUGUST [*to the* VAGRANTS]: Evening, all. Coming from work?

LONG ANNA [*in a high-pitched woman's voice*]: Where else, old good-for-nothing?

LIESKEN: Amadeus, you're bleeding.

LONG ANNA: Let him go ahead with his nosebleed, maybe he'll start talking sense out of his dreambook.

AMADEUS [*laying his hand anxiously over his heart*]: And it got cracked, Liesken; it keeps on dripping.

LONG ANNA: Let me lick on it once.

AMADEUS: Shush up; there's something more out there behind the dark. Just wait till it gets light.

AUGUST [*striking a match*]: Here's a light for you; we can take care of that.

[*To* LIESKEN.]

Stick your face in your Sunday hat, Liesken, Frederick's got his dangler hanging out again.

[DANGLING FREDERICK *mutters frightfully.*]

LIESKEN: I'm so scared, August. Let's go home to Mother.

LONG ANNA: Fraidy cat!

AMADEUS [*showing sympathy*]: You're right, it's time. Go home, the both of you. Such a little wheezer don't belong out in the street this time of night.

[*Above,* GRANDDADDY WALLBRECKER *coughs.* AUGUST *and* LIESKEN *turn into the narrow little street and enter their building.*]

I tell you, I can't stand this kind of life much longer. Dangling Frederick, what are you getting out of your life?

DANGLING FREDERICK [*muttering frightfully*]: I ain't getting nothing out of life, but it's got me to fool away the time with.

LONG ANNA [*jeering*]: What a rotten way to fool away the time.

DANGLING FREDERICK: Nothing for his fine-glazed fingers, but when it wants to play a joke on somebody, it gets me out of its bag of tricks.

[*He mutters angrily.*]

LONG ANNA [*laughing*]: The kitchen maids went running from the doors, and their hearts dropped into their britches.

[*He claps* DANGLING FREDERICK *on the shoulder and laughs in an even higher voice.*]

With you I go through this kind of show all the time.

AMADEUS: And why the police don't pick you up, Dangling Frederick?

LONG ANNA: They're laughing their own selves.

AMADEUS: What do you get out of acting dirty anyways?

LONG ANNA: And always peering out like that with the one eye in your head?

DANGLING FREDERICK: Red's what I always see, nothing but red.

[*He mutters frightfully.*]

AMADEUS: Old Mother Pius, she's got a medicine for it. She gets skulls out of the prison churchyard and rubs them to sugar.

[*All three laugh.* CARL *comes out of the house, whistling softly to himself, and sits down on the bench.* AMADEUS *continues speaking without noticing* CARL.]

Maybe she can help me, too.

[*He lays his hand with tender concern over his heart. Suddenly he notices* CARL.]

Evening. [*Sentimentally*] It's gotten cracked. It keeps clattering so inside there.

LONG ANNA [*jeering*]: He wants to consult your grandmother.

AMADEUS [*pointing to* FREDERICK]: She ought to bring him back to life, too. She knows her way around with the pennies like a specialist doctor, eh Carl?

CARL [*arrogant and rebuffing*]: Go look for work and your crazy ideas'll disappear.

DANGLING FREDERICK: I don't want to get richer.

LONG ANNA [*to* CARL]: Just don't act so stuck-up.

[CROATIAN YOUTHS *come along, crying loudly*.]

AMADEUS: What are you bawling for so late in the night? You could just as well bawl tomorrow.

CROATIAN YOUTHS: No sell nothing, nothing at all, boss beat us, hurt . . .

LONG ANNA [*to* CARL]: Pastor, take care of your congurgation.

[CARL *assumes a rebuffing dignity*.]

AMADEUS: Leave him be.

[*He reaches into his pocket. The* CROATIAN YOUTHS *exit*.]

LONG ANNA [*to* CARL]: How about it, you old skinflint, you church-changer, you pickpocket.

[*He tries to reach into* CARL'*s pockets*.]

Give us a look at the wallet you got from somewheres else.

[CARL *makes no reply but gives* LONG ANNA'*s arm a violent twist. He cries out with frightful shrillness.* AMADEUS *collapses.* DANGLING FREDERICK *takes a small whistle out of his pocket and blows it. He then goes off with a fixed stare, not waiting for results, and lies down on the riverbank opposite the building in which the Puderbachs live. At this point,* TWO ACCOMPLICES *approach from nearby. They believe, since* LONG ANNA'*s screeching and wailing make it impossible to understand him, that it is because of* AMADEUS *that they have been summoned, and they start to swear.* MOTHER PIUS *comes out of the house.*]

FIRST ACCOMPLICE [*pointing to* AMADEUS]: On account of this crazy boob?

SECOND ACCOMPLICE: It's the stinky one that's whistling for us.

[MOTHER PIUS *and* CARL *take* AMADEUS *into their house.*]

LONG ANNA [*pointing at* CARL, *to no avail*]: He's a murderer!

[*The* TWO ACCOMPLICES *finally understand what is going on. They threaten, show off their knives, and become very loud.* GRANDDADDY WALLBRECKER, *startled, comes to the upstairs window.*]

GRANDDADDY WALLBRECKER: Go to the devil, you drunken night owls!

TWO ACCOMPLICES: John's son's a murderer. Just let him show hisself again.

GRANDDADDY WALLBRECKER [*screeching*]: Amanda, call Carl to me.

[*He leaves the window, his bed is heard creaking, and he screeches sleepily.*]

I want my pipe [*imitating* LIESKEN] with the deer's head on it!

[*The men move off, threatening,* LONG ANNA *along with them.* GRANDDADDY WALLBRECKER, *softly.*]

Come tingalingaling . . .

[*The full moon shines, dazzling, in the sky. One of the attic windows in the Puderbachs' tenement opens softly. Little* LIESKEN, *with closed eyes and in her nightgown, comes out onto the roof without making a sound, takes a few steps toward the river where* DANGLING FREDERICK *is lying, and climbs back in through the window. While this is taking place,* DANGLING FREDERICK *slowly gets up on all fours and stares, glassy-eyed, at the roof. Meanwhile, some* SOCIAL DEMOCRATS, *passing by up in the woods, are singing a Social Democrat song in four-part harmony. The last words can be heard: "For our banner is red."*]

ACT 2

[*A blooming, well-cared-for garden with beds and rosebushes, and behind them a fountain on a small artificial elevation; in the background, mostly hidden from view, a summer house with windows of colored glass in various colors. To the right a vine-covered stairway leading into the old Sonntag mansion. In the left foreground a pavilion, with table, bench, and chairs under an awning. Between the garden fence and the neighboring wall runs a narrow lane leading into town. On the wall is a metal sign with the usual warning, but it is old and battered and its inscription is long since illegible.*]

MOTHER PIUS: Let me see him in with your folks. It's such a joy to an old grandmother's heart.

BERTHA [*condescending and affected*]: Our Mrs. Sonntag is ever so kind to him, and even Mr. Edward is respectful.

MOTHER PIUS: Just like you say—but ain't he worth it? Your young mister comes at five o'clock in the morning and drags him out of the nest and asks him all kinds of things for the exam.

BERTHA [*snippy*]: Carl's that smart?

MOTHER PIUS [*with superiority*]: When he's my grandson? [BERTHA *gives a cheeky laugh. She makes as though to leave* MOTHER PIUS, *setting the tray with the supper dishes on the bench, absentmindedly keeping the napkins under her arm.*]

Are you in such a hurry, Bertha? You usually like to tell me things, don't you?

BERTHA: I haven't got time.

MOTHER PIUS: Have you got your head full of your sweetheart, is that it?

BERTHA: Who says I've got a sweetheart?

[*She picks herself a camellia from the bed and in doing so drops two napkins.*]

MOTHER PIUS: Who says so? Just guess—the cards.

[BERTHA, *curious, places her arms akimbo.* MOTHER PIUS *picks up the two dropped napkins and complacently reads the names on the napkin rings. To herself*]

Like a babe in the woods.

BERTHA [*coaxing*]: Well, what do the cards all say then, Mother Pius?

MOTHER PIUS [*keeping* BERTHA *in suspense*]: Would you really like to know, Bertiekins?

[BERTHA *nods affectedly.*]

Your sweetheart's going to be untrue to you, but you're going to make a long journey over the ocean and you're going to meet a rich millionaire.

BERTHA [*astonished*]: Great balls of fire! Our Miss Martha dreamed about me on a ship two nights in a row.

MOTHER PIUS: You see!

BERTHA: But you told Augusta on Sunday that my sweetheart was a big strong man with a mustache.

MOTHER PIUS: I said that? Let me think a minute . . .

BERTHA [*affected*]: But he's short and has a blond goatee.

MOTHER PIUS [*fortune-telling, with humor*]: And he's of noble birth.

BERTHA [*amazed*]: Great balls of fire!

MOTHER PIUS: The dumb female, she got sore that the king of hearts wasn't next to her and she has to wait twenty years for one. And so she told you the wrong thing, out of envy. Nah, Bertiekins, how can you be so stupid!

BERTHA: I'll fix her for that!

MOTHER PIUS: Leave her be, Bertiekins, she's a poor critter with her wall eye and her crooked shoulder. Leave her be, Bertiekins.

AUGUSTA [*standing in the side door leading from the kitchen into the garden and speaking to* BERTHA]: Where are you anyways?

[*Catching sight of* MOTHER PIUS, *she hurries over to her.*]

MOTHER PIUS [*to* BERTHA]: I heard the missis calling, too.

[BERTHA *flounces into the house.* MOTHER PIUS *goes spryly to the summer house and bends over to be able to see through the cracks better. To* AUGUSTA]

I only saw him through the cracks. Now I've got to hurry; Liesken Puderbach's got the chicken pox.

AUGUSTA [*goggle-eyed, credulous*]: All the things you understand!

[MOTHER PIUS *takes her basket on her arm and offers* AUGUSTA *her hand.*]

Have you already spoken with our missis then?

MOTHER PIUS [*indicating the basket*]: That you can see from the dirty lace.

AUGUSTA [*goggle-eyed, credulous*]: All the things you understand!

MOTHER PIUS: A person's got to understand everything, the finest and the roughest.

[AUGUSTA *shakes her head in admiration.* MOTHER PIUS *turns around once more toward* AUGUSTA *with a deprecating manner and a devilish laugh.*]

Have you found a dandy boyfriend anyways, regardless of the cards?

AUGUSTA: Naw, it's too bad. Your cards are real devils, Mother Pius.

MOTHER PIUS: Then just come see me again sometime; maybe we'll get the upper hand over the magic, Augusta.

AUGUSTA: If I could make so bold.

[*Coughing is heard from the summer house.* AUGUSTA *and* MOTHER PIUS *turn toward it and listen, startled.*]

That's not Mr. Edward, that's Miss Martha. She spends too much time looking out the window at night.

MOTHER PIUS [*her interest aroused*]: Your young lady would do better to sleep.

AUGUSTA: She'd like to have you read the cards for her, too.

MOTHER PIUS [*cheerily*]: A countess has been to see me.

AUGUSTA [*gazing at her in admiration*]: If you won't tell, I'll show you a newfangled picture of Martha—stark naked like the first woman under the tree.

[MRS. SONNTAG *and* HENRY *emerge from the house unnoticed.*]

MOTHER PIUS: What, do you take Mother Pius for stupid?

AUGUSTA: Her friend, the mayor's daughter, she took her picture like that.

MOTHER PIUS: Go get it quick!

[AUGUSTA *hurries off through the side door;* MOTHER PIUS *calls after her.*]

I'll lay the cards out for you real fine, Augusta . . .

[MOTHER PIUS *notices the two approaching.* HENRY *goes up to the fence, receives the evening newspaper from a woman, and presses a coin perfunctorily into her hand, while* MRS. SONNTAG *proceeds toward the pavilion.*]

MOTHER PIUS [*not fazed by the situation*]: Excuse me, Mrs. Sonntag, ma'am, for still being here; I wanted to say adoo to my grandson.

[MRS. SONNTAG *nods in friendly condescension and proceeds to the right, looking at the roses.* MOTHER PIUS *comes up to* HENRY *and claps him familiarly on the shoulder.*]

HENRY: Damn it all, Mrs. Pius, how are you folks doing in these bad times?

MOTHER PIUS: You don't know anything about hard times, Mr. Henry.

HENRY: And you keep getting younger.

[BERTHA *comes out of the house to set the table.*]

MOTHER PIUS: You flatterer!

HENRY [*cynical, good-natured*]: Mrs. Pius, what do you think about us two?

[BERTHA *titters.*]

Just let the busybody laugh. She doesn't know anything about love.

[MRS. SONNTAG *strolls toward the pavilion.*]

MOTHER PIUS: Such a rich young gentleman and me?

HENRY: Damn it all, I'm serious, so help me God. I've got to have a smart wife.

MRS. SONNTAG: Mrs. Pius, don't let yourself be taken in by my son.

MOTHER PIUS: I like to make fun with him, Mrs. Sonntag, ma'am. Let him enjoy hisself.

HENRY: If you make a joke of everything, dear Mrs. Pius, we'll suit each other down to the last hair.

MOTHER PIUS [*not knowing how she should take it*]: Mr. Henry's got to marry a rich young lady. The grandma [*pointing to* MRS. SONNTAG] wants to rock babykins in her arms again.

[*She makes a rocking motion with her arms.*]

MRS. SONNTAG: Now leave Mrs. Pius in peace, Henry.

MOTHER PIUS: But you can come visit me in my booth at the fair on St. John's Day with your friends. This time I'm serving up [*giving* HENRY *a cynical nod on the sly*] an extra fine delicacy.

BERTHA [*aside to* MRS. SONNTAG *and* HENRY]: A two-headed child . . .

MOTHER PIUS [*finally noticing* AUGUSTA, *who has been waving at her vainly from the side door for some time*]: Evening, everybody, I got to be off to my folks!

[MRS. SONNTAG *sits down on the bench at the table, and* HENRY *remains standing beside her.*]

HENRY: The old gal's one of a kind!

[MOTHER PIUS *snatches the picture away from* AUGUSTA—*it is about four by six inches—and leaves by the gate in the fence.* AUGUSTA *remains standing, nonplussed.*]

MRS. SONNTAG: You're always teasing her, Henry.

AUGUSTA: Like teasing the wind.

[*She goes into the house.*]

HENRY: Fun's got to be, Mama Charlottakins.

MRS. SONNTAG: Does that give you so much fun?

HENRY: You say that so sadly.

MRS. SONNTAG: Oh, I wouldn't say that.

HENRY [*after a short pause*]: This year we're going to make a profit, Mama Charlottakins.

MRS. SONNTAG [*livelier*]: Are you deceiving me, Henry?

HENRY: By my rusty old saber.

MRS. SONNTAG: What a boy you are!

HENRY: Let's drink a nice little bottle to it, Mama Charlottakins!

[MRS. SONNTAG *shakes her head, laughing*.]

Too bad Pius's grandmother is gone. Are they still sitting in there?

[*He points to the summer house*.]

MRS. SONNTAG: One mustn't be too friendly with these people.

HENRY: At noontime she promenades past my office till I come out.

MRS. SONNTAG: Why?

HENRY: She loves me . . .

MRS. SONNTAG: Don't prattle nonsense, Henry.

[*He laughs*.]

Leave the poor old thing in peace; I don't want you teasing her, for Edward's sake. You know how he likes Pius.

HENRY: Pius knows the old bat down to a tee.

[BERTHA *brings out dishes with a cold supper*.]

MRS. SONNTAG: *Taisez donc!*

HENRY: But I'm not saying anything.

[*He goes toward the summer house;* MARTHA *is just coming out. They collide*.]

MARTHA: Did you ever give me a scare!

HENRY [*teasing*]: You can't scare an innocent person: Confess!

MARTHA: Jackass!

HENRY [*all at once speaking softly, with irritation that increases to a sudden outburst of anger*]: I want to tell you something. If I find out once more that you've been in my office while I wasn't there, you're going to get a couple of slaps in the face from me.

MARTHA [*a bit taken aback*]: But I didn't do anything there.

HENRY: You know Simon is my employee. I want him to respect us, do you understand!

[*Cheerful again.*]

Damn it all!

MARTHA: Mr. von Simon is always polite to me.

[EDWARD *and* CARL *come into the pavilion.*]

HENRY: I should hope so. [*Offering* CARL *his hand*] And I've honestly forgotten the stamps again.

EDWARD [*to* CARL, *putting his arm around* HENRY]: He sweats the whole day through for us, Carl. He's the most selfless person in the world.

[HENRY *pretends to be embarrassed, like a teenaged girl, which looks funny because of his husky build.*]

MARTHA [*going up to the table in the pavilion*]: Mama, my eyes are aching terribly [*opening them wide with affected gracefulness*] from looking up words.

MRS. SONNTAG: I've been admiring your perseverance for a long time.

[CARL *goes awkwardly to* MRS. SONNTAG *and bows deeply to her. She offers him her hand.*]

MARTHA: Mr. Pius wants to go home before supper, Mama.
MRS. SONNTAG: But why, Mr. Pius?
CARL: If I might take the liberty?

[MARTHA *offers him the chair next to her.* HENRY *sits down to her left.* EDWARD *sits by his mother on the bench.* BERTHA *serves the tea and waits on table.*]

MARTHA: Don't you think horn-rimmed glasses are dreadful on Mr. Pius, Mama? He looks like a country schoolteacher.
MRS. SONNTAG: Martha, don't prattle so much nonsense.

[CARL *is embarrassed.*]

I hadn't even noticed that Mr. Pius wears glasses.
CARL: Since just recently.
EDWARD: Please take them off once.

[CARL *hesitates.*]

I'm shortsighted too.
MRS. SONNTAG: Your fawn's eyes . . .
HENRY [*comically, imitating a teenager*]: I don't like this anymore; no one's paying any attention to me.

[BERTHA *titters softly;* MRS. SONNTAG *gives her a reproving glance.*]

You're thinking about Mother Pius, Bertha, eh? You've got some grandmother, Pius, marvelous!

[CARL *is embarrassed.*]

And I also believe she's a very clever woman?
EDWARD [*to* CARL]: With a delicious sense of humor.
MARTHA: Edward says she understands Latin.

MRS. SONNTAG: What day is your examination, Mr. Pius?

CARL: On Wednesday, a few days after St. John's Day, Madame Sonntag.

EDWARD: You're more stirred up about it than both of us and the senior class combined.

MRS. SONNTAG: My son tells me that you're concerned about your studies?

[CARL *is at a loss for an answer.*]

EDWARD: You were going to use your influence for his future career, weren't you, Mother?

MRS. SONNTAG [*nods kindly at* EDWARD, *then suddenly gazes at* HENRY, *who is reading the newspaper with interest*]: What interests you in the paper [*reproving*] while we're at the table?

HENRY: I beg your kind pardon, Mama Charlottakins.

MARTHA: Are you keeping your promise, Henry?

HENRY: My horse has to be the one that takes a fall.

MARTHA: You're always trying to put something over on me.

HENRY [*teasing*]: On the contrary, you've got to help carry the loss!

MARTHA: Jackass!

HENRY: Thanks!

MRS. SONNTAG [*to* HENRY]: You can't leave gambling alone after all.

HENRY: It is, as Mr. Schiller says, my way of taking a walk.

EDWARD: He does spend too much time in the office.

MARTHA: And you're fat, like the man who runs the shooting gallery over there.

CARL: Why don't you go riding, Mr. Sonntag?

MRS. SONNTAG: You do really have time on Sundays.

HENRY: The stallion shies when I mount without my uniform, children.

CARL: Walking tours would be good for you, too.

EDWARD: In the Tirolean Alps, eh Carl?

CARL: Up Schneerössl.

EDWARD: You should climb ten kilometers a day. It's true, it would do him good.

HENRY: I'm going to weigh myself in the shooting gallery right now. I think I've already taken off weight from your good advice.

[TWO LITTLE GIRLS, *daughters of the shooting gallery proprietor, stand unnoticed at the garden fence*.]

MRS. SONNTAG: You can't get a serious word out of him.

EDWARD: Just pack his suitcase, Mother.

[*The* TWO LITTLE GIRLS *disappear, unseen*.]

HENRY: Who's going to look out for the little ones, meanwhile?

MRS. SONNTAG: You do have an assistant. Martha was just praising him yesterday.

HENRY: She'd do better to concern herself with housekeeping.

MARTHA: Jackass!

HENRY: Thanks! Be glad you don't have a sister, Pius.

CARL [*somewhat shy, blushing unexpectedly*]: And I envy you for it.

MRS. SONNTAG [*smiling*]: Do you hear that, Henry?

[HENRY *claps* MARTHA *tenderly on the back. Pause*.]

And I'd go to the factory often.

HENRY [*teasing*]: Do you know where it is, as a matter of fact, Mama Charlottakins?

MRS. SONNTAG [*joking*]: How bad he makes me out to be!

MARTHA: Mr. von Simon is more energetic with the workers than you are.

HENRY: When I'm there.

[*Everyone laughs*. MARTHA *pouts*.]

On his account I had to fire my best worker, Willem.

MARTHA: He forced his way into the office, drunk, and wanted to kill Mr. von Simon.

HENRY: Yes, and I still don't know the whole story.

MRS. SONNTAG: As long as nothing happens to you, Henry.

EDWARD: They all like Henry. Workers have often said so to you, haven't they, Carl?

CARL: I hardly know all those people to speak to.

[MRS. SONNTAG *looks him over with distrust.*]

MRS. SONNTAG [*amused*]: Do you really want to become a *Protestant* minister, Mr. Pius?

CARL: Yes, Madame Sonntag.

MRS. SONNTAG: And your grandmother approves of it?

CARL: I'm in the habit of settling such serious questions by myself.

MRS. SONNTAG [*unconsciously adopting a condescending tone*]: Do you expect to make your way faster?

CARL [*like an upperclassman reciting*]: I came into conflict with the dogmas of the Catholic Church.

[MRS. SONNTAG *nods to* EDWARD *in agreement.*]

EDWARD: Oh, Mother, he wants to marry.

HENRY: I'm going over and bowl a few.

MARTHA: The little urchins were already standing at the fence before noon this morning. They have pigs' knuckles and sauerkraut today, their father said to tell the lieutenant.

HENRY [*to* CARL]: He was one of my men.

MRS. SONNTAG: They're the proprietor's children, then?

HENRY: I sometimes buy the little doll babies chocolate.

[*He stands and makes a long yawning motion with mouth and arms.*]

MARTHA [*jumping from her chair and speaking to* CARL]: Do you want to see the pillow I'm giving Edward for a graduation present?

CARL: Please show it to me.

[CARL *gets up, happy.*]

MRS. SONNTAG: But Martha, how childish. How can your fancywork interest Mr. Pius?

CARL: I used to like to do fancywork myself when I was a boy.

[MRS. SONNTAG'*s face shows disbelief.*]

EDWARD: It's a fact, Mother! Mother Pius showed me a big cross that he embroidered.

HENRY [*striding toward the house, his hands in his pockets, turning around as he goes*]: Adoo, everybody!

[MARTHA *and* CARL *stroll around one of the beds.*]

MARTHA: I embroidered a bouquet of camellias on it, copied from real ones.

CARL: You're a camellia yourself. [*Softly*] One would always like to ask you . . . And it's much more fitting for you to play with colored silk yarns than to help us two candidates study for our exams.

[*The last words fade away as they turn into the side path.*]

EDWARD: Mother, why aren't you friendlier to Pius?

MRS. SONNTAG: But my dear child, I take the greatest pains.

[*She places a coverlet around his feet.*]

EDWARD [*joking*]: When I'm up in heaven, will you come up evenings and close the star-window, dear little Mother?

MRS. SONNTAG: How you talk . . .

EDWARD: Oh, I still have a lot, a lot to take care of.

[*Smiling, he puts his arm around her shoulders.*]

MRS. SONNTAG: You should think more of yourself, all the hours of tutoring you've taken on for Pius! I'd rather give him the money.

EDWARD: That would embarrass him. I really enjoy it. Pius is too healthy to be patient.

[*Short pause.*]

He has powerful waves, Mother, that crash into one another.

MRS. SONNTAG: You're sorry for his pupils, I know you, Edward.

EDWARD [*smiling*]: Only superior justice is at work here.

MRS. SONNTAG: You see him poetically, Edward.

EDWARD [*joking*]: How could one who preaches heaven not be a poet?

[*Short pause.*]

What bothers you is that he's tedious and awkward.

MRS. SONNTAG: But I'm not requiring any man-of-the-world finesse of him.

EDWARD: Even the simple people around him respect his force of mind.

MRS. SONNTAG: His force of mind—child, child, these people respect only fists.

EDWARD: Think of Peter, James . . .

[MARTHA *and* CARL *come into view.*]

MRS. SONNTAG: You have no idea how distasteful it is to me to see him with Martha.

[EDWARD *raises himself up, distressed. He coughs lightly.*]

Do you want to go to bed, Edward?

EDWARD [*after a brief pause*]: Let us wander through the garden once again, Mother, withdrawn from the world, as though through a fragrant psalm.

MRS. SONNTAG: You make my heart heavy . . .

EDWARD: I don't want that. Your heart is a part of my heaven, and so I'll always be with you, Mother.

[MRS. SONNTAG *and* EDWARD *turn to stroll around the rosebushes.* CARL *and* MARTHA *come into the foreground and sit down on a bench before the fountain.*]

CARL [*shaking his head energetically; stern*]: I respect his faith.

MARTHA: But Mama cries all the time. He's determined to enter the strictest order. He'll go barefoot then, and his pretty curls will be cut off.

CARL [*envious*]: Is that the most painful part of it for you?

[*Pause.*]

But you were telling me, the doctors say it won't ever get that far.

MARTHA: You can't believe them anyway—and they haven't told Mama. His death would kill her.

CARL [*sarcastic*]: So according to that, your mother's death is certain.

MARTHA: Please don't make fun of it.

CARL: I'm in no mood to make fun of it.

MARTHA [*inquisitive*]: Has he actually become Catholic yet?

CARL: Ask *him.*

MARTHA: You're fresh!

CARL [*theatrically, like an upperclassman declaiming*]: And this is why I shall rid the world of the maternal bosom.

[MARTHA *makes a gesture of not understanding.*]

This is why I shall become a Protestant preacher.

MARTHA: I believe you'll shout insults dreadfully from the pulpit.

CARL [*sarcastic, joking*]: Bring down a rain of fire and brimstone on all the sinners.

MARTHA: But you once argued with Edward that there is no sin.

CARL: In the sense of Nature, there isn't any.

MARTHA: Then why do you want to punish it?

CARL: Because I can't enjoy it.

[*He turns abruptly toward* MARTHA.]

MARTHA [*startled*]: And to write such pious poems . . .

CARL: Were you able to translate them?

MARTHA: It was hard work; I looked up every word.

CARL: Later I'll send you a bunch of camellias every day. Give me one from your belt, please.

MARTHA: To remember me by.

CARL: They suit you, as the weapon suits the Amazon.

MARTHA: And they're just as dangerous.

CARL: Why don't you play "He loves me, he loves me not"?

[MRS. SONNTAG *and* EDWARD *are seen strolling through a tree-lined path toward the house.*]

MARTHA: I gave that up long ago.

CARL: You're sure of yourself.

[*He tries to kiss her hand.*]

You're playing with me, Martha.

MARTHA: If you touch my hand again, I'll hit you.

CARL: Go ahead.

[*Laughing in spite of herself,* MARTHA *picks a sprig from the bush and touches* CARL*'s hand with it.*]

MARTHA: Well, defend yourself!
CARL: How should I defend myself against a society girl?
MARTHA: You're a coward.
CARL: That's right.
MARTHA: Coward!
CARL: You're provoking me.

[MARTHA *laughs mischievously.* CARL *touches her hand lightly with his pencil.* MARTHA *laughs at him.* CARL *strikes out at her.*]

Forgive me—oh!

[CARL *tries to kiss her hand.*]

MARTHA: That was mean.

[*She hits back harder.*]

CARL [*parrying*]: Oh!
MARTHA: That was mean, here!
CARL: I'll burst out crying like a baby.
MARTHA: Ugh!
CARL: You're heartless.
MARTHA: And you're not, I suppose?
CARL: I couldn't help it.
MARTHA [*frivolous, childish, flirting*]: And if I give them all to you?

[*She reaches into her belt for the bouquet of camellias.*]

CARL: You'd be laying them on a grave now.

[HENRY *comes back through the garden gate and approaches.*]

MARTHA [*startled, to* HENRY]: Like a thief.
HENRY: With these feet [*pointing to them*] you'd have to be deaf.

[*He yawns aloud, starting on a higher tone and descending in pitch.*]

Pius, do you know a character named Amadeus?

[CARL *is still lost in thought.*]

He knows you.
CARL: Amadeus with the glass heart.
MARTHA: What are you doing back so soon?
HENRY: I'm tired.
MARTHA [*to* CARL]: Augusta knows his grandfather. He was a glass worker, and Amadeus interprets dreams.
HENRY: He just told me my fortune—that I'm going to die.
CARL [*ironically*]: The clarification of muddy waters.
HENRY: Nah . . . [*cynical, good-natured*] I dreamed of rotten eggshells. And for ten cents he had no intention of letting me live, either.
CARL: He's true to type.
HENRY: You've got to grant him that.
MARTHA: They say it's often just that kind of person whose predictions come true. Only don't tell Mama.

[HENRY *closes and latches the garden gate, then goes into the house, humming between his teeth.*]

I think he *is* a little afraid.
CARL [*laughing aloud*]: He's already forgotten all about it.

[*The cats yowl.*]

MARTHA: Like little children!

[CARL *says nothing.*]

White angora cats are heavenly.

[BERTHA *and* AUGUSTA *slip around the house, carrying letters, and climb over the fence.*]

CARL: Did you see your servants?
MARTHA: Well, they're human beings too.
CARL: Therefore they must obey.
MARTHA: Edward always says they're poor white slaves.
CARL: Edward is an idealist.

[*The cats yowl again.*]

MARTHA: That was the hoary old female.
CARL: I feel an uncontrollable excitement beginning again . . . [MARTHA *laughs mischievously, flirting*] Forget about the beasts!
MARTHA: Like drunken creatures . . .

[*They yowl again.*]

CARL: They lick too much on the sweet, bright flower cups.
MARTHA: There's always pollen on my blanket in the morning.
CARL: I can't sleep.
MARTHA: Because of the exam?
CARL: I have a harder one to pass each day.
MARTHA: My mama . . .

[*The two look up tensely at the upper window of the mansion.* CARL*'s arms sink heavily down.* MARTHA *breathes a loud sigh of relief.* MRS. SONNTAG *has disappeared from the window. Murmuring is heard outside the garden.*]

CARL: Martha!

[*He grabs* MARTHA *to him, but she pulls herself out of his arms and rushes into the house.* CARL *remains alone.* AMADEUS, DANGLING FREDERICK, *and* LONG ANNA *stop at the beginning of the lane.*]

LONG ANNA: You good-for-nothing. Two hours we scrunched ourselves in the corners by the doors while you was propheseeing, and now you give us such a crummy handout?

DANGLING FREDERICK: And you won't get me to go along and scare people no more, neether.

AMADEUS: I didn't ask you to go with me. And you, Frederick, you drive away the customers with your open trews.

LONG ANNA [*making up to* AMADEUS]: But I always went with you, and now you talk like that. [*Nudging him confidentially with his shoulder*] I guess it ain't jingled for a long time in your delicate heart?

AMADEUS: Oh there you are, but you got to leave me half a dollar.

[LONG ANNA *turns around and places himself before the wall.*]

Can't you see?

[*Points to the sign.*]

LONG ANNA: I got a free pass everywhere.

[BERTHA *and* AUGUSTA *return and try to jump quickly over the fence. They see the men and cry out.*]

AMADEUS: Now just don't holler so wild, you gentlemen's whorewomen.

LONG ANNA [*in a very high voice*]: Shall we?

BERTHA: Mr. Pius!

AUGUSTA: Help us!

[CARL *pays no attention to their cries for help.*]

One of them's grabbing me by the leg!

[BERTHA *and* AUGUSTA *cry out, one after the other. They finally get over the fence and run to* CARL.]

BERTHA: Did you see the three of them?
AUGUSTA: I can't anymore, I can't anymore, nah, I can't anymore.

[AMADEUS *laughs*.]

Did the mistress call for me, Mr. Carl?
CARL: I can't give you any information about that.

[DANGLING FREDERICK *mutters frightfully.* LONG ANNA *plays "O, du lieber Augustin, everything's gone, gone, gone . . ." on his concertina. They move along the lane toward town.*]

BERTHA: So stuck-up. Who do you think you are, Mr. Edward himself?
AUGUSTA [*good-natured*]: Leave him be, Bertha, it's his friend, eh Mr. Carl?
BERTHA [*suddenly speaking without affectation*]: Get yourself on home. Your grandma wants to sing her little grandson to sleep.
AUGUSTA: Quiet, Bertha, he's got some reason why he's sitting here.
BERTHA: But of course; the pink nightlight's already burning in Miss Martha's room.

[BERTHA *and* AUGUSTA *slip into the house through the cellar entrance. The cats yowl once again. In the distance are still heard the sounds of* LONG ANNA *playing "Everything's gone, gone, gone . . ."*]

ACT 3

[*Eight-thirty in the evening. The fair, crowded with* TOWNSPEOPLE, FACTORY WORKERS, CLERKS, SHOP GIRLS, SERVING MAIDS, *and* STREET URCHINS. *A carousel in left foreground. Behind the carousel and beside it on the right, the various booths. In the foreground stands the booth of* ROSA THE FAT LADY. *Next to it the shooting gallery booth, then the deep-sea diver booth, the honeycake booth, and so on. Opposite on the left, a little distance away, the diagonally placed booth of* MOTHER PIUS, *only a quarter of which can be seen. A painting of a mummified child with two heads is printed grotesquely on the blind. The carousel has a double circle of grotesque wooden animals: leopard with lamb, deer with tiger, lion with horse, stag with giant goose, etc. In carousel coaches that go up and down sit noisy* LOWER-CLASS WOMEN, *and by the iron pillars that hold up the roof of the carousel stand* WORKERS *and* SCHOOLBOYS, *competing for the ring, which hangs on a post not far from the carousel and is good for a free ride. The carousel is still turning slowly to the almost run-down tune "O, du lieber Augustin." The final tones: "Everything's gone, gone, gone, everything's gone . . ." Before the carousel stand* HENRY SONNTAG *and* LIESKEN PUDERBACH. *Each wears a blue pince-nez and holds a rubber ball in one hand.* HENRY *is somewhat tipsy. Around* LIESKEN'S *neck hangs a large gingerbread heart with the words "I love you." The two can be heard laughing amidst the tones of the carousel.*]

LIESKEN: For the life of me, I love to ride the merry-go-round!

[*She claps her hands.*]

I'll sit on the leopard and you on the lamb.

HENRY: That we'll do, little doll.

LIESKEN: If it would just finally hold still, Mr. Henry!

HENRY: You don't always have to say "mister" to me.

LIESKEN: What should I call you then?

HENRY: What you call your sweetheart, little doll.

LIESKEN: Him I call Mr. Edward; he's my royal sweetheart.

[HENRY *pretends amazement; he does not suspect the connection.*]

He's no one *you* know [*involuntarily scornful*].

HENRY: Is he just as handsome as I am?

LIESKEN: Carl Pius's friend, that's who he is.

HENRY: But a mustache this long [*twirls his mustache*] he surely doesn't have?

LIESKEN: Mr. Edward always shines out from his face.

HENRY [*somewhat cautiously; he knows now of whom she is speaking*]: I'd like to meet someone like that.

LIESKEN: Oh, but he wouldn't come here.

[*The carousel stops and the people jump off. Among others,* COARSE MEN AND WOMEN *get on, wild and shouting.* HENRY *jumps up with* LIESKEN *at a single bound.* MOTHER PIUS *stands suddenly before the carousel.* LIESKEN *is seating herself on the leopard, and* HENRY *already sits on the lamb.*]

MOTHER PIUS [*to* LIESKEN]: That I like to see, with such a nice gentleman, my little sweetie-heart.

LOWER-CLASS WOMAN [*to* LIESKEN]: Let me just take a bite of the sugar heart.

LIESKEN [*to* HENRY]: Naw, August's going to get it. He gawps his eyes out and he's too ashamed to go into the candy stores.

[*Short pause.*]

I can't wait till it starts!

[WORKERS *stamp their feet impatiently.* HENRY'S BUSINESS FRIEND, *wearing a gray top hat, comes up to the carousel with* TWO GIRLFRIENDS, *one on each arm.*]

BUSINESS FRIEND [*to* HENRY]: Well you old sinner!

[*The carousel moves.*]

HENRY: There's still time! Jump on!

[*They jump on.*]

STREET URCHIN: Take me along too, mister!

[*The music plays "O, du lieber Augustin" again.*]

MOTHER PIUS [*cynical; to them all*]: I wish you a pleasant honeymoon!

[*She hurries back to her booth. Other* GENTLEMEN IN GRAY TOP HATS—*acquaintances of* HENRY'S—*come along with numerous* GIRLFRIENDS *and jump onto the carousel as it gets under way.* WORKERS *push the* GIRLFRIENDS *roughly into the inner circle, since the* WORKERS *want to grab for the ring. The carousel goes around like a whirlwind.* DR. BRUNO VON SIMON *and* BERTHA *come out of* ROSA THE FAT LADY'S *booth and go toward the carousel.*]

BERTHA: Isn't that Henry?
DR. BRUNO VON SIMON: Where?
BERTHA: Wait a minute, you can see him again.

[DR. BRUNO VON SIMON *looks a bit startled.*]

What if Mr. Edward finds out? . . .

DR. BRUNO VON SIMON: Is the fool *your* father-confessor too?

BERTHA: . . . and our mistress?

DR. BRUNO VON SIMON [*looking through his small gold lorgnette, his composure restored*]: He can't sit up straight anymore.

BERTHA: It's all the same to me. I won't be working for others much longer.

DR. BRUNO VON SIMON [*seizing the opportunity and taking a deep breath*]: You must tell me everything that's in your heart, dear little pussycat.

[*He makes as though to turn around with her.*]

BERTHA: *He* won't stay here long. He goes riding every morning now at six o'clock.

[*They go into the deep-sea diver booth. The carousel slows down.* HENRY'*s voice is heard in passing.*]

HENRY: Again, little doll?

LIESKEN: For sure, dear Mr. Henry!

LOWER-CLASS WOMAN [*from a coach*]: Come on in here with me.

LIESKEN: Go on and stand by the pillar, then you'll get the ring.

STREET URCHINS [*shouting*]: The chimpanzee's busted out, the big chimpanzee's busted out!

[*Everyone panics. All mill around together. Almost all of the riders jump off the carousel.* LIESKEN *makes as though to do the same.*]

STREET URCHIN: The big chimpanzee with the little tail's busted out, busted out!

LIESKEN: Don't you hear? The wild monkey's busted out. It bites. I'm a-scared of animals. The teacher says the big animals go for children first.

[*The diver runs out of his booth and gesticulates with his iron head and iron fists, which looks extremely funny.* HENRY *holds* LIESKEN *fast.*]

MOTHER PIUS [*coming up to the carousel*]: Stay where you are; it's nothing but a fake come-on from the circus people.

LIESKEN: And is it really not true, dear Mother Pius?

HENRY [*nods*]: No. Have you chilled that little bottle, Mother Pius?

MOTHER PIUS [*cynical, sad*]: And myself with it.

[*The people who jumped off the carousel come back toward it. Two* LOWER-CLASS WOMEN *stroll by, arm in arm.*]

FIRST WOMAN [*to* HENRY]: Why don't you take me? You're going to break that life-sized plaything you've got there.

SECOND WOMAN: Why do you think they call him "little doll" Henry?

[*The* GENTLEMEN, *including the* BUSINESS FRIEND *and his* TWO GIRLFRIENDS, *laugh gaily.*]

HENRY [*to* LIESKEN]: What they don't want from good old Henry, eh Liesken?

GIRLFRIEND [*to* BUSINESS FRIEND]: We want to go in and see the Fat Lady. [*To the other* GIRLFRIEND] Looky, Minna, she's got a beard like a fella.

[*The carousel moves again, without playing. Only a few children remain, scattered between* HENRY *and* LIESKEN.]

HENRY [*uncertain because he is so tipsy*]: Liesken, isn't it playing?

LIESKEN: It's already late in the night. Mother Pius says the police'd come otherwise.

HENRY: Then we'll see about getting off too.

[*He has* LIESKEN *climb from the leopard onto his back, jumps off the carousel with her, halloos, drops her to the ground, lifts her up again, drops her again, lifts her and drops her once more, catches her up, and bounds through the crowd with her.* MOTHER PIUS *comes toward them as far as the deep-sea diver booth. The* GENTLEMEN *have gone ahead with their* GIRLFRIENDS; *they stop at the shooting gallery and shoot.*]

MOTHER PIUS [*somewhat enviously to* HENRY *and* LIESKEN]: Like a pair of noisy children.

[*Another crowd of* WORKERS *appears.*]

LIESKEN: I'm a-scared my father'll come and fetch me.
HENRY: I'll hide you in my overcoat, little doll.
LIESKEN: He'll take away my dollar for saving in the bank.
HENRY: Then I'll give you a gold one, little doll.
LIESKEN: You're that rich?

[MOTHER PIUS, HENRY, *and* LIESKEN *walk on.*]

WOMAN WORKER [*with incredulous amazement*]: Puderbachs' little one!

[*Her mouth opens in a wide grin.*]

MOTHER PIUS: Well, and what of it! The child helps me here.

[*They turn to the left.* DR. BRUNO VON SIMON *and* BERTHA *come out of the deep-sea diver booth.*]

DR. BRUNO VON SIMON: You mustn't always say my name so loudly, little pussycat, that's not fair.
BERTHA [*offended*]: Oh, I know how to behave. [*Imitating the way* MARTHA *moves*] You want to be rid of me, don't you, Bruno?

DR. BRUNO VON SIMON [*irritated*]: Of course not. But you certainly should have told me about the crowd that would show up here. Think of the consequences if one of my workers surprises me here.

BERTHA: But our Henry always goes to the fair.

DR. BRUNO VON SIMON: *Trés bien!* And the workers know what to think of him, too.

BERTHA [*sullen*]: Then we could have stayed at your place to begin with.

DR. BRUNO VON SIMON: That we can still make up for.

[DR. BRUNO VON SIMON *tickles her surreptitiously in the side.* BERTHA *shakes her head. He pushes her slowly forward past the carousel toward the downstage exit.*]

When are we going to get married, little pussycat?

BERTHA [*conciliated*]: I thought after Christmas; that long I'm willing to stay. The mistress had Miss Martha ask me what I'd like to have.

DR. BRUNO VON SIMON: Ask for soft pillows as a present [*whispering something else in her ear*] with a dainty pink heaven up above . . .

[BERTHA *acts affectedly embarrassed.*]

And it's nothing doing beforehand?

BERTHA: I'm a respectable girl. [*Affectedly*] I wouldn't dare go home anymore.

DR. BRUNO VON SIMON: Not even for my sake?

[*He tickles her in the side again. They make a turn and disappear from view.* DYERS, *whose hands have been stained different colors by their work—* AUGUST PUDERBACH *is among them—* WEAVERS *in striped smocks, and other* WORKERS *in blue work shirts come across the fairground.* MOTHER PIUS *steps into the foreground again.*]

AUGUST [*to* MOTHER PIUS]: Where is she?

MOTHER PIUS: Liesken or my child mummy?

AUGUST: Her!

MOTHER PIUS: Look for yourself.

AUGUST: But your booth's already closed up.

MOTHER PIUS: Do you think I let it stand open till first thing in the morning?

[AUGUST *jumps onto the carousel and grinds the organ, which gives off a few last muffled tones of "O, du lieber Augustin." Then he sits on the stag and sucks at a long stick of licorice.* DR. BRUNO VON SIMON *returns alone, spying on* HENRY. A LOWER-CLASS WOMAN *approaches him.*]

LOWER-CLASS WOMAN [*to* DR. BRUNO VON SIMON]: Treat me to a round in the shooting gallery. I'd like to get me a pocket knife.

WILLEM: Listen, if you have anything to do with *that* one, I'll knock yer teeth right out of yer face.

DR. BRUNO VON SIMON [*recognizing him, afraid*]: Cool down, I'm not going to snatch her away from you.

WILLEM: You skinny little shrimp, who was it brought me down in the world if it ain't you?

[*Threatens.*]

DR. BRUNO VON SIMON [*trembling*]: Aren't you Willem?

WILLEM: That's my name.

DR. BRUNO VON SIMON: Why did the director fire you, anyway?

[*Looks at him through his lorgnette.*]

WILLEM: Just take the glass down off your nose. The main thing is I recognize you, you no-good seducer!

DR. BRUNO VON SIMON [*trembling and humble*]: Cool down, Willem!

WILLEM [*to the bystanders*]: I even said to my sister: If I ever get that one between my fingers!

AUGUST [*jumping comically off the carousel*]: I wanted to suck my licorice stick down to the end. [*To* DR. BRUNO VON SIMON, *with buffoonish spite*] His sister, you got her on your conscience. Well, she can wait a long time till I take her now, you filthy worm.

WILLEM: My sister Laura wanting to marry you? The likes of you?

[WILLEM *spits on* AUGUST. DR. BRUNO VON SIMON *tries to get away, but the* GENTLEMEN *detain him with questions*.]

AUGUST: I'm not getting married at all, and to yer kissed-out Laura for damn sure not.

[WILLEM *gives* AUGUST *a slap. The* GENTLEMEN *come downstage and drag* DR. BRUNO VON SIMON *with them*.]

DR. BRUNO VON SIMON [*to the* GENTLEMEN]: It's getting to be high time to leave. *Choquant! Choquant!* Shocking!

ONE OF THE GENTLEMEN: You don't know how to joke with these people.

DR. BRUNO VON SIMON [*scornful, affected, dusting himself off with his fingertips*]: I should hope I don't!

BUSINESS FRIEND: Did someone snitch that nice little thing away from you?

GENTLEMAN [*indicating* HENRY]: The director knows how to get along with people better.

[HENRY *staggers into the foreground, very drunk, holding* LIESKEN *by the hand. She is also very tipsy, and her cheeks and eyes are burning*.]

HENRY [*to* LIESKEN]: Do you like me, little doll?

[LIESKEN *nods and tosses her head, making her hair wild and disheveled*.]

DR. BRUNO VON SIMON: *Choquant!*

GENTLEMEN [*in a friendly manner*]: Let's take him home.

HENRY: Go home? Top hats off! Liesken, do you hear, they want to transport me home.

MOTHER PIUS [*softly and confidentially in* HENRY'*s ear*]: Just go on and get away from here. The skinny little toothpick [*indicating* DR. BRUNO VON SIMON] ain't up to no good.

HENRY: When will you be confirmed, Liesken?

LIESKEN: A bosom I got like two little heads of spring lettuce.

GENTLEMEN [*serious, urging*]: Sonntag, come along now!

DR. BRUNO VON SIMON: *Choquant!*

HENRY: What did you say?

DR. BRUNO VON SIMON [*pulling him roughly by the arm and speaking in a commanding manner*]: You will follow me without further ado!

HENRY [*in a firm tone, as though suddenly sober*]: Who's the master, I or you?

BUSINESS FRIEND [*to* DR. BRUNO VON SIMON]: Don't provoke him now!

DR. BRUNO VON SIMON [*bold, believing himself protected by the* GENTLEMEN]: In this case, I'm the master.

HENRY [*staggering, in an outburst of sudden anger*]: Soldiers, comrades, who is the lieutenant in command, he or I?

[*Clusters of* WORKERS *suddenly gather around* HENRY. DR. BRUNO VON SIMON *feels a catastrophe coming; trembling from head to toe, crestfallen, he seeks safety behind* HENRY'*s tall, broad-shouldered* BUSINESS FRIEND *and the other* GENTLEMEN.]

WORKER: He was a good lieutenant.

SECOND WORKER: He come and drunk with us to the emperor's birthday just like one private with the others.

THIRD WORKER: Let's give him a cheer.

WORKERS: Long live our good old lieutenant! Hurray! Hurray! Hurray!

WILLEM [*threatening* DR. BRUNO VON SIMON]: You no-good!

[DR. BRUNO VON SIMON *does not dare to leave the scene or even move*.]

HENRY [*roaring*]: Fall in!

[*The* WORKERS *and others from the crowd form into columns as though drilling. The* GIRLFRIENDS *look on with curiosity.* AUGUST *places himself at the head of the battalion on the left, putting on a helmet he has made out of newspaper. He takes a pounding and shoving because of his clumsiness.* HENRY *reviews his regiment, staggering, sends one to the rear, puts another at the head of the column, etc. Curses loudly now and then*.]

HENRY [*roaring*]: Straighten ranks! Damn it all!
WILLEM: First thing, the militia's got to rush the enemy.

[AUGUST *makes as though shooting, seeking out the trembling* DR. BRUNO VON SIMON.]

LIESKEN [*sassy*]: There he is!
HENRY: And the June bugs are lying in ambush.
WILLEM: And the bobbin boys'll play the music to make the stallions gallop just so.

[*All laugh uproariously, and the* WORKERS *whom* HENRY *has drilled have a good time with him, like ungainly overgrown boys playing soldiers*.]

Let's go, Lieutenant, sir, I'll be your noncom.
HENRY [*roaring*]: Regiment left, forward march!

[LIESKEN *runs along next to* HENRY, *drumming with her hands and marking the beat with her lips. The* WORKERS *drill for a few steps, from downstage toward the center of the fairground. Suddenly noticing* DR. BRUNO VON SIMON, *they make as though to throw themselves on him like mad dogs*.]

Halt! I'll cut the enemy down to size myself.

[WILLEM *slips past* DR. BRUNO VON SIMON *and binds his hands with his lorgnette chain as though before his field commander.* DR. BRUNO VON SIMON *groans in fear. The* GENTLEMEN *do not come to his aid. They are enjoying themselves, watching the proceedings with curiosity.*]

WILLEM: Don't let him kill you with his saber, Lieutenant, sir!

[*Roaring with laughter, he points at* DR. BRUNO VON SIMON'*s slender walking stick.*]

AUGUST: Here we go, boys.

[WILLEM *loosens the chain from* DR. BRUNO VON SIMON'*s hands. The* BUSINESS FRIEND *pushes through the crowd of excited* WORKERS *to* HENRY, *but in his drunken state,* HENRY *does not hear his friend's quiet words. He picks up a piece of chalk from the ground and draws a large circle below his heart.*]

HENRY: So, young fellow, you're not allowed outside that terrain. Otherwise, it's too bad for me.

[*They all laugh. Only* LIESKEN *is afraid, holding onto* MOTHER PIUS.]

LIESKEN [*her sensuality aroused*]: He'll kill Henry.

[DR. BRUNO VON SIMON *is bewildered.* HENRY *sways toward his friends.* DR. BRUNO VON SIMON *tries to flee, but the* WORKERS *grab him.*]

ROSA THE FAT LADY [*peering out from her booth*]: Come on in here to me, little gentleman!

[DR. BRUNO VON SIMON *breaks free for a moment. The* WORKERS *pursue him.* AUGUST *springs onto his back like a cat, but* DR. BRUNO VON SIMON *succeeds in throwing him off. They race across the fairground one after the other toward the exit.*]

HENRY: Stick him in the lookout tower, for all I care!

[*The* GENTLEMEN *support the thoroughly exhausted* HENRY *to take him away. To* LIESKEN *and* MOTHER PIUS]

Sweet dreams, Marthie! Good night, Mama Charlottakins.
BUSINESS FRIEND: If she heard that!

[*The crowd disperses, the booths close up,* MOTHER PIUS *runs back into her booth.* LIESKEN *stands all alone in the foreground, sits down once more on the leopard on the carousel, strokes it, and then jumps off.*]

ROSA THE FAT LADY [*sticking her head out of the window*]: What's his name, your charming cavalier?
LIESKEN: That's none of your business.

[HENRY, *surrounded by the* GENTLEMEN, *can still be seen on an elevation behind the fairground, on the way home.* DANGLING FREDERICK, AMADEUS, *and* LONG ANNA *drift past the carousel, crossing the fairground.*]

DANGLING FREDERICK: Let us now cleanse the garden from the sinning.

[*He murmurs malevolently.* LONG ANNA *makes as though sweeping. He wears a long, rustling paper apron, a ladies' nightcap with fluttering ribbons, and a fat nose with warts.*]

AMADEUS [*pointing to* HENRY]: There goes my death candidate.

[MOTHER PIUS *comes back from her booth. In one hand she has a basket, in the other the child mummy. Its second head, fabricated out of rags, swings down from the body.*]

MOTHER PIUS [*to* LIESKEN]: I'll be hanged if that wasn't your cantankerous old father.

[LIESKEN, *her head hanging from weariness, starts as* MOTHER PIUS *holds the mummy out toward her.* MOTHER PIUS, *cynical.*]

Hold onto your twin, will you!

[*She attaches the head back onto the body.* ROSA THE FAT LADY *grins from the window.*]

Just come along quick now, otherwise [*indicating* ROSA THE FAT LADY] Rosa'll put the touch on me again, and Mother Pius can't say no.

[*As they start quickly across the fairground,* LIESKEN *stops, suddenly embracing* MOTHER PIUS *around the hips.*]

LIESKEN: And I thank you very much for everything, dear Mother Pius.

[*They hurry on.* ROSA THE FAT LADY *lets down the green-and-yellow-striped blind of her booth. As it descends, the curtain falls.*]

ACT 4

[*In the workers' section, as in the first act. Chimneys steam and smoke in the distance on the other side of the river. The river is agitated and colored a dark red.* FACTORY WORKERS *of both sexes are on the way to work. Boys pull milk carts and children run to the bakeries to bring home breakfast. Over the bridge toward the Piuses' little house comes* EDWARD.]

EDWARD [*catching sight of* LIESKEN, *who is on her way to the bakery*]: Liesken!

LIESKEN [*running to him, overjoyed*]: Mr. Edward! Mr. Edward!

EDWARD: Where are you going so early?

[LIESKEN *is still too happy to speak. She holds* EDWARD'*s hand fast and keeps jumping up and down.*]

Are you so very happy, then, little one?

LIESKEN: For sure!

EDWARD: Look here!

[*He swings a rolled-up picture high in the air.*]

Come, we'll sit down here on the bench.

[*They sit down on the bench in front of the Piuses' house.* EDWARD *unrolls the picture.*]

LIESKEN: It's from England, huh?

[EDWARD *nods.* LIESKEN, *admiringly*]

Is that ever painted pretty!

EDWARD: Which of the doll mothers do you like the best, Liesken?

LIESKEN [*happy*]: The one in the middle. She's got eyes as big as yours.

EDWARD [*stroking her hair*]: You should hang the picture on the wall, little one.

LIESKEN: It's going to hang over our bed, and the old Lord Jesus'll fly off to our old man, with his weepy red eyes.

EDWARD: But Liesken . . .

LIESKEN: He looks at you like our father when he's preaching about the sinful world.

EDWARD: But it takes a devout painter to paint our savior as fair as he was.

LIESKEN [*somewhat bold*]: My mother says you might buy us a gold frame for the picture.

EDWARD: Did your mother say that?

LIESKEN [*realizing her boldness, crestfallen*]: Well, anyways!

EDWARD [*tender, kind*]: But you didn't go to see the little Christ child yesterday, Liesken. I'm very sad about that.

LIESKEN [*shaken*]: You mustn't be sad. I'd rather stay my whole life long in the church, lying on the stone, three hundred and sixty-five days, [*deliberating*] and all the hours and the minutes.

EDWARD [*moved*]: Our dear Mother loves you especially, Liesken.

LIESKEN: But I'm dressed so shabby.

[*Looks down at her dress.* WORKERS *greet* EDWARD *respectfully.*]

EDWARD: Our dear Mother doesn't look at that. She told me your little heart is heavenly blue, Liesken, and she wants so much for it to stay pure.

LIESKEN: A little heavenly blue heart . . . have you ever seen one like that?

[CHILDREN *call* LIESKEN.]

FIRST CHILD: Liesken!
SECOND CHILD: Liesken!

[*They run off again.*]

EDWARD: Only once. It belonged to a little tiny angel, who carried it very carefully in its hands, wrapped in a little silk cloth.
LIESKEN: But then it couldn't beat anymore, could it?
EDWARD: Of course. It beat very softly, each beat a pearl.
LIESKEN: Really?
EDWARD: And the little angel could always see it. And so must you too take good care of your little heart. Do you understand me, Liesken?
LIESKEN [*enraptured and amazed*]: Yes . . .
CHILDREN: Liesken, it's six-thirty! We're telling you again!
LIESKEN [*coming back to reality*]: I got to go now, Mr. Edward.

[GRETCHEN STOMMS *approaches the two somewhat boldly and whispers something in* LIESKEN'*s ear.*]

He's not *that* one.

[LIESKEN *turns bashful and makes as though to run off with* GRETCHEN.]

EDWARD: But you can still give me your hand before you go.
LIESKEN: My father'll thrash me if I dillydally.
GRETCHEN [*acting grown-up*]: She gets her allowance today.

[EDWARD *nods, going along with the importance of this fact.* LIESKEN *leaves him self-consciously. The two children run off, their arms around each other's waist.* GRANDDADDY WALLBRECKER *comes out, wearing old-fashioned green-embroidered slippers, the new pipe in one comer of his mouth. More* WORKERS *pass* EDWARD.]

WORKER [*pointing brutally to* EDWARD]: It won't be long now till he'll be biting the dust.

GRANDDADDY WALLBRECKER [*catching sight of him*]: Looky there, young mister, so early in the morning.

[*Not waiting for an answer, stretching up toward the dormer window.*]

Carl, get up, you lazybones, you big lout, get up! Amanda!

EDWARD [*trying to calm him down*]: Let them sleep in peace, Grandfather.

GRANDDADDY WALLBRECKER: Come tingalingaling!

[*He urges* EDWARD *to sit down on the bench again.*]

EDWARD: What do you think, Grandfather, shall I light me a pipe too?

GRANDDADDY WALLBRECKER [*striking a sulfur match on the house wall*]: You're looking poorly again, even if you do have all the comforts of life. Where the devil once gets a toehold! . . . What am I saying, the devil? Wallbrecker, you're a stupid blockhead. What kind of Satan could be inside *you?*

EDWARD [*mischievous*]: And who is it that could conquer that one, Grandfather?

GRANDDADDY WALLBRECKER: You're a saint, you're the holy Laurentius, and you got to drink coffee with us or you'll insult my daughter Amanda.

[*He gestures toward* AMANDA, *who comes out of the house with a table and places it before the bench.*]

AMANDA: Such an honor, Mr. Edward, sir!

[*She places the table before the bench and offers him her hand. To* GRANDDADDY WALLBRECKER.]

Where's that Carl?

GRANDDADDY WALLBRECKER: He's still sleeping. You call him.

[AMANDA *goes into the house.*]

Well, he wants to be a pastor now. Don't hold it against him, dear Mr. Edward.

[AMANDA *comes back with coffeepot, cups, bread and butter, and so forth. The light grows steadily brighter.* WORKERS *of both sexes, including* DYERS *with bright green, red, and yellow hands and pale faces, pass by. To some of the* WORKERS]

Good day to you all!

WORKERS: Up already too?

AMANDA: If the young mister would . . .

CARL [*interrupting her*]: I'll be right down.

AMANDA: If the young mister would give us the honor and drink a cup of coffee with us?

EDWARD [*kindly*]: I'm really thirsty, dear lady of the house.

AMANDA: I wouldn't have dreamed that the young mister might come today, or I'd have ground an extra measure of coffee.

CARL [*heard from above*]: I can't find my collar-stud anywhere.

MOTHER PIUS [*peering out of the little dormer window*]: What do I see—[*stepping back from the window again*]. Just hold still now. It ain't as though I could still pick you up in my arms and dress you.

[*All below laugh.*]

GRANDDADDY WALLBRECKER: I'm so stupid in the head.

AMANDA: Well, you're already an old man, Daddy.

[MOTHER PIUS *comes out of the house*.]

MOTHER PIUS [*to* EDWARD]: Just keep your seat and make yourself at home.

[EDWARD *coughs*.]

GRANDDADDY WALLBRECKER: There, he's letting hisself be heard from.

EDWARD [*coughing harder*]: The old devil dragon, eh Grandfather?

MOTHER PIUS: The old doctors are fooling around practicing their cures on you, but Mother Pius'll put Mr. Edward on his feet. Every morning and every evening you've got to drink a little cupful from the young wheatseed. I'll tell your servants.

EDWARD: That may very well be beneficial, Mother Pius.

GRANDDADDY WALLBRECKER: And just now when the moon's full, it ought to help the most.

MOTHER PIUS [*domineering and scornful*]: Don't meddle in my practice, Granddaddy Wallbrecker.

EDWARD [*smoothing things over*]: All medical people take that badly, Grandfather. After all, we're only laymen.

GRANDDADDY WALLBRECKER [*bursting with suppressed laughter*]: Come tingalingaling, come tingalingaling . . .

CARL [*fresh, vigorous, acting like an upperclassman, pathetic*]: I greet you, man of God, putting up with our food and drink.

EDWARD [*beaming mischievously*]: Peace unto your house, my brother.

[GRANDDADDY WALLBRECKER *speaks earnestly to* AMANDA, *the actual words not heard.* MOTHER PIUS *pours herself coffee and butters bread for* CARL. EDWARD *lays an envelope in* AMANDA'*s lap*.]

From my mother.

GRANDDADDY WALLBRECKER [*inquisitive*]: Let me see!
AMANDA [*pushing her father back roughly with her elbow*]: Nah, your mother's good as an angel.

[*A fat tear flows over her cheek.*]

GRANDDADDY WALLBRECKER [*nodding along, confirming* AMANDA*'s words as she speaks*]: Come tingalingaling, come tingalingaling, ting, ting, ting, ting!

[CARL *and* EDWARD *converse in low tones. Noise comes from the side street, from the room on the top floor in which the Puderbachs reside. A group of children gather before the house, listening.*]

MOTHER PIUS [*speaking more loudly*]: Maybe Mr. Edward will drink one more little cup?

[*The noise abates.*]

EDWARD [*nodding to* AMANDA]: It's unusually well brewed; I'd like to tell our Augusta the recipe.
MOTHER PIUS [*acting friendly to* AMANDA *for* EDWARD*'s benefit*]: It does taste good today, Amanda.
AMANDA: Daddy, run quick and get some sugar out of the bag.

[*He gets up slowly.*]

Go on and hurry it up a little!

[*The noise from the side street increases in volume again. Crying is heard and the sound of breaking china.* WORKERS *of both sexes, curious, join with the children at the entrance to the side street.*]

Go on over there, Carl; you know how to get along with that two-faced thinks-he's-a-saint. You *are* an authority, after all.

CARL [*harshly*]: Leave me alone!

[EDWARD *is embarrassed.*]

AMANDA: What kind of rough talk is that!

[*The noise abates.* GRANDDADDY WALLBRECKER *comes back, carrying the sugar in his red handkerchief as though in a bag.*]

Are you crazy, Daddy?

[CARL *and* EDWARD *laugh.*]

MOTHER PIUS: I'm not going to say another word.

GRANDDADDY WALLBRECKER: What should I do, then? I slop it all over with the spoons [*to* AMANDA] and I get it into the porridge anyways like this.

CARL [*enjoying himself*]: I'm a witness! Granddaddy blurts out the pure truth!

AMANDA: Don't believe it, Mr. Edward. [*Indicating* GRANDDADDY WALLBRECKER] He's always dreaming.

MOTHER PIUS [*magnanimous, hypocritical*]: What do you say, Wallbrecker, I take me a spoonful in my little cup?

[EDWARD *slaps* MOTHER PIUS *on the shoulder.*]

GRANDDADDY WALLBRECKER: I ain't blowed my nose in it yet today.

[*All laugh heartily. But the noise comes frightfully from the house in the side street.*]

AMANDA [*pleading*]: Either you go or I do.

CARL [*pitilessly*]: Let him give her a good thrashing once.

GRANDDADDY WALLBRECKER: You want to be a pastor, Carl—I said it right off, you got to have helpers.

[GRANDDADDY WALLBRECKER *stands up*.]

MOTHER PIUS: On account of that trashy woman over there we're letting our breakfast be ruined.

[GRANDDADDY WALLBRECKER *is on his way over to the house*.]

EDWARD: Stay here, Grandfather, Carl will restore peace and quiet.

[*But* GRANDDADDY WALLBRECKER *doesn't let himself be stopped*.]

MOTHER PIUS [*jealous*, *pointing to* GRANDDADDY WALLBRECKER]: He's doing it to rile me up.

AMANDA: Go on quick and run after Granddaddy, Carl.

CARL [*snapping*]: You go and stand by your friend!

[CARL *restrains* EDWARD, *who unobtrusively starts to get up*.]

He'll be right back, safe and sound.

[GRANDDADDY WALLBRECKER *approaches*.]

Salve Caesar! Instead of the laurel wreath, his cap on his head and Liesken's present in his trap.

[*All laugh*, *and no further noise is heard*.]

GRANDDADDY WALLBRECKER: I got them all quiet again, children. Just keep your seat, Mr. Edward.

[*He disregards the fact that* EDWARD *has remained sitting in his chair*.]

AMANDA [*gossiping*]: Just what's to become of Liesken?

EDWARD: Let me get on the road to recovery first.

MOTHER PIUS [*sly*]: Just keep your hands off.

CARL: The apple falls not far from the tree. Like older brother, like younger brother.

MOTHER PIUS [*cynical, half to herself for her own amusement*]: But Mr. Edward's no connoisseur!

EDWARD: My sister shall take the child under her wing.

MOTHER PIUS: Your miss princess sister?

EDWARD [*nodding proudly*]: Isn't she a princess, Carl?

[CARL *blushes and is embarrassed.*]

MOTHER PIUS: I like her so much; she's the living picture of her mama.

GRANDDADDY WALLBRECKER [*in a confirming tone*]: Come tingalingaling, come tingalingaling, ting, ting, ting, ting!

[*Men pass by again, the* TWO ACCOMPLICES *who came to* LONG ANNA*'s aid on the first night.*]

Get your head over heels out of here.

FIRST ACCOMPLICE [*sarcastic*]: Are you having a good breakfast?

GRANDDADDY WALLBRECKER: Carl, did you hear that?

MOTHER PIUS [*to* CARL, *fearful that he might start a fight*]: Just don't get riled up over them, Carl, they ain't worth it.

CARL [*confused*]: I didn't hear anything.

GRANDDADDY WALLBRECKER: Maybe you could spare me an evening chat some time, Mr. Edward. Twenty-five years I sat at the loom with Liesken's granddaddy, [*weepily*] and the winding sheet was still too small for the both of us.

CARL: Mother, give me my cap!

EDWARD [*kind, mischievous, to* GRANDDADDY WALLBRECKER]: We'll still smoke many a pipe together, Grandfather.

[*All laugh; only* GRANDDADDY WALLBRECKER *nods seriously.*]

GRANDDADDY WALLBRECKER: Now I'm living off the mercy of my daughter and that one [*pointing to* MOTHER PIUS].

MOTHER PIUS: You bet I *am* generous to you!

AMANDA: If he'd only leave off the smoking so much.

CARL: For working—that's what the females are there for!

[AMANDA *grabs* CARL*'s cap through the window and puts it on his head.*]

MOTHER PIUS [*laughing*]: You sassy bulldog!

GRANDDADDY WALLBRECKER [*to* CARL]: You, you're still young, but I'm an ailing old war horse. [*Coughing and talking to himself*] I proper forgot how to neigh.

[*He makes to get up and spit.*]

AMANDA [*to* GRANDDADDY WALLBRECKER]: Go hide yourself quick, don't you see?

[GRANDDADDY WALLBRECKER *quickly bends over behind the bush by the house. The* PRIEST, *returning from a walk in the woods, comes over the meadow to the left; he has a swinging gait. He pays no attention to the group in front of the house.*]

EDWARD: Why should Grandfather hide from the gentle priest?

MOTHER PIUS [*pointing to him*]: Like a little processional boat over the Protestant sea.

EDWARD: He's very unhappy about your apostasy, Carl.

CARL [*sarcastic*]: No one has ever made so much over my soul.

EDWARD: What do you say about it, Mother Pius?

MOTHER PIUS: That you'd do better to listen to our Luther again. What do you want to sail around on your own for?

EDWARD [*to* CARL]: Mothers!

AMANDA: Get up, Daddy, we got to get to the meadow.

GRANDDADDY WALLBRECKER [*sighing, to* EDWARD]: To lay out the washing.

[EDWARD *gets up, too.*]

MOTHER PIUS [*to* EDWARD]: Come on and stay a little longer with Mother Pius, Mr. Edward.

EDWARD: The examination comes tomorrow; I still have to do some mathematical calculations.

MOTHER PIUS: What all they don't want, the schoolmasters. In my day it wasn't half so bad.

CARL [*sarcastic*]: That's why you never got to be a pastor, too!

EDWARD [*offering his hand to* GRANDDADDY WALLBRECKER *and* AMANDA, *as they wait hesitantly. The two go into the house*]: We're all plow horses. Are you coming with me, Carl?

[CARL *nods.*]

MOTHER PIUS: With your slip-slops on your feet, boy?

CARL [*crestfallen*]: I really would have gone off that way. I was thinking about something. [*To* EDWARD] My boots are at the cobbler's.

MOTHER PIUS [*to* EDWARD, *as to a small boy*]: Your mama will be getting anxious—I know her.

[MOTHER PIUS *shakes her finger admonishingly at* EDWARD. CARL *accompanies him to the corner;* EDWARD *waves once more to* MOTHER PIUS, *who calls in through the window.*]

Give me my Valencia lace and my lace collars. They're in the vase on the cupboard so the pussycat can't play with them.

[GRANDDADDY WALLBRECKER *hands out the lace and points into the distance where, at the edge of the woods,* DANGLING FREDERICK, LONG ANNA, *and* AMADEUS *are walking round and round a street-light, which is still not completely out.*]

GRANDDADDY WALLBRECKER [*in a silly tone of voice*]: There go the three archangels almost out of sight, blowing out the lantern's light.

MOTHER PIUS: Are you starting to rhyme too, like Carl?

[CARL *returns;* MOTHER PIUS *to him*]

It won't be too much longer that one'll keep a-going.

GRANDDADDY WALLBRECKER [*nodding along with her words, in agreement*]: Ting, ting, ting, ting.

CARL: For him I'd give up a piece of my healthy lungs.

[*Pause.*]

MOTHER PIUS: Say, Carl, which do you like better, me or him [*looking off in the direction* EDWARD *took*]?

CARL [*laughing*]: You must be dreaming, Grandmother, that I'm the little Carl in your lap.

MOTHER PIUS: That's just the way it seems to me.

CARL: You?

GRANDDADDY WALLBRECKER: Come tingalingaling!

MOTHER PIUS: Did you think your grandmother's never been sad?

CARL: Grandmother, what is it?

[MOTHER PIUS *sits silently for a little while, her head sunk on her breast. In the distance,* DANGLING FREDERICK, LONG ANNA, *and* AMADEUS *disappear into the woods.*]

AMANDA [*calling*]: Where are you anyways, Daddy?

GRANDDADDY WALLBRECKER: I got to stay with Mother Pius a while longer; she's got wedding ideas.

MOTHER PIUS [*flaring up*]: You old sinner.

GRANDDADDY WALLBRECKER: If I'm a sinner, then we should of got married.

MOTHER PIUS: You! You spineless old buck!

CARL: Shut your traps; I've got to work.

GRANDDADDY WALLBRECKER [*getting a carpet-beater*]: Just wait; I'll make it quiet for you.

[AMANDA *pulls her father away from the window. He is still heard talking, importantly.*]

In the examination he's got to get ahead.

[CARL *takes notebook and book, inkwell, and penholder out of his briefcase and begins to leaf through the book.* MOTHER PIUS *irons the lace expertly and remains silent, deep in thought.*]

CARL [*somewhat teasingly*]: You know, I believe Granddaddy was right.

MOTHER PIUS: An old woman like me?

CARL [*teasing her*]: With your young heart!

MOTHER PIUS [*getting down to business*]: All the Piuses have had hot blood, and you too, Carl, you see, and your grandmother knows that.

[*She carefully draws* MARTHA'*s picture from her leather bag and holds it up to* CARL, *who is incredulous and taken aback.*]

Your burning flame!

[CARL *blushes deep red, trembles, grabs the picture.*]

You rascal, give it back, quick!

[CARL *puts it into his wallet. Short pause.*]

She's gawping her eyes out after you.

[*Short pause.*]

CARL: Who says so?
MOTHER PIUS: Me!
CARL: That's a lie.
MOTHER PIUS: Everybody says so in the neighborhood.
CARL: Women's gossip. [*Short pause, then beseeching, excited*] Who gave you this, Grandmother?
MOTHER PIUS: Ain't it enough that you've got it next to your skin, Carl?
CARL [*suddenly happy*]: Grandmother! [*Kissing her on the mouth*] You're a devil!
MOTHER PIUS: And all Mother Pius gets for reward is cusses.

[*Short pause.*]

You're crying!
CARL [*repressing his excitement*]: That's what you think.
MOTHER PIUS: What are you shaking for then?
CARL: I'm afraid I'll flunk the examination. [*Suddenly harsh*] You females bother me!

[*Short pause.*]

MOTHER PIUS: Carl, I got something real private to tell you. No one must hear it.
CARL: Leave me in peace.

MOTHER PIUS: Have a talk with your mother-in-law.
CARL: What?
MOTHER PIUS: When you've passed the examination.

[CARL *ponders*.]

She won't refuse you, believe Mother Pius.

[*Short pause*.]

You're gaping at me like I was making a fool of you.

[CARL *becomes tense*.]

A lusty man the likes of you, Carl—and the fine families like to strengthen their hothouse blood from time to time with the real thing.

[CARL *remains tense*.]

Don't you often read in the papers where the countesses carry on with the serving men?
CARL [*naively*]: Behind their mothers' backs?
MOTHER PIUS: The old ladies always know what's going on. [*Slyly*] Mama Sonntag knows about all the goodies and the cigarettes Martha stuffs into your coat pockets, too.
CARL [*defiant*]: Who told you that she does?!
MOTHER PIUS: I can smell it in the mist, Carl. Nah, you're still like a little rooster!

[AUGUST PUDERBACH *and other* DYERS, *with their varicolored hands, enter from the side, talking with one another as they return from the factory. They stop in front of the Piuses' house*.]

AUGUST: They're striking again.

MOTHER PIUS [*annoyed*]: And you?

WORKERS [*to one another*]: They ought to hang the troublemakers.

CARL: That's what I say, too.

AUGUST: For once we agree.

[AMANDA *comes back from around the house on the right. She has heard the last words.*]

AMANDA: You still do like Carl, August. You're even parting your hair on the side like him on Sundays.

ONE OF THE WORKERS: What are we getting out of this striking mess?

AUGUST: Three and a half dollars less a month. As far as I'm concerned, the working hours wasn't too long.

MOTHER PIUS: I'll say that for you, you *are* a hardworking boy—but what can you do at home, with your puffed-up, two-faced father?

AUGUST [*to* CARL]: The pastors, they don't strike, eh Carl? Maybe I'll put my saddle on another horse too, one of these days.

CARL: Shut your trap!

ANOTHER WORKER: What are we going to do, Mother Pius? We can't go home like this.

MOTHER PIUS: It ain't for you to be your brothers' keepers.

ONE OF THE WORKERS: What should we do against all them Social Democrats? We're all Social Democrats, but that don't mean we got to act stupid.

MOTHER PIUS: Nah, that it don't.

SAME WORKER: What do you advise us, Mother Pius?

AMANDA: Just go on back to your bosses and let them know what's going on.

ANOTHER WORKER: Nah, selling out our brothers, that we won't do.

CARL [*condescending, brutal*]: Kill your bosses, the way they do it in Russia!

SECOND WORKER: And then?

MOTHER PIUS [*laughing*]: Then you'll be the owner, August.

ONE OF THE WORKERS: We'd rather stay workers than be made the bosses over them all.

MOTHER PIUS: I'd change places with them in a minute. You stupid old sheep, wherever they lead you, you gobble up your feed!

ONE OF THE WORKERS: She's right.

ANOTHER WORKER: My boy'll drown in our sweat [*pointing at the river*] before I let him become a dyer.

ONE OF THE WORKERS: Can you lend us something, Mother Pius?

ANOTHER WORKER: Just take a peek into your bag.

MOTHER PIUS: I don't have an extra penny from one day to the next. Carl's got to have a whole pair of trews on his behind at the university, you know.

[LIESKEN, *who has returned from getting the bread, runs to* AUGUST; *he and the* WORKERS *move on in order to confer.* GRANDDADDY WALLBRECKER *comes coughing over the meadow and rests by the bridge. He carries his sack of washing on his back. From the side street trampling and cursing are heard.* WORKERS *approach* PIUS's *house*.]

MOTHER PIUS [*snatching up* CARL's *books and her lace*]: Get in the house quick, Carl; I got to stay neutral if the Old Nick hisself asked me for advice.

[GRANDDADDY WALLBRECKER *sees* LIESKEN, *who still stands in front of the Piuses' house*.]

GRANDDADDY WALLBRECKER: Liesken!

LIESKEN [*conspiratorially to* MOTHER PIUS]: Should I help again today, Mother Pius?

[*But* MOTHER PIUS *is already in the house and has not heard* LIESKEN'S *question. The workers disperse.* LIESKEN *goes toward the side street.* GRANDDADDY WALLBRECKER *calls, but* LIESKEN *apparently does not wish to hear him; he gives the whistle that has become a signal to her. Now* GRANDDADDY WALLBRECKER *stands before the house.*]

GRANDDADDY WALLBRECKER: Nah, how the child has changed! Amanda, my back is breaking!

[*He goes into the house.*]

ACT 5

Scene 1

[*A sort of garden room in the Sonntag family mansion. On the right the door leads to the hall, from which the front door is clearly visible. On the left, a wide window, which reflects the garden. Many climbing plants and flowers decorate the room. Near the window is a lavender leather sofa on which* MRS. SONNTAG *and* EDWARD *are sitting.* MRS. SONNTAG *holds an open book absentmindedly in her lap, upside down.* MARTHA *is engaged in removing the crape from* HENRY*'s picture. The family members wear black, as do the servants.*]

MARTHA: Augusta keeps hanging it around the picture.
MRS. SONNTAG: Why are you taking it off?
EDWARD [*lovingly*]: I want him to have something with more life in it, dear Mother.
MARTHA [*to* EDWARD]: How do you like this fresh green?

[EDWARD *nods in appreciation.*]

MRS. SONNTAG [*in a melancholy tone*]: I grieve that he ever lived.

[MARTHA *finishes decorating the picture and then sits down by the window and works at embroidering camellias on silk in an embroidery frame. Her movements are restless, expectant.*]

EDWARD: That you can doubt his honor even for an instant!

MARTHA: But Dr. von Simon says too, an innocent person doesn't run away from life.

EDWARD: It's not for the manager to take the liberty of judging our brother, especially not to his employer's sister.

[MRS. SONNTAG *motions to* MARTHA *to remain silent. Short pause.*]

He was a soldier; how else could he have acted in a case like this, where he could never prove his innocence?

MRS. SONNTAG: I thought he had long since forgotten that time.

EDWARD: But Mother, the soldier was in his blood, just as victory lay within Achilles.

MRS. SONNTAG: How you try to glorify him, Edward!

MARTHA: He looked dashing in his fancy braid and parade helmet.

EDWARD [*interrupting* MARTHA]: He should have stayed a soldier, Mother, even after Papa's death.

MRS. SONNTAG: You say that so reproachfully. Should I have been expected to run the factory?

EDWARD: Mother, you're upset.

MRS. SONNTAG: He had to promise Papa at the time to take over the direction.

EDWARD: I wouldn't have given him the promise if I'd been Henry.

MRS. SONNTAG: You? [*Amazed*] That I know my children so little. A substitute could certainly have been found among our relations.

MARTHA: The way you keep on talking to each other so seriously—it's already sad enough in our house.

MRS. SONNTAG [*in a melancholy tone*]: And I'm no company for you, either.

EDWARD: Soon you'll be rid of me.

MRS. SONNTAG: I hoped that you'd stay now, Edward?

MARTHA [*speaking almost simultaneously*]: Will you sometimes bring a monk home with you?

[*Mother and son smile.*]

EDWARD: How do you come to be thinking that?
MARTHA: I'd like to meet someone truly pious sometime.
MRS. SONNTAG [*sad, mocking*]: You're not pious enough for her.
EDWARD: Children and fools . . .

[*Short pause.*]

MARTHA: Mama, do you think one could wear pink to the registry office?
MRS. SONNTAG [*interrupting* MARTHA, *shaken*]: That you can find it in your heart, Edward.
EDWARD: If you loved God, Mother, you wouldn't try to shake my resolve.
MRS. SONNTAG: I don't love God.
EDWARD: Because you seek him with human feelings.
MRS. SONNTAG [*in a melancholy tone*]: I have no others.
EDWARD [*putting his arm around her*]: And yet you suffer inhumanly, little Mother.

[*Short pause.*]

I'd like, for as long as I'm with you, to take the place of Father and Henry. Why do you smile so strangely?
MRS. SONNTAG: That you can never do, child.
EDWARD: Even if I tried my very hardest?
MRS. SONNTAG: You simply wouldn't be able, thank God.
MARTHA: I once saw two monks in the Cologne cathedral. Their heads were shaved, like criminals', and later they went off barefoot through the snow.
MRS. SONNTAG [*sighing*]: You won't last a year in the Franciscan Order, Edward.
AUGUSTA [*cautiously opening the door*]: Mr. Pius is here and wants to speak to the missis all alone.
MRS. SONNTAG [*to* EDWARD]: He means you, of course, Edward.
AUGUSTA: Nah, he says clear as can be, the missis.

[MRS. SONNTAG *gets up, shrugging her shoulders.* AUGUSTA *whispers in* MARTHA's *ear.*]

Your intended's back again, too.

[MARTHA *looks inquiringly at* EDWARD, *who has heard nothing, however, and she leaves the room, humming softly.* AUGUSTA, *imitating* MRS. SONNTAG, *puts a coverlet over* EDWARD's *feet.*]

EDWARD: In this heat, Augusta?
AUGUSTA: If Mr. Edward would like, I'll keep him company a little while.

[EDWARD *nods kindly.*]

For the life of me, I like to hear tell of the Lord Jesus.

[EDWARD *nods.* AUGUSTA *sits down and takes her wide blue knitted stocking out of her pocket.*]

You mustn't keep looking at Henry, or he won't get any peace.
EDWARD: And it was actually my turn.
AUGUSTA: That don't make any difference. Just see, Mr. Edward, [*in a tone of joyful anticipation*] after the mourning comes the wedding.

[EDWARD *looks at her questioningly.*]

I don't mean you, heaven forbid, or the dear Lord God would have to make hisself a daughter too.

[EDWARD *smiles.*]

I mean Martha.

BERTHA [*coming sullenly into the room with a pitcher of milk and a glass on a tray and speaking to* AUGUSTA]: And I don't care about following you around anymore and bringing what you're supposed to take.

[*She leaves the room.*]

AUGUSTA: The silly thing acts as stuck-up as a fine young miss.

EDWARD: She's looked very disconcerted these past few days.

AUGUSTA: Given her notice to Mama Sonntag, she has. She's going to America.

EDWARD: So?

AUGUSTA: I think Mother Pius told her so, fortune-telling, from the cards.

EDWARD: Mother Pius is just fooling you—but she *is* a smart woman, I gather?

AUGUSTA: You, you're always looking up into heaven.

EDWARD: No, isn't she a smart woman?

AUGUSTA: Depends on how you look at it. Out of her slyness comes creeping crazy things.

EDWARD: That's absolutely new to me.

AUGUSTA [*after a short pause*]: I could confess everything to you, Mr. Edward.

[*She picks up a stitch dropped as she spoke.*]

EDWARD: Go ahead, Augusta!

AUGUSTA: I told Mama Sonntag a lie last week.

EDWARD [*repressing a smile*]: What, then, Augusta?

AUGUSTA: I didn't really oversleep; I was in the mortuary. I wanted to say adoo to dear Mr. Henry.

EDWARD: *That* my mother wouldn't have forbidden you, Augusta.

[A GROUP OF BOYS *with wild berries in pans ring the doorbell, knock, and murmur.*]

AUGUSTA [*closing the door to the hall*]: And what do you think, who do I see there—Old Lady Pius! Her eyes was staring like a skull, and she went [*speaking ever more softly*] round and round the corpse, without stopping, and singing she was, [*sings in a very low voice, almost bass*] "O, du lieber Augustin, everything's gone, gone, gone."

EDWARD: What kind of a story are you telling there, Augusta?

AUGUSTA: Don't let it bother you. Carl's granddaddy, he said to me a long time ago, Mother Pius, she's the merry-go-round we're all sitting on.

[MRS. SONNTAG *comes into the room, upset; her face looks absolutely livid. As she enters, the* GROUP OF BOYS *is seen thronging in front of the front door. The largest holds a small oil lamp in his hand.*]

AUGUSTA: Them boys makes me all nervous.

[*Imitating* MRS. SONNTAG, *she gets up slowly from her chair and goes cautiously out of the room.*]

GROUP OF BOYS: Stingy! Stingy!

MRS. SONNTAG: Of course you know it already.

EDWARD [*still stirred up from* AUGUSTA*'s story; nods questioningly in the negative*]: You're shuddering as though you'd walked over a dung heap.

MRS. SONNTAG: You really don't know, Edward?

EDWARD: Sit down next to me, poor, poor little Mother.

MRS. SONNTAG [*after a pause*]: Have you forgotten, Pius was here.

EDWARD: Ah, yes, what did he want?

MRS. SONNTAG [*tonelessly*]: Martha.

[*Short pause.*]

EDWARD: I would have been more startled if it had been the manager.

MRS. SONNTAG [*disconcerted*]: You should have seen him, the bashful boy—he became impertinent, I tell you, Edward. And in addition, he's drinking.

EDWARD [*pausing briefly*]: I imagined he visited us so often on my account.

[*Short pause.*]

I've become an egotist during my illness.

MRS. SONNTAG: But Edward, he could count himself fortunate to be allowed to visit you.

EDWARD: How trivial you take our friendship to be, Mother.

[*The boys become so loud that they are heard in the closed room.*]

MRS. SONNTAG [*very disconcerted*]: Augusta must send the children away.

[*She rings.*]

EDWARD: A young bronze apostle figure is Carl Pius in temptation.

MRS. SONNTAG: You are a fanatic.

EDWARD: And yet illness does teach us to sing a wiser song.

[*Short pause.*]

What did you say to him?

MRS. SONNTAG: I reminded him first of his youth.

EDWARD: And?

MRS. SONNTAG [*recalling*]: That Martha would be an old maid before—but when he became impertinent—I showed him the door.

[EDWARD *bows his head.*]

AUGUSTA [*cautiously entering the room, her red cheeks aglow, and leaving the door half open*]: Like two turtledoves, the two in the garden . . .

[MRS. SONNTAG *is disconcerted.*]

EDWARD: That certainly would be an impertinence . . .

[*The* GROUP OF BOYS *keep up an uninterrupted begging.*]

AUGUSTA: Let's buy a liter of the wild berries from the boys, then they'll quiet down.

[*Without waiting for an answer, she takes money from* MRS. SONNTAG'*s wallet, in the basket with the house keys.* MARTHA *and the manager come into sight in the garden.* EDWARD *turns his head toward the window.* MRS. SONNTAG *pulls herself together.*]

MRS. SONNTAG [*in a choked voice*]: They should tell you themselves, Edward.

[*Short pause.*]

EDWARD: You couldn't betray your son Henry any more shamelessly.

[*Short pause.*]

My poor brother, a soldier trying to escape, he went to his death in desperation . . .

MRS. SONNTAG: When you speak like that you admit his guilt.

EDWARD: It doesn't become you, Mother, to try to win me over by betraying him.

MRS. SONNTAG: I don't understand what you actually have against Dr. von Simon.

EDWARD: The same thing you have against him, Mother, and that's why you didn't dare tell me about the catastrophe yourself.

MRS. SONNTAG [*somewhat ominously*]: I'm not afraid of my children, not even of you, Edward.

[*Short pause.*]

EDWARD: Have you forgotten the suspicion you brought against him just yesterday?

MRS. SONNTAG [*haughty*]: It was only this morning that I really took a good look at him.

EDWARD [*mocking*]: Can it be that you're still daydreaming over his languishing eyelashes even after what's happened?

MRS. SONNTAG [*sobbing aloud*]: I feel, Edward, that I was too unselfish toward you.

EDWARD: Mother, dearest Mother, for what reason do you want to sacrifice Martha's young soul?

MRS. SONNTAG. The fact that Henry was angry with him lately has deeper causes.

EDWARD: But we do have eyes and ears, Mother.

MRS. SONNTAG [*stiffly*]: I wish, as a matter of fact, that we had begun inviting Dr. von Simon into our home sooner.

EDWARD: Are you still avoiding my question, Mother?

MRS. SONNTAG: At that time, Edward, you were much too young to be initiated into business affairs.

EDWARD: But we did live more luxuriously than we do now; Papa gave one party after the other.

MRS. SONNTAG: That was just it. Henry often enough praised his horse luck, as he put it, that he had found a man like Dr. von Simon.

[*Short pause.*]

We can consider ourselves lucky that he's taking Martha.

EDWARD: It certainly isn't any sacrifice for the man.

[AUGUSTA *opens the door hesitantly, holding a large bunch of roses in her hand; amidst the foliage is a card. She tries to inform* MRS. SONNTAG *with gestures.*]

MRS. SONNTAG: Isn't it so, Augusta, that Dr. von Simon is indeed the right man for Miss Martha?

[AUGUSTA *opens her eyes wide in amazement and then smiles contentedly.*]

AUGUSTA: From the young miss, the mayor's daughter . . .

[*She puts the bouquet tenderly into a vase.*]

EDWARD [*sarcastic*]: You don't usually consult your servants.

MRS. SONNTAG [*to* AUGUSTA]: You may go.

AUGUSTA [*reaching into her apron pocket*]: And this, I'm supposed to give this to the missis from the big tall fellow out there, and he wishes you a long life.

[MRS. SONNTAG *takes the envelope absentmindedly, plays with it, and finally lays it on the table.*]

AUGUSTA [*to* EDWARD]: I believe it was Liesken's brother, the fellow with the long nose and the dyed-green hands. He's got his pants rolled up over the knee.

[AUGUSTA *remains standing by the half-open door, unnoticed.*]

EDWARD [*resuming the conversation*]: All of that is still no cause to sell one's daughter.

MRS. SONNTAG: Should Martha perhaps become a store clerk?

EDWARD [*like an upperclassman declaiming*]: Rather than lie in a paramour's bed.

MRS. SONNTAG: You're exaggerating, Edward. I ask you, sleep on it a night.

EDWARD [*with biblical rage*]: I say unto you, woman, defile not our house.

MRS. SONNTAG [*collapses, weeping, then says softly*]: You are impertinent, like Carl Pius.

AUGUSTA [*cautiously coming back through the doorway, goggle-eyed, kindly, lying*]: The bell keeps ringing . . .

EDWARD: That one always comes to you right on cue.

AUGUSTA: I can't see Mama Sonntag crying. [*Approaching her, kind-hearted*] Mrs. Sonntag, ma'am . . .

[EDWARD *struggles with himself.* MARTHA *comes into the room in high spirits.* DR. BRUNO VON SIMON *hangs back uncertainly from the half-open door as he catches sight of* EDWARD.]

MRS. SONNTAG: Martha, leave us alone for another moment.

[MARTHA *obeys, pouting; a moment later, smiling graciously at her fiancé, she disappears again with him.*]

EDWARD [*tender but firm*]: Do you have anything more to say to me?

AUGUSTA: Look at him, Mrs. Sonntag, ma'am. He's got a halo round his curls.

[MRS. SONNTAG *nods with infinite sadness.*]

He don't belong in the sinful world.

[MRS. SONNTAG *solemnly nods in agreement.* AUGUSTA *points to the front door.*]

God help us, that big lummox of Puderbachs' is still standing in front of the door and watching.

EDWARD: Is Liesken with him?

MRS. SONNTAG: But Edward . . .

AUGUSTA: You better not concern yourself with the poor child or *you'll* get under false suspicion too, like Henry.

[EDWARD, *exhausted, coughs harder.* AUGUSTA, *inoffensively.*]

He often asked me himself if Mr. Edward was trying to get somewheres with Liesken.

EDWARD [*thunderstruck; after a short pause*]: Mother, did you know that?

MRS. SONNTAG [*sympathetic*]: I know *you*, Edward . . .

[EDWARD *walks isolated and lonely from the room, as though crossing a mountain.* MRS. SONNTAG *looks after him sadly. She absentmindedly picks up the envelope from the table and goes to the window, which the engaged couple are approaching.* MARTHA *looks, astonished, along the garden fence.*]

MARTHA: Just think, Mama . . .

[MRS. SONNTAG *barely listens.*]

Bertha just came out of the house and went past the fence in my jacket and hat, and her things are hanging on my hook on the coat rack.

DR. BRUNO VON SIMON: May I kiss the respected Mama's hand?

[*Brushes with his lips the hesitantly proffered hand.*]

MRS. SONNTAG [*flustered*]: I still just can't get used to the idea.

[AUGUSTA *waits at the far end of the room. She cannot comprehend the situation. She leaves.* MARTHA *pouts. She takes a camellia from her belt and fastens it over* DR. BRUNO VON SIMON'*s heart.*]

DR. BRUNO VON SIMON: You're going to decorate me like a dandy, little pussycat.

[MRS. SONNTAG *opens the envelope apathetically; she takes out the nude photograph of* MARTHA, *starts violently, cannot understand, regards it from all angles. She summons* MARTHA *to her at the window and holds up the back side of the photograph to her.*]

MRS. SONNTAG: Martha, do you know this handwriting?

MARTHA [*with spirit*]: That's Pius, his heavy paw.

AUGUSTA: [*entering conspiratorially*]: Mr. Edward's sitting in his room and peering at hisself in the mirror.

MARTHA: But he pasted it over so that he wouldn't grow vain.

[MRS. SONNTAG *locks the photograph away in her desk.*]

DR. BRUNO VON SIMON [*aside to* MARTHA]: It's high time you got out of here, little pussycat.

MRS. SONNTAG [*apathetic, then brightening and speaking to herself, but with her head turned toward the two at the window*]: I'll bring joy to his heart.

MARTHA [*somewhat snippy*]: What are you planning to do, Mama, go with him into the monastery?

[AUGUSTA *goes solicitously out of the door behind* MRS. SONNTAG, *expressing with gestures her answer to* MARTHA'*s question: "For heaven's sake, no!" The engaged couple disappear, into the garden.*]

Scene 2

[*In the same workers' section as in the first act.*]

[EDWARD *knocks on the door of the Piuses' house.*]

AMADEUS: Just knock hard; Old Lady Pius don't sleep in the night anyways; she's got to confer with Satan.

LONG ANNA: And up there where Wallbrecker sleeps, the window holes are stuffed up.

DANGLING FREDERICK [*nudging* EDWARD *with an empty stare*]: I got a dry throat, mister.

LONG ANNA: You dead mole, what do you know about being thirsty?

DANGLING FREDERICK [*to* EDWARD]: The both of us is on the way to heaven.

[*He mutters frightfully.* EDWARD *gives him a coin.*]

LONG ANNA [*regarding it scornfully*]: You don't need to give me any of that, Frederick!

DANGLING FREDERICK: You old swine!

AMADEUS: If you want to speak to Carl, mister, he's in the pub and he's swilling off one rotgut after the other.

[EDWARD *becomes agitated.*]

And August is sitting by him and chomping sugar out of his pocket and swilling right along with him.

[EDWARD *moves in the direction of the pub.* AMADEUS, *instinctively*]

I'll get him out, you better stay here.

DANGLING FREDERICK: Bootlicker!

[EDWARD *holds* AMADEUS *back.* LONG ANNA *cries out suddenly as he did on the evening when* CARL *twisted his arm.*]

AMADEUS: What's the matter with you, Long Anna?

[LONG ANNA *whimpers in a falsetto voice.* DANGLING FREDERICK *mutters malevolently.*]

Your sleeve's hanging down against your body like your grandmother's bellpull.

[LONG ANNA *squeaks something inaudibly into* FREDERICK'*s ear.*]

DANGLING FREDERICK: You old swine!
AMADEUS [*to* LONG ANNA]: You did go a little too far.
LONG ANNA: Me?
AMADEUS: Yeah, you did. He's been soaking in rotgut ever since.
LONG ANNA: Heeheeheehee!
AMADEUS: That's making me sad, sad's what it's making me. Otherwise he don't booze it up at all.

[LIESKEN'*s father comes home, through the little side street from the direction of the inner city. He is thus not seen but is only heard as he pushes the house door open with a crashing blow of his fist.*]

AMADEUS: I feel the noise here [*putting his hand over his heart*].
DANGLING FREDERICK [*muttering malevolently*]: He's coming from the Bible study class.
LONG ANNA [*nudging* EDWARD *in the shoulder and squeaking out scornfully in falsetto*]: That was her father . . .

[DANGLING FREDERICK *mutters frightfully.*]

AMADEUS: Howled, she did, when they took her off to the reform school, like she was a madame's lap poodle on the way to the slaughterhouse.

[EDWARD *is agitated.*]

LONG ANNA: In that place they'll thrash her black and blue from one end to the other for her playing around.

[*Short pause.*]

It's me your brother should of took.

DANGLING FREDERICK: An old swine like you?

[EDWARD *is agitated.*]

The little one understands finer than you. In her nightgown she goes walking on the roof right under the moon. I was lying there watching, my own self, and grabbing for the little firefly.

AMADEUS [*sadly, to* EDWARD]: I seen her once, too.

LONG ANNA: Early in God's morning, after it happened, [*pointing to his arm*] she laid down by me over there on the riverbank.

AMADEUS: I liked the nice little critter.

LONG ANNA [*pointing to his arm*]: I just ain't supposed to tell the policemen about Carl, that she was his girlfriend. Heeheeheehee!

DANGLING FREDERICK: Lying swine, you snuck away for fear of Carl's big fat fist.

LONG ANNA: Looks like you peek out from under your patch.

[CARL *and* AUGUST *come reeling arm in arm from the pub.* CARL *looks completely changed.* AUGUST *carries* CARL*'s old upperclassman's cap impaled backward on a stick.* DANGLING FREDERICK, AMADEUS, *and* LONG ANNA *laugh.* CARL *catches sight of* EDWARD.]

CARL: Evening, Edward, how's my sweetheart Marthibilikins? She does want to marry me, yeah, yeah! [*Talking to himself in his grandmother's tone*] Carl, do you love your grandmother? [*Short pause, then in a tone of blissful drunkenness*] I do love you so much, Edward.

AUGUST [*envious, and also staggering*]: Leave the miserable fellow be, Carl. He's going to get his hair cut off.

AMADEUS [*to* AUGUST]: Come on and show my two business associates the holy Saint Eva out of your wallet, August.

[AUGUST's *wallet hangs out of his pants pocket.*]

EDWARD: That's Pius's wallet.

[*The wind begins to rise.*]

AMADEUS: A saying in Latin is written on the backside.
EDWARD [*taking hold of* CARL *from behind*]: Help me, Amadeus.
AMADEUS: I can't grab ahold of him from beneath or my glass heart will smash to smithereens. [*Mournfully*] It's already got a crack.
LONG ANNA: Take me in the middle, drunken brothers.

[*He pushes* EDWARD *away, who falls staggering on* DANGLING FREDERICK's *breast.* LONG ANNA *pushes himself in between* CARL *and* AUGUST.]

DANGLING FREDERICK: The pair of us deathbirds is joined together.

[CARL, LONG ANNA, *and* AUGUST *go reeling over the bridge and out of sight. The night wind wails like a child.* EDWARD *shivers. He knocks once more, softly, on the door of the Piuses' little house.*]

GRANDDADDY WALLBRECKER [*opening his little window and screeching*]: I'll drive them away this time, the spooks in the night.

[*He pours down an enameled pot full of water.*]

DANGLING FREDERICK [*muttering malevolently*]: I'm going to lay me down and sleep under the bush.

[EDWARD *heads toward home, his head bowed.*]

ARTHUR ARONYMUS AND HIS ANCESTORS

From the Childhood of My Beloved Father

A Drama in Fifteen Scenes

CHARACTERS

Moritz Schüler, *landowner*
Henrietta, *his wife*
Their twenty-three children:

1. Heinrich Menachem
   Elfrieda, *his wife*
   Oskar, *their son*
2. Simeon
3. Julius
4. Fanny
5. Katharina
6. Elisa
7. Berthold
8. Alex
9. Ferdinand
10. August
11. Dora
12. Eleonora
13. Albert
14. Bettina
15. Arthur Aronymus
16. Margareta
17. Lenchen
18. Karl

19. Max
20. Meta, *twin*
21. Louisa, *twin*
22. Meyerchen
23. Titi

Rabbi Uriel, *chief rabbi of the Rhineland and Westphalia, father of Henrietta Schüler*

Ephraim, *the rabbi's servant*

Cantor *of the synagogue*

Chaplain Bernard Michalski, *a Catholic priest*

Narcissa *and* Ursula, *his two little nieces*

Bishop Matthias of Paderborn

Altmann, *night watchman*

Wholesale Merchants

Kern, *a Rosicrucian, and* Young Kern, *his sixteen-year-old son*

Angel of Death

Poor Jews

Nathanael Brennessel, *itinerant laborer*

Lemmle Tsilinsky, *peddler*

Three Perlmutters, *junk dealers*

Josefchen, *their nephew*

Willy Himmel *and* Caspar, *eight-year-old friends of Arthur Aronymus*

Christmas Tree Seller

Villagers of Gaesecke

Mr. Paderstein *and his wife*, Milchen, *friends of the Schüler family*

Hugo Paderstein, *their young son*

Miss Paderstein, Mr. *Paderstein's elder sister*

Mr. Vogelsang *and his wife*, Alvina, Mrs. *Paderstein's parents, from Elberfeld in the Wupper Valley*

Dr. Engelbrecht Vogelsang, *apothecary, their youngest son (born long after their other children)*

Alfonso Kissingen (Dr. Faust), *a traveling wine salesman*

Alexander *and* Siegfried Ostermorgen, *the seventeen- and eighteen-year-old sons of Mr. Schüler's old friend*

Jewish Gardener in Paderborn

Christian Gardener in Paderborn

Henry Filigran, *overseer on the Schüler estate*

Mamsell, *cook*

Clara, *parlor maid*

Fanatical Man *and* Woman

Maids, milkmaids, male servants, beekeeper, and gardener on the estate

NOTE ON PRONUNCIATION: The diminutive ending –*chen* on several names is unaccented and pronounced "khen"; for example, Lenchen is pronounced "LAYN-kh'n."

Scene 1

[*The little village of Hexengaesecke begins at the large, fenced garden of the Schüler mansion, with its elegant flight of broad steps leading up to the entrance. A warm August night with full moon and stars. On all sides are hedges clipped into animal forms. The action takes place about 1840. Near the manor house is an old well.* CHAPLAIN MICHALSKI, *walking cheerily toward the village from the highway, rests in front of the garden. He hears* ALTMANN, *the night watchman, snoring.*]

ALTMANN [*wakes with a start, then sleepily*]: Hey, Brennessel, already back from making the rounds?

[CHAPLAIN MICHALSKI *remains silent.*]

Up and away just yesterday. [*Imperiously*] All I've got to do is hang around in the world at night, man!

[*Pause.*]

Huh?

[*Recognizes* CHAPLAIN MICHALSKI.]

CHAPLAIN MICHALSKI [*raises his hands, pretending to beg*]: One more little quarter hour granted to the chaplain to look up from the beautiful green world into the—?

[*He points to the sky.*]

ALTMANN [*confused*]: I—[*looking for his horn, which has slipped to his back*] horn-ox that I am!

[CHAPLAIN MICHALSKI *helps him find his horn.* ALTMANN *kisses* CHAPLAIN MICHALSKI*'s hand.*]

But certainly, as long as it pleases the reverend chaplain.

[ALTMANN *blows his horn very softly and carefully.*]

So my children [*indicating all the houses in the village, last of all, sentimentally, the many windows of the mansion*] don't open their little eyes.

CHAPLAIN MICHALSKI: You take care of our dear village like a father.

ALTMANN: That's good to hear and specially from your chaplainship.

[CHAPLAIN MICHALSKI *plucks a small sprig from the branch hanging luxuriantly over the fence.* ALTMANN, *amazed*]

Look at that—?

CHAPLAIN MICHALSKI [*pointing questioningly to himself*]: Can it be that you're thinking of turning me in for stealing foliage, Altmann?

ALTMANN [*naively trusting*]: I? Why, I snitch the plums from the trees myself.

CHAPLAIN MICHALSKI [*with a lively and indulgent laugh*]: This wild little sprig was just growing toward me, asking to be picked and enjoyed.

ALTMANN: That's just the way it is!

[*Short pause. He points to the mansion.*]

The grandfather rabbi from Paderborn is visiting.

CHAPLAIN MICHALSKI [*eagerly*]: The famous scholar?

ALTMANN: Scholar? He's a rabbi! Madame's father.

[*He sets his horn to his lips.* CHAPLAIN MICHALSKI *reminds him not to wake his children.*]

I'm blowing shofar—in his honor.

[*He gives a hoarse blast.*]

NATHANAEL BRENNESSEL [voice from offstage, fluting as though on a syrinx]: *Tekia! Shevarim! Terua!*

ALTMANN [*to* CHAPLAIN MICHALSKI]: *I didn't* do it wrong—[*Both hearkening*] Come out of that hollow tree trunk, Nathanael!

[*He blows again, very hoarsely.*]

CHAPLAIN MICHALSKI: But what do you know about blowing shofar?

ALTMANN [*evasively*]: I even know how to blow Catholic and—other things.

CHAPLAIN MICHALSKI: And do you also know why shofar is blown in the synagogue?

ALTMANN: Does the reverend chaplain know?

CHAPLAIN MICHALSKI: In order to coax the new year in, Altmann.

ALTMANN: Yo! [*He blows again, hoarsely but softly, on his horn; then, scrutinizing* CHAPLAIN MICHALSKI]: And the old year—where is it now?

[CHAPLAIN MICHALSKI *shrugs his shoulders questioningly, with an ironic smile.*]

The Catholics, by your leave, count time from the birth of Christ, but we—I mean the Jews—keep having to carry the old year back through the Great Flood to the beginning of the world.

CHAPLAIN MICHALSKI: You're an expert in world history!

ALTMANN: And only then do we—I mean the Jews—coax the

new year in, when the used-up one is gone home [*instructively*] into the beginning.

CHAPLAIN MICHALSKI: And who taught you to blow shofar, then?

ALTMANN [*evasively*]: I know how to blow Catholic and—other things.

CHAPLAIN MICHALSKI [*smiling to himself*]: Can you really be a Jew? Just think—

ALTMANN: Half ways—from my father's side; but my mother—was a nun. [*To himself*] That's what comes from all that chattering in the dark, where you can hardly find your mouth.

CHAPLAIN MICHALSKI: Are you ashamed of your old religion, Altmann?

ALTMANN: Not for myself, Reverend Chaplain, but the Catholics are ashamed—because of me—so I blow Catholic, and when he's visiting, [*points up to the mansion*] for him, Jewish.

CHAPLAIN MICHALSKI: But doesn't this confusion trouble you in your dignity as a human being?

ALTMANN: That you have to give up. A day laborer—[*corrects himself*] a simple night watchman—darn well can't afford to put on airs like that.

CHAPLAIN MICHALSKI [*reflective, kind, sympathetic*]: Your secret will remain between us, Altmann. Go on blowing as you will, but don't blow it anymore for me.

ALTMANN: Altmann always had a weakness for the chaplain—[*looking up abruptly as a window opens in the house*]. One moment—one little moment—one little teeny moment—and then I'll put the chaplain to bed and blow him to sleep.

CHAPLAIN MICHALSKI: Me?

ALTMANN [*his gaze fixed on the window*]: Night owls have been wandering around on the paths lately.

[CHAPLAIN MICHALSKI *stretches his strong arm toward* ALTMANN.]

Quiet a second! Ssh! [*Continuing absentmindedly*] If you were to be—by such a night spirit—

CHAPLAIN MICHALSKI [*notices* FANNY *framed in the window and keeps preventing* ALTMANN *from looking upward*]: But I'm still young.

[ALTMANN *is perplexed.*]

Just look!

[*Holds his arm under* ALTMANN'*s nose.*]

ALTMANN [*distracted*]: That's amazing, by darn, on what *you* get to eat! Excuse me, Chaplain, but in the scholars' school the only thing they get to gulp down is learning.

[FANNY *leans out of the window, between flowered curtains.* CHAPLAIN MICHALSKI *continues to act disinterested.*]

CHAPLAIN MICHALSKI: Why, that's the very thing to strengthen a man!

ALTMANN [*ignoring the answer, ecstatically*]: Fanny! [*Looking intensely up at the window*] That's the fine lady Altmann would have married if he'd been a gentleman.

CHAPLAIN MICHALSKI: What?

ALTMANN: Fanny's the eldest of the sisters. [*Devotedly mawkish*] Now the lark is trilling out into the night—

[*He holds his hand behind his ear.* CHAPLAIN MICHALSKI *looks upward, smiling ironically.* ALTMANN, *somewhat jealous, looks* CHAPLAIN MICHALSKI *over.*]

She would have been something for you, too. [*Watching him closely*] But the priests have to stay virgin, eh?

CHAPLAIN MICHALSKI [*severely*]: Altmann!

[FANNY *leaves the window.*]

ALTMANN: Excuse me, Reverend Chaplain.

[*Short pause.*]

Twenty-three children and one grandson and the whole family partied around one coffeepot together on the lawn this afternoon.

CHAPLAIN MICHALSKI: When *do* you rest up from the night, then?

ALTMANN: Moritz and I are from the same hometown, so he always gives me something extra beside the bare wages I get from my job.

[CHAPLAIN MICHALSKI *nods.*]

Only Simeon, the second when you count from the beginning, dassn't see it.

[ALTMANN *never takes his eyes from the upstairs window.*]

She's gone again. Now she comes, now she goes—

CHAPLAIN MICHALSKI: Squire Schüler is said to be a generous, honorable man.

ALTMANN: For the most part, yes. That's why I like to sleep by his gate. [*Stealing another look upward*] And specially Henrietta, his wedded wife, [*in singsong tone*] so rounded and mounded like the golden moon [*lustfully*] up there in its bed of clouds.

[*He sits down again on the boundary stone.*]

Or would the chaplain please to sit here?

[FANNY *recognizes* CHAPLAIN MICHALSKI *and leans far out of the window. Her hand can be seen reaching behind her for a light-colored scarf, which she lays over her shoulders coquettishly. She throws a rose out over the garden, but it catches in the thorns of the fence.* CHAPLAIN MICHALSKI *picks it up.* ALTMANN *has not seen this byplay.*]

CHAPLAIN MICHALSKI [*to* ALTMANN, *self-controlled and raising his voice*]: Refresh yourself the rest of the night with this perfume, Altmann [*giving him the rose*].
ALTMANN: Where did that come from?

[FANNY *closes her window audibly.* ALTMANN, *disappointed*]

Now she's gone from the stage—and she won't be back today. What's the matter with her all of a sudden? She comes, she goes, she comes, she goes; what's the matter with her all of a sudden?

[CHAPLAIN MICHALSKI is *repelled by* ALTMANN'*s confidences. He starts to move on,* ALTMANN *hesitantly following.* ALTMANN *stops again for a moment.*]

He has twenty-three children to feed, has Moritz, out of one till, and all the guests and their families.

[*They continue walking.*]

First Menachem Heinrich was given to him. He's his firstborn. He was a perfect little squire, the crown prince in his cradle. Then came Simeon [*he singsongs the names like a schoolboy*] and Julius, Fanny, Katharina, Elisa, Berthold, Alex with his weak lungs, Ferdinand, August, Dora, Eleonora, Albert, Bettina, Arthur Aronymus, Margareta, Lenchen, [CHAPLAIN MICHALSKI *is counting the names*] Karl, Maxie—the apple of his father's eye—the twin Metas, like two little sugar dollies, little Meyerchen, and last of all—Titi.
CHAPLAIN MICHALSKI: Well, you've certainly memorized the poem without any mistakes.

ALTMANN: What else have I got to do all night?

CHAPLAIN MICHALSKI: It is indeed a nice bouquet of names.

ALTMANN: But the fifteenth of the children, Arthur Aronymus—you can't get rid of weeds—he won't behave like he wants him to.

CHAPLAIN MICHALSKI: How do you mean?

ALTMANN: Well, yesterday the boy rode through Hexengaesecke on Prell's donkey in a pair of paper pants cut from the local news rag, and his two ne'er-do-well school pals—Willy and Caspar are their names—right after him to spur the lazybones on.

CHAPLAIN MICHALSKI: Priceless!

ALTMANN: But you should have heard his father sound off, Chaplain, when the confounded little devil came sneaking home with the ads on his rear end.

[ALTMANN *sets the horn to his lips once more and blows hoarsely into it.*]

NATHANAEL BRENNESSEL [*teasing offstage voice*]: *Tekia! Shevarim!* [*Trilling*] *Terua!*

ALTMANN: Come out of that well, y'ole billy goat!

[CHAPLAIN MICHALSKI *and* ALTMANN *turn across the highway toward the square before the Catholic church. All is perfectly still. The hour of one strikes from the church tower.*]

Scene 2

[*In the small garden of the synagogue in Paderborn.* RABBI URIEL *rests on a simple bench, his fine hands motionless in his lap, one placed upon the other. His lips continue moving devotedly as though in prayer.*]

EPHRAIM [*pointing to a cluster of men, including four Jewish* WHOLESALE MERCHANTS, KERN, *and* YOUNG KERN, *before the iron fence of the garden*]: They won't take no for an answer, Rabbi.

RABBI URIEL [*gently*]: And why should they?

[*With a hospitable gesture he invites them to come in.*]

EPHRAIM: I saw the rabbi's soul still hanging on the worship service.

[*The men remain at a pious distance before the high priest. One of the* WHOLESALE MERCHANTS *begins to speak.*]

FIRST MERCHANT: Rabbi, we started out early in the Lord's morning, each from his own city and yet all for the same purpose.

SECOND MERCHANT: And laid our course in the Almighty's hand.

THIRD MERCHANT: Like great migratory birds—

FOURTH MERCHANT: We allowed ourselves no rest.

KERN: I joined the Jews, Reverend Priest, [*puts his arm around his son*] I and my son.

FOURTH MERCHANT: He is August Friedrich Kern, the Rosicrucian and world-famous astrologer.

[RABBI URIEL *applauds soundlessly.*]

WHOLESALE MERCHANTS [*together*]: What free time he has in the evenings he spends with us, submerging himself in the study of the Kabala.

KERN [*bows before* RABBI URIEL]: It is written: Simeon ben Yochai injured himself. Two of God's saints were consumed in a supernatural light because of their knowledge. Only Rabbi ben Akiva returned unscathed from the metaphysical paradise of the Kabala.

[*All murmur a pious Hebrew passage.* RABBI URIEL *repeats it, then kisses his fingertips to them in greeting. He signals to* EPHRAIM *to bring the second bench, by the wall, for the guests.* YOUNG KERN *helps him. They all sit down next to one another, opposite* RABBI URIEL.]

RABBI URIEL [*after a pause*]: What do the beloved pilgrims desire of me?

KERN: Make use of your influence in Parliament, Mighty One in Israel.

SECOND MERCHANT [*indicating* KERN]: He has been driven to you, as we have, by the approaching danger . . .

THIRD MERCHANT: That threatens our people.

FIRST MERCHANT [*devoutly*]: Your pleading, Rabbi Uriel, can reach the ear of the Eternal One.

THIRD MERCHANT: It reaches into his heaven.

WHOLESALE MERCHANTS: Amen!

[*From the synagogue the last line of the worship service is heard.* RABBI URIEL *points to the dome of the synagogue.*]

RABBI URIEL: The Shema Yisroel still glows on my lips that have comforted the God-fearing Jews of Paderborn; a divine whisper still blows over my old priest-heart.

[*The men bow their heads before* RABBI URIEL.]

FIRST MERCHANT [*devoutly*]: Mighty One!

SECOND MERCHANT: Thou falcon!

THIRD MERCHANT [*to* KERN]: His mind soars above Sinai.

FOURTH MERCHANT: Tearing at God's robes!

[YOUNG KERN *wants to say something, but his father motions to him to remain silent.* RABBI URIEL *notices.*]

RABBI URIEL: Well, boy, with what pious tidbit did you think to gladden the old rabbi?

YOUNG KERN [*sharply*]: My father is afraid that my word still sounds too childish for your table.

RABBI URIEL: And yet, Uriel's sorely plundered rabbi-heart longs not for idle trifles but to be hung with the playing of children.

[YOUNG KERN *approaches* RABBI URIEL *and kisses him on the cheek.* RABBI URIEL *claps his hands, then to* EPHRAIM]

You tell them, Ephraim, what the rabbi is—tell them.

EPHRAIM: The rabbi is—

RABBI URIEL: Tell them!

KERN: *Shema* in Israel.

EPHRAIM [*hesitantly*]: The rabbi is a child.

[*The* CANTOR *enters the little garden. Since* EPHRAIM *does not notice his waving, he steps carefully behind* RABBI URIEL*'s bench and whispers something in* EPHRAIM*'s ear. He exits.*]

The rabbi is a child; I must remind the rabbi of it two or three times a day, "The rabbi is a child." In the morning when the rabbi gets up, "The rabbi is a child!" And evenings when the rabbi lies down to sleep, "The rabbi is a child." And I must keep telling the rabbi, "The rabbi is a child."

KERN: In truth, a holy child in Israel. Such an ancient child the rabbi seems to me, going back to the origin of all, a simple child, a child fallen from the stars onto our futile world.

FIRST MERCHANT [*devoutly*]: A child fallen from the stars! And that is why a light shines forth from him.

SECOND MERCHANT: The rabbuni!

THIRD MERCHANT: And his countenance lifts the darkness of confusion!

FIRST MERCHANT [*kneels before* RABBI URIEL]: Rabbi Uriel!

[*Pause.*]

FOURTH MERCHANT [*to the others, energetically*]: *Le temps s'enfuit!*
SECOND MERCHANT [*to* FOURTH MERCHANT]: Begin!

[RABBI URIEL *nods his head, inviting them to begin.*]

FOURTH MERCHANT [*passionately*]: Our daughters will be burned at the stake!

SECOND MERCHANT: In the medieval tradition.

THIRD MERCHANT: With its horrors.

FIRST MERCHANT: Witch hunting has come alive again.

THIRD MERCHANT: Out of the rubble of the centuries.

SECOND MERCHANT: The flame will consume our innocent Jewish sisters.

FIRST MERCHANT [*questioning*]: And keep their souls from ascending to God, Rabbi?

KERN: Enlightened monks, a few of them, are rising up and preaching from the church pulpits, admonishing the Westphalian Christians who have been bitten by the devil.

SECOND MERCHANT: What can a shepherd do, even several watchmen, against a rabid flock?

RABBI URIEL [*rises up, intense*]: Moses became a nation, and his arm smote the blinded Amalekites.

[*Pause.*]

FOURTH MERCHANT: From hour to hour the hatred of the Christians for us Jews grows stronger, especially in the villages and market towns of Westphalia.

THIRD MERCHANT: No Jewish house that isn't marked with the blood of the daughter.

FOURTH MERCHANT [*impatiently*]: What action will the rabbi take? The days are hectic and the nights sleepless.

KERN: Like the Jew, the Christian too respects the high priest of the Rhineland and Westphalia.

SECOND MERCHANT: Your voice penetrates into the blood, Rabbi.

FIRST MERCHANT: Your word strengthens those who have strayed from the way, Rabbi.

[RABBI URIEL *ponders.*]

YOUNG KERN: We Rosicrucians tell one another of the rabbi's miraculous deeds.

FIRST MERCHANT [*devoutly*]: In truth it is so. [*Laying his hand over his heart*] The rabbi's mere appearance and tranquility bring hope—

YOUNG KERN [*listens intently; questioningly*]: They say that Rabbi Uriel can take his heart out of his breast and set its red marker at God-east—

RABBI URIEL [*firmly*]: I conferred in Parliament with Archbishop Matthias of Paderborn.

[EPHRAIM *nods confirmation of* RABBI URIEL'*s words.*]

FOURTH MERCHANT [*impatient and stern*]: The result?

EPHRAIM [*lovingly smoothes* RABBI URIEL'*s beard. Suddenly the words wrench themselves vigorously from his mouth*]: He fasted all week long, the rabbi, yet his holy voice roared through the barriers of cold procedures, swirling upward through the expanses of the Parliament.

RABBI URIEL [*gazes long at his servant; then firmly*]: For I was filled only with the single thought, how to help my tortured people.

KERN [*discreetly*]: They say of Matthias that he is a fanatic Catholic.

RABBI URIEL: He is a good-tempered, likable prince of the church, who walks in enlightenment.

WHOLESALE MERCHANTS [*eagerly*]: And his answer to Israel?

RABBI URIEL: He considers the aberration of his Christians to have no further significance.

FOURTH MERCHANT: What? And the danger threatening to turn the ancient and venerable soul of Israel to ashes once again?

SECOND MERCHANT: Just a topic of discussion to him?

RABBI URIEL [*in assent*]: A resurrected fragment!

FOURTH MERCHANT [*sarcastically*]: With little devil's ears and tail, weak on its legs but able to survive long enough to be driven away by the coming Christmas season.

YOUNG KERN: With little devil's ears and tail, ha, ha.

[KERN *admonishes him to keep quiet.*]

RABBI URIEL: From the essence welling forth out of this prince of the church, I, your rabbi, drew uprightness! To comfort you, my dear men.

THIRD MERCHANT: And how does our great rabbi privately regard the comfort granted to him by the church prince?

FOURTH MERCHANT [*in a superior tone*]: And the resurrected memory of anno 1600.

RABBI URIEL: As it was offered to me, my dear friend.

FOURTH MERCHANT [*in a superior tone*]: And does our rabbi feel so strengthened by the Host?

RABBI URIEL [*severely*]: Even elderly children dislike being the target of barbed sarcasm.

[FOURTH MERCHANT *bows,* RABBI URIEL'*s reply having hit home.*]

It seems to me that the archbishop knows his children.

[*The* CANTOR, *gesticulating, motions to* EPHRAIM *to come over to the wrought-iron fence of the little garden. The conversation continues.*]

CANTOR: I cannot awaken the children.

FIRST MERCHANT [*devoutly*]: Just as the rabbi cannot awaken *us*, the children of Israel.

[*He admonishes the rest of the men with his finger. Pause.* RABBI URIEL, *with great power, stretches his arms toward heaven in a mighty gesture.*]

RABBI URIEL: The One, the Only, God over us. He has tested the willingness of his servant's heart to sacrifice.

[*The men rise, deeply moved, bow before* RABBI URIEL, *and leave one after the other, bowing once more at the garden gate.*]

EPHRAIM [*lays* RABBI URIEL'*s prayer shawl, which has slipped off, around his shoulders*]: Two children, the cantor says, are asleep on the last bench in the sanctuary.

RABBI URIEL: Look after them, Ephraim. Your abba can find his way inside alone.

[*But* EPHRAIM *leads* RABBI URIEL *into the house, then returns, hurrying through the garden into the synagogue. It grows steadily darker.*]

Scene 3

[*In* RABBI URIEL'*s small conference room. A long, heavy table with high-backed chairs around it. On one of the chairs sits* RABBI URIEL, *lost in thought, his back to the door leading into his private apartment. On the table stands the Sabbath candelabrum with burning candles. On the wall hangs a very large family picture of his daughter* HENRIETTA *with her husband and all of their twenty-three children.* EPHRAIM *comes into the conference room from the neighboring apartment. Before he closes the doors,* ARTHUR ARONYMUS *and* LENCHEN *are seen standing in the doorway.*]

EPHRAIM [*admonishing* ARTHUR *and* LENCHEN *to go back into the next room*]: Grandpa will be back on earth in just a little while. Meanwhile, eat your porridge like good children!

[*He shuts the door quietly and approaches* RABBI URIEL. *He is very frightened at* RABBI URIEL'*s paleness.*]

The long conversation after the service has tired the rabbi.

[*Short pause.* EPHRAIM, *amazed, notices a disappearing figure.*]

But I didn't let this beggar in.

[*Without opening the door, the figure disappears from the room as though it had gone through the wood.*]

Shema.

RABBI URIEL: He was no beggar, Ephraim, he was the Eternal One's messenger of death.

EPHRAIM [*paralyzed*]: *Shema Israel—*

[*He hurries into the next room.*]

ARTHUR AND LENCHEN [*heard indistinctly*]: Is Grandpa back on earth yet?

[EPHRAIM *returns to the conference room.*]

RABBI URIEL: Did you see him too, Ephraim, the Lord's death messenger?

EPHRAIM [*bewildered*]: Your servant Ephraim—dreamed—

RABBI URIEL: You have been more to me than a servant, my Ephraim mine, and only to spare you did I keep secret what happened.

[*He strokes* EPHRAIM's *hands.* EPHRAIM *listens with total devotion.* RABBI URIEL *is transfigured but acutely present in this world as well.*]

We were coming out of the Parliament as the Eternal One sent his angel of death to me.

EPHRAIM: We left the great white building early, the chief rabbi of the Rhineland and Westphalia and his servant.

RABBI URIEL: And took our modest meal. But as it grew dark, you, my faithful friend, lovingly wrapped the rabbi's body in festive silk, smoothed the pious skin of the white draperies.

[EPHRAIM *smiles and kisses the hem of* RABBI URIEL'*s prayer shawl.* RABBI URIEL *rocks his upper body in devotion.*]

The Lord Sabaoth demanded of his servant the favorite among his grandchildren—

EPHRAIM [*rises, deeply frightened, and carefully opens the door to the next room; quietly to* ARTHUR *and* LENCHEN]: Grandpa will be back on earth in just a little while.

RABBI URIEL: With the most beloved, living gift the Lord thought to test the willingness of his servant's heart to sacrifice.

[EPHRAIM *raises his arms protectively.*]

And all my pleading that he be satisfied with the soul of his servant—have mercy, Sabaoth—slid off from the majesty of the Lord like dust from the wings of his dark angel.

[*Suddenly* RABBI URIEL *rises up with a violent gesture.*]

Then I tried to trick the Eternal One, our God!

[EPHRAIM *is horrified.*]

In glowing terms I praised the weakest one among the grandchildren to the Holy Angel, the sixth of the twenty-three, whose soul, a gossamer thread delicately attached to our earthly world, jeopardized even so by every breath of air, already threatens to quiver out of existence.

EPHRAIM [*fearful, hesitant*]: Was the Lord's messenger satisfied, rabbi?

RABBI URIEL: The heavy beating of his wings terrified me. Your rabbi trembled—

EPHRAIM [*holds out both hands with the fingers spread wide apart*]: And?

RABBI URIEL: He accused me of deceiving Adonai!

EPHRAIM [*with faith in* RABBI URIEL]: Only the devil dares to accuse the rabbi of deceit. It was the devil, on angel wings.

RABBI URIEL: Even you, Ephraim, believe in this unworthy power?

[*He kisses* RABBI URIEL'*s hand repentantly.*]

I fought with the venerable angel in mysteries the rest of the night.

EPHRAIM [*speaking as though in a ballad*]: And so the rabbi's lips were bleeding in the morning.

RABBI URIEL [*closes his eyes, overcome, remembering the hour*]: I bargained with Him—the rabbi of smitten Israel, a dealer in human beings, with the buyer! "Be satisfied with my soul, fling the tortured thing into *sheol.* But pluck not from my stem the laughing red grape still throbbing gaily on the vine, innocent and unfermented."

EPHRAIM: Amen.

RABBI URIEL [*after a short pause; pleading*]: "Take my firstborn grandson instead of the boy; take the God-fearing squire! Be satisfied with Simeon Mordechei! Take Julius Ahasuerus! Take Fanny, the flower of the Westphalian meadow. Take Katharina, her father's pride! Take Elisa! Berthold, the lively young man! Take Ferdinand! Take Dora, still not quite grown up! Augustus! Eleonora! Albert! Bettina! Margareta! Take the twins, two identical almond seeds in their golden shell! Take the gentle Lenchen; bear her up to God! Take Karl! Max, the apple of his father's eye! Be satisfied with Meyerchen! Even take from its mother's arms the tiniest child, just born, [*even more intensely, almost shouting*] only give him up, Arthur Aronymus, my heart's favorite!"

[EPHRAIM *dries* RABBI URIEL'*s moist eyes and cheeks.*]

ARTHUR [*from the next room*]: Grandpa!

[*He tramples impatiently with his feet.*]

LENCHEN: Grandpa!
EPHRAIM [*happy at the sudden brightening of* RABBI URIEL]: It was these two sleeping in the synagogue.

[*The* ANGEL OF DEATH *is visible to* RABBI URIEL *for a brief moment. He leans over him, stands behind his chair.* RABBI URIEL'*s face shines with bliss, for the* ANGEL OF DEATH *has whispered a blessed message into his ear.*]

They'll divert their Grandpa.
RABBI URIEL [*still elated from the* ANGEL OF DEATH'*s words*]: What is it?
EPHRAIM: The children!

[RABBI URIEL *smiles weakly, claps his hands softly.* LENCHEN *and* ARTHUR *rush into the conference room.*]

RABBI URIEL [*bending over them, very tired*]: Where have you come from?
ARTHUR [*in a singing tone, like* RABBI URIEL]: From Hexengaesecke!
LENCHEN [*in the same tone*]: From Hexengaesecke!
RABBI URIEL: And your dear mother?
ARTHUR [*merrily*]: We climbed aboard with coat and hat, hoo-ha, up to where the coachman sat.
RABBI URIEL [*caressing* ARTHUR *and* LENCHEN]: You little run-aways!
ARTHUR: Grandpa!
LENCHEN: Grandpa!

[EPHRAIM *sets* ARTHUR *and* LENCHEN *on* RABBI URIEL'*s knees*.]

RABBI URIEL: And your dear mother, does she know about your journey?

ARTHUR [*evasively*]: Mother says to look out, look out for Lenchen.

RABBI URIEL [*to* EPHRAIM]: You ask the children.

[*His head sinks wearily back into the chair*.]

EPHRAIM [*with emphasis*]: Pay close attention to what Ephraim asks you. Does your mama know that you traveled from Gaesecke to Paderborn in the mail coach to your grandfather rabbi?

ARTHUR: It was so bright!

RABBI URIEL [*somewhat impatiently*]: Does your mama know about it?

EPHRAIM: Who sent you?

RABBI URIEL [*with a happy sigh*]: The Almighty—to gladden his servant once more with the sight of the boy.

[EPHRAIM *bows deeply*.]

ARTHUR [*to extricate himself from the unusual and serious situation, imitating his father*]: My father says to my mother, "In one day the rabbi in Paderborn, with his ideas on raising children, undoes my eight long years of struggling to make this child into a person."

EPHRAIM [*to* RABBI URIEL, *both of them smiling*]: He's afraid his grandpa will send him back home to Gaesecke with his little sister. Is that it, Arthur Aronymus?

ARTHUR [*energetically*]: Precisely.

RABBI URIEL: You runaways, you!

[*Kisses the two children and rocks them wearily on his knees*.]

ARTHUR [*as he and* LENCHEN *throw their arms impetuously around* RABBI URIEL*'s neck*]: We wanted to ask Grandpa something about Dora. Is she really a witch?

RABBI URIEL [*distressed*]: Who told you that?

ARTHUR AND LENCHEN: She's to be burned.

RABBI URIEL: *Shema Yisroel!* And your mother kept this monstrous danger from me?

EPHRAIM [*to himself*]: It is truly raining fire on the rabbi today.

RABBI URIEL [*to* EPHRAIM]: And now I understand the brave little traveler, my beloved Arthur Aronymus, and what drove him to Grandpa.

ARTHUR [*very comically and in strong local dialect*]: Actually we came because it's as cozy with you as with Father Abraham.

[*He embraces* RABBI URIEL *again tempestuously.* RABBI URIEL *and* EPHRAIM *smile.*]

LENCHEN: Dora's got a St. Vitus's dance.

RABBI URIEL [*aside to* EPHRAIM]: An illness children often get at puberty.

ARTHUR: Oh, always Dora!

EPHRAIM [*suspiciously*]: Maybe this unruly child has just tried to play a little joke on Grandpa with his witch story?

RABBI URIEL: He's old enough and rational enough, for all his pranks, to know that this sorrowful news could tear Grandpa apart heart from soul!

ARTHUR [*begins to cry loudly*]: The witches sit on the animal hedges all the time at night. A real fat one with staring eyes always sits on the one that's cut like a calf. I showed her to Lenchen myself, didn't I, Lenchen?

LENCHEN [*nodding meaningfully*]: This fat.

[*Draws a circle in the air.*]

ARTHUR: And two or three of them sit on the stag a lot, together, and gobble up his antlers.

[*Both children laugh uproariously.*]

LENCHEN: And, Grandpa, when I was on my way to the mail coach with Arthur Aronymus this morning, a witch that staggered like our Dora was sitting on the big pink hawthorn that's cut like a rooster.

RABBI URIEL [*to* EPHRAIM]: How this superstition poisons the children's imagination! [*To* himself] And Matthias thought the aberration insignificant?

EPHRAIM [*to* ARTHUR, *to divert* RABBI URIEL]: But I'll bet the little rascal broke something at home? [*To* LENCHEN] You tell Grandpa and Ephraim about it.

LENCHEN [*looks questioningly at* ARTHUR]: He always runs into Mother's room with muddy shoes and boomph! into her sewing basket so the threads go flying.

EPHRAIM: And what else?

LENCHEN: And Arthur Aronymus built a tower for us two and set it on the flower shelf in front of his window.

ARTHUR: Since I'm going to court Lenchen later so she won't have to marry an educated man.

LENCHEN: And as Father passed by, a block from the tower fell from high above down onto his freshly brushed—

ARTHUR: Chimney!

LENCHEN: Then he got an assignment from Father, as punishment. A hundred times he was supposed to write "I beg Father's pardon." And that was really a bore for him!

EPHRAIM: And then you two took off, you little rogues!

RABBI URIEL [*to* EPHRAIM]: It was the Lord's will.

ARTHUR: Precisely! And later I and Lenchen will live in my tower in the clouds—and always rain!

EPHRAIM: Let the little children leave you no more, Abba.

[*Behind* RABBI URIEL'S *high-backed chair the* ANGEL OF DEATH *is again visible to* RABBI URIEL. *A faraway look suddenly comes into his eyes. He presses the boy to him and blesses him.* ARTHUR, *to free himself from the seriousness of* RABBI URIEL'S *action, jumps into the middle of the room onto the carpet,* LENCHEN *behind him. They join hands, form a little circle, hop and dance, and sing the witches' rhyme.*]

ARTHUR AND LENCHEN:

Maria, Joseph, it's ringing tonight
Bimmel la bammel,
Wash yourself in Christ's blood white,
Bimmel la bammel!
If the Eucharist damns your sin,
Bimmel la bammel!
Pull your witch's tail in
And be damned to hellfire pain,
Hellfire pain, h, h, hellfire pain.
But Jesus our savior, we thank him all
For redeeming our souls from eternal fall.

RABBI URIEL [*very disturbed over this song; softly to* EPHRAIM *as he is about to stop the children after the first line*]: Let them alone. Evil too serves to inspire children's play.

EPHRAIM: I'll put the two of them to bed on the parlor couch.

RABBI URIEL: First hand me our precious Torah.

[EPHRAIM *takes it from a shelf on the wall.* RABBI URIEL *smiles.*]

What was it Kern said? The "ancient child"—

[*He embraces the Torah ardently.*]

Almighty God, as I cherish the Torah, so turn the light of thy countenance on Arthur Aronymus, my dearly beloved.

[ARTHUR *notices the* ANGEL OF DEATH, *whom he has also unwittingly seen before, while playing, behind his grandfather's chair. He tears himself away from* EPHRAIM'*s hand and stops transfixed before the conference room door, his lips parted.*]

EPHRAIM [*unsuspectingly, to the children; pointing to* RABBI URIEL, *who has closed his eyes*]: Now don't disturb your grandpa while he's napping!

[*All three go into the next room.*]

RABBI URIEL: The Lord Sabaoth has heard his servant.

[RABBI URIEL *has died.*]

Scene 4

[*The Catholic church, with its two towers, stands upstage, on the church square. Next to the church is a small structure in which* CHAPLAIN MICHALSKI *lives. Christmas trees for the approaching holidays fill the marketplace, as well as little stalls with Christmas decorations and all sorts of other wares. Schoolchildren wearing schoolbags on their backs romp and slide over the frozen ground of the marketplace past* POOR JEWS *(Westphalian Jewish men), among them the Galician peddler* LEMMLE TSILINSKY. *His hands hang as though he were a lamb standing on its hind legs.* ARTHUR, WILLY HIMMEL, *and* CASPAR *throw off their schoolbags, draw circles, and play marbles.*]

WILLY: If I win the fat one today, you'll never get it back, I'm telling you!

CASPAR: Did Fanny give it to you or did Lenchen?

ARTHUR: You clowns!

WILLY: All right, let's go!

CASPAR [*after they have been playing*]: I almost had it won. [*To* WILLY] What do you keep shoving me for?

WILLY [*points insolently to the poor peddler* LEMMLE TSILINSKY]: Hepp! Hepp! Hepp!

ARTHUR: Look at that; he forgot to turn off his nose.

CASPAR: Come on, give me your paw; make it snappy!

[WILLY *gets up from the ground, makes as though to give* LEMMLE *a marble, then takes it back teasingly*.]

LEMMLE: What do you want with me? Leave me in peace!

CASPAR: Hepp! Hepp! Hepp!

WILLY, CASPAR, AND ARTHUR: Hepp! Hepp! Hepp!

WILLY: Take your Sabbath cover off your head!

LEMMLE [*as all three shout*]: How is mine little hat bothering you—you village boylet?

POOR JEWS [*who have followed* LEMMLE]: Get out of here, you miserable urchins, or you'll get your ears boxed.

[WILLY, CASPAR, *and* ARTHUR *jump quickly aside, stick their tongues out at the* POOR JEWS, *and notice* CHAPLAIN MICHALSKI, *who has seen and heard everything from behind a stall. They cannot avoid running directly into his arms. He catches all three*.]

WILLY [*embarrassed*]: That Jew did sock us, Father.

CHAPLAIN MICHALSKI: So?

ARTHUR: Caspar just wanted to give him his mib.

CHAPLAIN MICHALSKI [*smiling to himself*]: Ah! Then that's very ungrateful of the poor peddler—or?

CASPAR: And we also wished him good day.

[*Winks at his friends*.]

CHAPLAIN MICHALSKI: So you wished him good day?

ARTHUR: Something like good day.

CHAPLAIN MICHALSKI: Hmm, now, I'm curious to know what "something like" you three wished him. Well?

WILLY, CASPAR, AND ARTHUR [*crestfallen and subdued*]: Hepp! Hepp! Hepp!

CHAPLAIN MICHALSKI: That certainly didn't give him any reason to hit you, for do you know what that means? [*Points to* ARTHUR]

CASPAR: He can't know that.

CHAPLAIN MICHALSKI: Why not, then?

WILLY: He's a Jew himself.

CHAPLAIN MICHALSKI: Then you two boys answer me.

[*They open their mouths wide like two helpless sparrows.*]

Hepp! Hepp! Hepp! means good news for the Jews: that Jerusalem is not lost.

CASPAR, WILLY, AND ARTHUR: We won't ever shout at him again.

CHAPLAIN MICHALSKI: And do you know in what country Jerusalem is?

[*Waits.*]

In the Promised Land.

[*All three pretend to listen with great interest.*]

So, what do we understand by "hepp, hepp," Willy?

[WILLY *racks his brain, nonplussed.*]

Caspar, you tell them.

CASPAR: I did know it a minute ago.

CHAPLAIN MICHALSKI [*to* ARTHUR]: And you, my son?

ARTHUR [*abruptly*]: Gaesecke is not *perdu*.

CHAPLAIN MICHALSKI [*smiling*]: When you get into my class, then we'll talk about many things that you little ne'er-do-wells seem to be still too little to understand. And now, home, quick, or your soup will get cold.

WILLY [*quietly to* ARTHUR]: There's your father.

CASPAR [*quietly to* WILLY]: All dressed up.

ARTHUR [*to* CHAPLAIN MICHALSKI]: Our twins, the Metas, it's their birthday today, so we're not eating till one o'clock on account of Menachem.

CHAPLAIN MICHALSKI: So?

ARTHUR: He's coming on the mail coach from Erwitte.

WILLY AND CASPAR [*referring to* HEINRICH MENACHEM]: That's his oldest brother, and he's Arthur Aronymus Schüler. And my mother says I can go around with him because he has light brown hair and he's the right sort.

CHAPLAIN MICHALSKI [*pats* ARTHUR *on the head*]: I'll call on your mother during the Christmas season, Willy. Tell her that, my boy.

WILLY: Yes, I will, Father.

CHAPLAIN MICHALSKI: Now let's look at the holy trees nicely gathered together and see which of them is the tallest.

[LEMMLE *has parted company with his companions before reaching the other side of the square. Returning, he catches sight of* CHAPLAIN MICHALSKI *and tips his hat timidly.* CHAPLAIN MICHALSKI *offers him his hand and keeps his eye on the children.*]

Now, my dear brother, and do you feel at home in our village?

WILLY [*softly to his friends*]: Holy strawsack!

CHAPLAIN MICHALSKI [*smiles, for he has heard the exclamation*]: Or do you suffer from the lack of understanding of our adult—or even of our little—fellow citizens?

LEMMLE [*touchingly childlike*]: The schoolboylings, if they'd just leave me in peace, kindest Mister Chaplain. Your policemen were telling me, if I stick mine curls under the hat and change the long coat [*looking down at his caftan*] from mine father—of blessed memory—for a new-style frock coat, then I have peace.

CHAPLAIN MICHALSKI: If you like those clothes, keep on wearing them in honor, Lemmle Tsilinsky.

LEMMLE: How is it you know me?

CHAPLAIN MICHALSKI [*keeping the children in his eye*]: I certainly know a hardworking man like you by name, dear Tsilinsky.

LEMMLE [*lowering his eyes to conceal his emotion at the seldom heard praise*]: Mister Chaplain, I must tell you, whether you want to hear it or not—I always have a secret joy when I see you. And that you, of all people, should give me, poor Jew, such praise, poor Tsilinsky would never in his dreams have imagined.

[*With tears in his eyes he kisses* CHAPLAIN MICHALSKI'*s hand and goes on his way, as unpretentiously as he came.*]

CHAPLAIN MICHALSKI: Do you boys see how few words it takes to raise a person up?

[*The boys are embarrassed.*]

CASPAR: Mother and Father go to church every Sunday at six.

CHAPLAIN MICHALSKI [*to* WILLY]: And your dear mother?

WILLY [*nods, then somewhat gloatingly points to* ARTHUR]: His father and mother are—Semites.

CHAPLAIN MICHALSKI [*to* ARTHUR]: So you are little Arthur Aronymus from the big mansion's garden over there? And where do you stand in the long line of sisters and brothers?

CASPAR: The twenty-fourth.

ARTHUR: I don't even have that many!

CHAPLAIN MICHALSKI: Well?

ARTHUR: I'm precisely the fifteenth, Bernard!

CHAPLAIN MICHALSKI: Who told you, then, that the chaplain's name is Bernard?

[*He sends* WILLY *and* CASPAR *home, admonishing them.*]

ARTHUR: My sisters. They always call when you pass by, "Come quick! Bernard's coming, Bernard's coming!"

CHAPLAIN MICHALSKI [*flattered; he can hardly bite back his laughter*]: That honors me deeply, little Arthur Aronymus.

ARTHUR: Especially Fanny. [*Imitating her*] "Oh, why couldn't the chaplain happen to be a Jew?"

CHAPLAIN MICHALSKI: Oh!

ARTHUR [*imitating his sister* KATHARINA]: "What a *malheur,*" Katharina said then.

CHAPLAIN MICHALSKI: Oh!

ARTHUR: And Elischen said, since she's educated, "Fanny, how illogical you always are! A Jew *can't* be a Catholic priest or a Catholic priest a Jew." Then Fanny said, "Hush!"

[ARTHUR *stops to deliberate and keeps swallowing.* CHAPLAIN MICHALSKI *covers his face to hide his laughter.*]

"Do you know," said Fanny, "whom Bernard looks like?" And they all thought. Then Fanny said, "He looks like the great elector Conradin von Hohenstaufen." Then Elischen said, "How uncultured, Fanny! Conrad was a crusader and not an elector, for he went off to the holy war from 1680 till 1725. Take note of that, sister!"

CHAPLAIN MICHALSKI: Priceless! [*Pats* ARTHUR *on the head.*]

CHRISTMAS TREE SELLER: The little fir in the pot [*lifts it up*] is just right for the chaplain's parlor. To the chaplain for half price?

CHAPLAIN MICHALSKI: God bless you, dear friend.

CHRISTMAS TREE SELLER: Schülers' Aronymus will carry it into your parlor for you. The Jewish child can enjoy the little Christmas tree, at least part of the way.

CHAPLAIN MICHALSKI [*takes the little tree, but* ARTHUR *deliberately takes it from him to carry*]: There it stands on his shoulder now.

ARTHUR: Now we'll play porter.

CHAPLAIN MICHALSKI: It isn't too heavy for you?

ARTHUR: A little tiny tree like my mother's rubber poplar.

[CHAPLAIN MICHALSKI *tries to put a small coin in* ARTHUR'S *pocket*.]

Naa, I wouldn't take anything for this!

CHAPLAIN MICHALSKI: There are so many children in your family. Do you have a favorite little sister among them too, as I do?

ARTHUR [*after a pause*]: Don't you know our Lenchen? [*Confiding*] She's my fiancée. I'm two whole years older, you see. Lenchen likes marzipan so much. That's why the two of us go to visit Mrs. Greenbaum all the time, the health commissioner's wife, in Lippstadt.

CHAPLAIN MICHALSKI [*in the same confidential tone*]: But doesn't Mrs. Health Commissioner Greenbaum notice that the two of you only come for the marzipan?

[*Acts very interested; they stop frequently*.]

ARTHUR: Just the opposite. She always calls out, "Ah, it's nice that you two are visiting me again," and then she says, "My son has sent me fresh marzipan from Königsberg again, too." And when we've eaten it up, then we both stand there a little longer, because I and Lenchen are thirsty, till she says, "And what does your mother have going these days?"

[CHAPLAIN MICHALSKI *looks questioning;* ARTHUR *looks up at him naively*.]

The coffee pot, when company comes.

CHAPLAIN MICHALSKI: Priceless!

[MISS PADERSTEIN *stops curiously before the two figures approaching through the marketplace and regards them through her lorgnon.* CHAPLAIN MICHALSKI *and* ARTHUR *have arrived in front of* CHAPLAIN MICHALSKI'*s little house next to the church. The entrance is on the side. He lifts the small tree from* ARTHUR'*s shoulder.*]

CHAPLAIN MICHALSKI: You will accept a piece of chocolate from Father Bernard?

[ARTHUR *blows a shrill blast on his metal whistle and runs off.*]

Scene 5

[*In the garden of the Schüler mansion. The maid* CLARA *is setting the table for afternoon coffee in the jasmine arbor; it is enclosed in tinted glass walls for the winter, and a small wood fire burns inside.*]

NATHANAEL BRENNESSEL: Just look—our little house mother!

CLARA [*seeing him on the highway and motioning him into the garden; reproachful, sarcastic*]: Mr. Never-Tired—

NATHANAEL BRENNESSEL: *You* go out journeying, little lady; it's exactly the journeying that offers such a good opportunity to *relax*.

[*Whistles with puckered lips.*]

As Wolfgang already said it when he wrote to his Mrs. Councilor mother [*affectedly*] from Italy back to Weimar.

CLARA [*mimics him sarcastically*]: "—offers such a good opportunity"? Try your line on some other female. Dawdling and flirting don't make the potatoes grow round.

NATHANAEL BRENNESSEL [*his honor touched; affectedly*]: I must beg you most politely, little lady.

CLARA: You know what I mean, Mr. Brennessel.

[*He comes close to her and tries to embrace her.*]

Do you want to ruin me the way Wolfgang did Friederike?

[NATHANAEL BRENNESSEL *giggles.*]

Look here—our Katharina lost this just now as she was called to the beehives by the beekeeper.

[CLARA *shows him a ribbon with a little heart-shaped locket.*]

NATHANAEL BRENNESSEL: For a queen's honeymoon. [*Somewhat lustfully*] I saw her outside with the bee man, Clairkin.

CLARA [*regards the little heart, humming*]: Look at it, Brennessel. [*Swinging it to and fro*] His intentions toward the young lady are honorable. [*Whispering*] The Vogelsang parents got here yesterday. That impresses me, Brennessel!

[*He pretends to wipe tears from his eyes.* CLARA, *sympathetically*]

I *know* that *you* don't have any parents, Nattykin.

NATHANAEL BRENNESSEL: And that's why I'm so footloose too; that's my inborn weakness, my Sweetie Clairkin.

CLARA: Madame is coming!

[*Behind* MRS. SCHÜLER *is her husband, both of them in best clothes and best spirits. It is too late for* NATHANAEL BRENNESSEL *to disappear.*]

MRS. SCHÜLER [*to him*]: Brennessel, here you are as though summoned!

NATHANAEL BRENNESSEL: I hope so, most honored Madame.

MRS. SCHÜLER: You can help beat the rugs. Will you? [*To* CLARA] Have him first—

MR. SCHÜLER [*abruptly*]: Well?

[NATHANAEL BRENNESSEL *removes his hat and bows to the ground with it.*]

MRS. SCHÜLER: —go to the kitchen for a little snack.

[*She nods kindly to him. He and* CLARA *exit.*]

MR. SCHÜLER: You spoil people, Henrietta; the man is used to grazing in the open.

SIMEON [*who has come into the arbor*]: The man gets his wages, and that's enough, Mother.

MRS. SCHÜLER: In my parents' house, no one went away hungry.

SIMEON [*to his father*]: In matters of economy you just can't tell Mother anything.

[JULIUS *comes into the arbor.*]

MR. SCHÜLER [*rather unpleasantly struck by his second son's pronouncement*]: In household matters we'll let Mother have the last word.

JULIUS [*cleans his lorgnon; sniffing*]: It smells of cheesecake—or am I wrong?

MRS. SCHÜLER: Katharina baked it last evening with the cook.

MR. SCHÜLER [*unwittingly somewhat jealous of* KATHARINA'S *impending engagement*]: A wonderful girl, upon my soul, the doctor can congratulate himself.

SIMEON: How far have the discussions with his parents gotten?

MRS. SCHÜLER [*looking up toward the bay window on the side of the house*]: Ssh—

SIMEON: I ask because they'll be here any minute.

MRS. SCHÜLER [*pointing to her husband*]: Father has declared himself willing to buy their son a medium-sized apothecary.

SIMEON: What does Mother say to that?

MRS. SCHÜLER: We must leave these questions to Father's greater experience.

MR. SCHÜLER [*obviously gratified by his wife's answer*]: I can only give you the same advice, my son Simeon.

JULIUS: I'm surprised by the brand-new brother-in-law's knowledge of modern literature. He can recite all of *Faust*, part 1 and part 2, by heart!

SIMEON [*ignoring* JULIUS]: In these hard times, too.

MR. SCHÜLER: These are not the worst of times. It is simply that the happiness of my daughter Katharina lies close to my heart. My wonderful girl!

JULIUS [*swelling as though giving a lecture; excitedly*]: Part 2! He recites it by heart! Do you, Respected Parents, grasp what intensity of understanding is involved in this achievement?

SIMEON [*sarcastically*]: But the brand-new brother-in-law seems on no account to be a Werther.

MR. SCHÜLER: Who knows—since he loves my little girl.

[MRS. SCHÜLER, *touched by her husband's sentiment, strokes his hand.*]

SIMEON: Idealists—

MR. SCHÜLER [*pulling himself together*]: If only the whole troop doesn't interrupt our conference—

MRS. SCHÜLER: I've sent Elischen and Fanny with all of the children to Varresbeck to drink milk and hunt for blueberries. The children won't let themselves be disturbed so easily when they're picking berries.

SIMEON [*carefully*]: If you please, Father, I've asked Menachem, our eldest brother, to gather information on the Vogelsangs.

[*Short pause.* MR. SCHÜLER *jumps up angrily; his face grows red. But the* VOGELSANGS *are already approaching and the* PADERSTEINS *with them.*]

Yes, they really are among the wealthiest families in the Wupper Valley.

[MR. SCHÜLER *rises, self-controlled, goes to meet his guests like a grand-seigneur, and leads old* MRS. VOGELSANG *courteously into the arbor. The others follow them.* MISS PADERSTEIN *enters the garden.*]

MRS. VOGELSANG [*played by a very thin man; she has gray stubble on her cheeks, is dressed tastelessly in lilac and green silk, and speaks in strong local dialect*]: Vogelsang couldn't be awakened, and of course I couldn't go to sleep with him snoring. He's been ruining my rest like that ever since our wedding.

MR. VOGELSANG: Alvinkin, you're telling tales out of school again.

[*Everyone laughs to be polite, including* MR. SCHÜLER. *Only* SIMEON *still calculates, absentmindedly.*]

MR. SCHÜLER: The cheesecake baked by our Katharina will taste all the better to Madame Vogelsang.

MISS PADERSTEIN [*curious*]: Well, have you come to an agreement?

MRS. PADERSTEIN [*putting her foot in her mouth*]: Engelbrecht is making a good match.

MRS. VOGELSANG [*slyly*]: Easy does it.

MRS. SCHÜLER [*her honor aroused on her daughter's behalf*]: My daughter?

[MR. SCHÜLER *diplomatically ignores the byplay for* KATHARINA'S *sake.*]

MRS. VOGELSANG [*kicking her husband's foot under the table as she holds up her coffee cup*]: You know all about porcelain, don't you, Vogelsang?

MR. VOGELSANG: Top quality, Schüler, genuine Sévres. Why do we keep calling one another Madame and Monsieur—parents of the bride and groom.

MR. PADERSTEIN [*feasting, he crows*]: Raise your filled cups! So, Moritz and Wilhelm, Henrietta and [*indicating his mother-in-law*] Alvina.

MRS. VOGELSANG: Well, easy does it, son-in-law.

MR. SCHÜLER [*reserved and severe*]: *Eh bien*, Madame Vogelsang.

MRS. VOGELSANG [*feeling the suddenly chilled atmosphere; joins in slyly*]: Dear Engelbrecht, all the ladies in Elberfeld are after him.

MRS. PADERSTEIN [*making another faux pas*]: I should say so. He's got all of them—

MRS. VOGELSANG [*breaks in, horrified*]: —nice and clean with his incomparable copyrighted shampoo.

MISS PADERSTEIN: What's it called?

SIMEON [*sarcastically*]: It's named after Katharina.

MRS. PADERSTEIN [*matter-of-factly*]: That's a good idea!

MR. SCHÜLER [*energetically*]: Before our children come, I suggest we take care of the matter at hand.

MRS. VOGELSANG: I say so too.

[*Scratches her whiskers.*]

MR. VOGELSANG [*familiarly*]: Well, Moritz? [*To his wife*] We'll come to agreement all right.

JULIUS [*his honor aroused on behalf of his sister; spiritedly*]: With the horse trade, eh?

MR. SCHÜLER: All right, I declare myself willing to buy a medium-sized apothecary, namely the vacant one in your sister-city Barmen. I love my daughter Katharina and want her to be happy.

MISS PADERSTEIN [*enviously*]: She's always been wild about pharmacists, ever since the pharmacist's assistant here in Gaesecke whitened her red hands with bran.

MRS. VOGELSANG [*with a sigh of relief*]: Bravo, Moritz! [*Suddenly familiar*] See, Vogelsang, such fatherly love impresses me!

[MR. VOGELSANG *has tears in his eyes. His wife, with dignity*]

Control yourself, Vogelsang. [*Letting the words drop casually*] The whole world stood open to our boy—

MISS PADERSTEIN [*rather enviously*]: Katharina will close it off in a hurry, once and for all.

SIMEON [*ice cold, disregarding her remark*]: Then I advise you, Madame Vogelsang, not to close it behind him yet.

[*Chilly pause.*]

MR. VOGELSANG [*reproachfully*]: See how your love for Engelbrecht has gotten you into a fix again, Alvinchen.

MRS. PADERSTEIN: Mother doesn't mean it that way.

MRS. VOGELSANG [*burns her tongue on the hot coffee*]: Children, the coffee, the coffee, the coffee.

[MRS. PADERSTEIN *treads on* MRS. VOGELSANG*'s foot.*]

MR. VOGELSANG: A first-rate mocha.

MRS. VOGELSANG [*holding her abdomen with both hands*]: I'm not used to it so black, kiddies!

[*She groans and gets up quickly to rush off to a certain place.*]

MR. VOGELSANG: Will Alvinchen find it all right?

[MRS. SCHÜLER *hurries after her, rather disgusted; in the meantime* MR. VOGELSANG *takes a stroll on the gravel path.*]

MR. PADERSTEIN [*crowing*]: In Barmen the children won't have anything to fear from old lady Vogelsang, Schüler!

[*The engaged couple come through the gates onto the garden path, deep in conversation. Without noticing the silent relatives in the arbor, they climb the broad stairway arm in arm.* KATHARINA *leans comically on* ENGELBRECHT*'s shoulder.*]

MISS PADERSTEIN [*enviously*]: Why do you suppose he didn't choose pretty Fanny?

[MRS. SCHÜLER, *agitated, steps back into the arbor from the side entrance of the house.* MRS. VOGELSANG *breathes sighs of relief, her hands on her abdomen as after an operation.*]

MR. SCHÜLER: Get hold of yourself, Mother. [*Pointing to the young couple*] For their sake let's let seven be an even number.

MRS. VOGELSANG: Have you seen our two children—as though they weren't even on earth. I like Katykin *even* better from one minute to the next. A charming child!

[*Short pause.*]

You must be exhausted, Henriettchen, after the serious conference? Y'know what, lie down on the sofa in the front parlor and stretch out your limbs. Meanwhile we'll take a walk in the garden. Come on, Moritz! Be chivalrous and offer me your arm.

[*Controlling himself, he politely does so.*]

MRS. VOGELSANG: Follow his example, Vogelsang.

MRS. SCHÜLER [*calling her husband to her as she stands by the stairs*]: Moritz, you put up with anything in your blind love for Katharina, once she's cried on your shoulder—

MR. SCHÜLER: She's a serious girl, Henrietta, she knows what she wants. And anyway, the old fool is seventy and won't live much longer. Katharina will soon be in the clear.

[MRS. SCHÜLER *goes into the house. Meanwhile* MRS. VOGELSANG *has been strolling with her husband on the garden paths.* MR. SCHÜLER *takes a letter out of his wallet and reads it once again before returning to the arbor, where* MISS PADERSTEIN *is awaiting him. Refolds the letter.*]

Another exaggeration!

[ELISCHEN *comes through the garden gate.*]

ELISCHEN [*excitedly*]: Where is Mother?
MR. SCHÜLER: What do you want with Mother?
ELISCHEN: Fanny left our group and is sitting at Prell's with a Dr. Faust.

[*All of the children come through the gate singing Goethe's "Heidenröslein." They are returning from the city. Between* FERDINAND *and* BERTHOLD *is* DORA, *fidgeting restlessly; then the twins, hand in hand. Behind them* ALBERT *wheels the ailing* ALEX *in a little wagon. Then come* ELEONORA *and* AUGUST, BETTINA *and* MARGARETA, ARTHUR *holding* LENCHEN *by the hand, and finally* KARL *with* MEYERCHEN *and* TITI. *They notice their father and proceed warily up the stairs into the house.*]

MR. SCHÜLER [*benevolently, almost in* MRS. SCHÜLER'*s good-natured tone*]: Just keep cheerful, children!

[*Returns to the arbor.*]

MISS PADERSTEIN: Your procession, Moritz.

[*He nods absently. She, coyly*]

You used to call me by my first name, Moritz. Call me Milchen again now that we're relatives.

[ELISCHEN *returns to the arbor.*]

MR. SCHÜLER [*to* ELISCHEN]: What were you saying just now about your sister Fanny?

ELISCHEN: She left our group and is sitting with a foreign monsieur in the wine garden at Prell's.

MR. SCHÜLER: I'll send Julius right away.

[ELISCHEN *exits.* NATHANAEL BRENNESSEL *is on his way out of the garden.*]

Go get me the local paper from the news dealer, Brennessel!

[NATHANAEL BRENNESSEL *comes to the arbor in one bound.* MR. SCHÜLER *puts a coin into his hand.* NATHANAEL BRENNESSEL *spits on it three times, tips his hat several times in thanks.*]

MISS PADERSTEIN [*watching*]: Maybe it's in the paper already.

MR. SCHÜLER: Does Miss Paderstein know about the reported pogroms in Erwitte and the neighboring market towns?

[*Mechanically reaches for his wallet and the disquieting letter from* MENACHEM.]

MISS PADERSTEIN: Today is the first I've heard about it.

MR. SCHÜLER: Then what did you mean? What news were you speaking of? Please be so good as to speak clearly and openly.

[NATHANAEL BRENNESSEL *hands* MR. SCHÜLER *the paper through the foliage of the arbor and exits.*]

MISS PADERSTEIN: It is rumored in the village that you intend, Moritz, to have your son Arthur Aronymus baptized.

MR. SCHÜLER [*paralyzed*]: Either you have made that up or someone has taken you in with this rumor, not a hair of which is true.

MISS PADERSTEIN [*laughing scornfully*]: Aren't you aware, then, Moritz, that the two of them jump over the animal hedges together, trying to outdo each other, the chaplain and your Arthur Aronymus? Why, the unruly boy carried his Christmas tree from the marketplace into his parlor just a few days ago.

MR. SCHÜLER [*stands up*]: Then I'd just like to awaken my Henrietta.

MISS PADERSTEIN: She knows about it, and did she keep it from her husband? [*Slyly*] In your place I'd be very offended by that, Moritz.

MR. SCHÜLER: Offended? On the contrary, I respect this fresh young clergyman, and let his friendship be a lesson to me from now on to take more pains with my boy's upbringing—this friendship with which he singles out my dear Arthur Aronymus, whom I have neglected.

[FANNY, *sneaking past into the house, sees her father.*]

Fanny! You come at just the right moment.

[*He places her arm in his and, glad to be rid of* MISS PADERSTEIN, *draws* FANNY *into the house.* MISS PADERSTEIN *blows her nose in a small embroidered handkerchief, picks up her lorgnon, and looks for her relatives in the garden.*]

Scene 6

[*In* CHAPLAIN MICHALSKI'S *little house. A decorated Christmas tree. His two little nieces,* NARCISSA *and* URSULA, *kneel in the niche before a small altar, under the cross on which Lord Jesus hangs. Lighted candles, a wax heart consecrated to Mary, fir boughs and flowers decorate the room.*]

ARTHUR [*outside the half-open door of the parlor, holding a bouquet in his hand*]: Mother said I mustn't climb in the window today—even if it were open.

CHAPLAIN MICHALSKI: That must be because of the lovely bouquet of flowers in the elegant lace wrapper.

[*Draws* ARTHUR *inside.*]

ARTHUR: For the festive occasion, my mother said. [*Catches sight of the tree*] Ahhh! Control yourself, boy, my mother said, so that the chaplain can see you've had a good upbringing.

[*Suddenly notices the two nieces, who are saying the last verses of the Lord's Prayer.*]

NARCISSA AND URSULA [*together*]: And forgive us our debts as we forgive our debtors. And lead us not into temptation but deliver us from evil. Amen. [*Both rise.* URSULA *approaches* ARTHUR.]

CHAPLAIN MICHALSKI: Now children, all shake hands! [*Turning toward his nieces*] This nice boy is my little friend Arthur Aronymus, and these good little girls, dear Aronymus, are my nieces Ursula and Narcissa. Come closer, all of you; let's look at the Christmas tree first of all.

[ARTHUR *stands rooted to the spot, subdued.*]

You're so quiet all of a sudden; what is it, my boy?

ARTHUR [*in dialect*]: I've got a funny feeling.

[*Looks around him.*]

CHAPLAIN MICHALSKI [*leading them to the tree*]: Now let's sing "O Christmas Tree" together.

URSULA: And then Uncle Bernard will give us presents.
NARCISSA: Dear Uncle Bernard!

[*Puts her arms around his neck.*]

CHAPLAIN MICHALSKI [*patting* ARTHUR *on the head*]: Or do you know what? You go stand in the corner and all three close your eyes, and when I call "Open your eyes!" the Christ child will have been here and brought presents.
URSULA, NARCISSA, AND ARTHUR: Oh yes!

[CHAPLAIN MICHALSKI *takes from the cupboard two dolls, two little Testaments bound in velvet, a little set of blocks, and a top and places the presents on the table under the tree. Then he gets three plates filled with Spekulatius cookies, apples, oranges, and nuts. Last of all, he pulls a hobby horse out from behind the desk.*]

URSULA [*to* ARTHUR, *softly*]: I can see everything, between my fingers!
ARTHUR: I don't see a thing.

[CHAPLAIN MICHALSKI *hears and smiles in amusement.*]

NARCISSA: I'm so excited, Uncle Bernard.
CHAPLAIN MICHALSKI: Eyes open!
CHILDREN: Aaaaaaaah!
CHAPLAIN MICHALSKI: Take Arthur Aronymus in the middle, you two girls, and go up to the Christmas tree table.

[URSULA *is about to fall upon the presents.*]

Not so impatient, Ursula.

[URSULA, NARCISSA, *and* ARTHUR *look at their presents with cries of joy.*]

URSULA: Narcissa, should we trade? I'd rather have the pink doll.

[ARTHUR, *overjoyed at the wonderful hobby horse, has forgotten everything else around him.*]

CHAPLAIN MICHALSKI: Now let's sing.
NARCISSA [*in a very fine high voice*]: "O Christmas tree—"
ALL: "O Christmas tree, how green are all your branches—" [*They sing all of the first verse.*]
ARTHUR [*to* CHAPLAIN MICHALSKI]: We just learned this song in our singing lesson.

[*He beams with joy.*]

CHAPLAIN MICHALSKI: I just heard about that from the little Christ child.
ARTHUR: I always have to sing it alone in school. The teacher says that really gives him a good laugh and does his lazy intestines good.
NARCISSA [*raising her finger*]: Isn't that a sin, for his teacher to laugh at a holy song, Uncle Bernard?
CHAPLAIN MICHALSKI [*shaken*]: A very great sin, my child. Now quick, back to the Christmas presents the Christ child brought you.
NARCISSA [*overjoyed*]: Dear, dear Uncle Bernard.

[*She takes her doll on one arm and embraces* CHAPLAIN MICHALSKI *with the other.*]

CHAPLAIN MICHALSKI: In truth, you are a real child of God.
URSULA [*to* NARCISSA]: Do trade with me; I'll give you my blue and you give me your pink.

[ARTHUR *jumps onto his nag and rides. His eyes flash.*]

CHAPLAIN MICHALSKI: You should build him a stall, Arthur Aronymus.

[CHAPLAIN MICHALSKI *watches the children, deeply moved.*]

ARTHUR [*abruptly throws his arms around his neck*]: Thank you, dear Uncle Bernard.

URSULA [*to* NARCISSA]: Let's see your plate [*to* ARTHUR] and yours.

NARCISSA: Fine, isn't it?

URSULA [*to* ARTHUR]: You've got a candy frog; I and Narcissa don't. [*To* CHAPLAIN MICHALSKI] Why does Arthur Aronymus have a candy frog?

CHAPLAIN MICHALSKI: It came hopping onto his plate, no doubt about it.

URSULA: How odd.

CHAPLAIN MICHALSKI: But we don't want to keep the chocolate in the big pot waiting any longer. My housekeeper is going to celebrate Christmas Eve with her daughter and her grandchildren, and she won't warm it up again. And now that you've got your presents, take your places around the table like three well-behaved children.

[*Before* CHAPLAIN MICHALSKI *stands the largest cup, with "Bernard" in gold letters. In two baskets are sweet anise bread and cake. The two little girls ceremoniously arrange their wide skirts as they sit down so as not to crush them.* ARTHUR *still regards his hobby horse, deep in thought. Then suddenly, with one motion, he is sitting on the chair between the little girls.*]

Now Ursula, Narcissa, you'll be ladies of the house one day, so pass the cakes.

[*He fills the cups.*]

NARCISSA: I want to be a nun, a very devout one, in black robes.

CHAPLAIN MICHALSKI: And you, Ursula?

URSULA: I want to get married and have a lot of children, and then there'll be pudding and saffron sauce every day. [CHAPLAIN MICHALSKI *and* ARTHUR *laugh.*]

CHAPLAIN MICHALSKI: And our Arthur Aronymus? Just what does he want to be?

[ARTHUR *smiles, embarrassed.*]

Probably a master builder.

ARTHUR: Oh yes. I just didn't know what it's called.

CHAPLAIN MICHALSKI: By the way, I wanted to ask you: how is your sick sister, Dora?

ARTHUR: Simeon said, "The doctor is just studying around on the child. He will soon have swallowed up all your money, Father—the quack." And Julius said, "Send for Professor Eisenbart from Paderborn. He's the doctor for over five hundred *incurable* patients."

[CHAPLAIN MICHALSKI *bites back his laughter. Suddenly a stone is thrown against the window, and someone sings maliciously outside: "A Christian child should be having that, out with the chaplain's Jewish brat!"* CHAPLAIN MICHALSKI *hurries to the window; the slanderer has vanished.*]

ARTHUR [*raising his finger*]: May I say something?

CHAPLAIN MICHALSKI: Certainly, my boy.

ARTHUR: He always sings in summer when they gather the windfall fruit in our garden into their sacks. My mother says, poor people like to eat fruit too.

CHAPLAIN MICHALSKI [*disturbed*]: Did you children understand the evil man?

URSULA [*fibbing*]: I understood everything, Uncle Bernard.

[ARTHUR *is absorbed with his hobby horse. He pulls it to him at the table and feels that he should confirm* URSULA*'s words*.]

ARTHUR: Precisely.

NARCISSA [*pensively*]: I didn't understand it—

CHAPLAIN MICHALSKI [*putting more cake on the children's plates*]: Now feast on, my dear little guests, or the Christ child won't invite you to the chaplain's again next year.

ARTHUR [*to* URSULA]: Your cup's empty already.

URSULA [*to* ARTHUR]: Well, go ahead and finish yours. [*Points to* NARCISSA] She's always such a prude.

ARTHUR: Stop nudging, will you?

URSULA: Uncle Bernard, I'm still so thirsty. [*He refills her cup*] It tastes yummy, Uncle Bernard.

[*A second stone strikes the window. The same song, somewhat farther off, this time sung by several voices.* CHAPLAIN MICHALSKI *hurries again to the window and opens it.* NATHANAEL BRENNESSEL *comes across the square.* CHAPLAIN MICHALSKI *recognizes him. On his arm he holds a small decorated Christmas tree*.]

NATHANAEL BRENNESSEL: There they go.

CHAPLAIN MICHALSKI: Do you know the people by name?

NATHANAEL BRENNESSEL: The criminals? Naa. [*Holding up the little tree and saying a bit affectedly in a flute tone*] From Sweetie-Clairkin. She trimmed a little tree for Nathanael. [*Moving along*] I wish the chaplain a happy Christmas Eve.

[*Exits*.]

CHAPLAIN MICHALSKI [*comes back from the window, forgetting to shut it completely, and sits down with the children again*]: Now you may all pick something off the tree to end our celebration.

NARCISSA: The beautiful silver star, please, please.

[CHAPLAIN MICHALSKI *returns to the window he has forgotten to close.*]

URSULA [*to* ARTHUR]: Pick me the red ball, quick, that one there!
ARTHUR: Naa.
URSULA [*pointing toward* CHAPLAIN MICHALSKI]: He won't notice now.

[*She stretches* ARTHUR's *arm upward.*]

But quick.

[ARTHUR, *as though bewitched, picks the ball.*]

CHAPLAIN MICHALSKI [*comes upon them; to* ARTHUR]: But you don't want to be a pushy little Jewboy, do you?

[*Horrified by the remark that has escaped his lips.*]

ARTHUR [*instinctively shaken to the core; comes to abruptly, then grows apathetic, and suddenly calls out tearfully and terribly sadly*]: I want my mother.

[*Pause.* CHAPLAIN MICHALSKI *is deeply shaken.* ARTHUR *swings himself abruptly onto the hobby horse and rides, wild and reproachful.*]

Now I'll be home soon.
CHAPLAIN MICHALSKI [*feeling deeply guilty, he seizes* ARTHUR *in the midst of his galloping ride, lifts him from the horse, and kisses him on the mouth. Then he takes the wax angel from the crown of the tree*]: For Lenchen, your little sister.

[ARTHUR *smiles wearily and apathetically and lets the angel be slipped into his pocket. Without even looking out for his presents, he flees from the parlor and out of the* CHAPLAIN's *little house, across the marketplace toward home.*]

CHAPLAIN MICHALSKI [*in despair*]: Go to bed in the next room, Ursula and Narcissa, so that you'll be rested for the journey home tomorrow.

[NARCISSA, *instinctively comforting, strokes his cheek and goes into the next room with* URSULA. CHAPLAIN MICHALSKI *takes his rosary from beneath the flowers on the altar and kneels before it.*]

Forgive me, poor sinner, Jesus Christ, for this poisonous mollusk [*tears flow over his face*] washed to the shore of my lips by the blood of generations.

[*His eyes are tightly closed. After a while he rises and blows out the candles on the Christmas tree.*]

Scene 7

[*In the bedroom of* ARTHUR *and several of his brothers. Two beds on the right wall* (FERDINAND'S *and* BERTHOLD'S), *two on the left wall* (ARTHUR'S *and* MAX'S). *Two medium-sized washstands, two wardrobes, several chairs, a small desk with school notebooks, ink, etc., and a table, also covered with school things. It is Christmas morning, early.* ARTHUR *is still in bed, sleeping restlessly. Now and then he groans and speaks tearfully in his dreams. From outside, the Christmas bells are heard ringing clearly through Hexengaesecke. The children are all up and playing in the garden. Nearby, the maid* CLARA *is heard scolding at the back entrance to the garden.*]

CLARA: I'll get the overseer, Monsieur Filigran, this minute if you don't get out—and on Christmas morning.

VILLAGERS OF GAESECKE [*in garden; mimicking* CLARA]: Monsieur [*nasally*] Filigran— The airs you put on when you talk! It even beats Madame Schüler. Just go get him, Monsieur [*nasally*] Filigran.

CLARA: There wasn't a pear or an apple left over for us servants in the kitchen. Every day you've grazed away all the windfalls from the orchard where the richest trees are. [*Fibbing*] The Madame says so too.

VILLAGERS OF GAESECKE: You claim Madame Schüler said that? What we did was sweep away the rotten windfalls! Our children are hungry for undamaged fruit, you stingy wench!

CLARA: Rotten fruit? Tell that to someone dumber than I am. It's the apple that falls from the branch that tastes the best! And it doesn't lie very long in the grass. You see to that, you vultures. [*Fibbing*] The Madame says so too.

VILLAGERS OF GAESECKE: We'll tell her what you said.

[*They leave the garden, threatening and muttering. Up in the bedroom,* ARTHUR'*s dream is projected on the wall. The dream (seen as a film):* ARTHUR *and his grandpa,* RABBI URIEL, *wander through the streets of Paderborn, past the old-fashioned biblical houses with peaked roofs. Many of the houses have an arabesque resembling a long, pointed nose in the middle of a face. In many of the houses, great mouths gape open between the windows; one of them gulps out at them.* RABBI URIEL *keeps stumbling over his long beard; he is very ancient, much older than in real life.* ARTHUR *too has white hair, and he carries the little wax angel from the Christmas tree in his hand. Suddenly they encounter* LEMMLE TSILINSKY, *who greets them both politely.* RABBI URIEL *waves him to a stop and asks him, "Are all of the children polite to you now?"* LEMMLE *nods, and* ARTHUR *says to him, "I won't say bad things to you anymore." Two black wings grow onto* RABBI URIEL'*s shoulders, growing ever larger, and* ARTHUR *begs him, "Dear Grandpa, please stay on earth." Suddenly a very tall man comes riding on his hobby horse—and then* FANNY, ELISCHEN, ARTHUR, *and* KATHARINA *are looking out of the window of a very old house. And* FANNY *says, "That is the elector von Hohenstaufen."* KATHARINA *says, "Where?"* ELISCHEN *says, "How uncultured, Fanny, shame on you, he's not called elector but Conradin, the crusader." Then* CHAPLAIN MICHALSKI *laughs, with the utmost arrogance, and on his ear dangles the red Christmas tree bub-*

ble that ARTHUR *was supposed to snitch for* URSULA. *Then suddenly comes a lightning bolt from on high and strikes* ARTHUR *directly in the heart. And afterward a clap of thunder. Simultaneously with the thunderclap the parlor door slams shut. The dream ends.* FANNY *enters, followed by* ELISCHEN *with a superior smile. Then* KATHARINA, *holding the hand of* DORA, *who has St. Vitus's dance and keeps up a restless movement.* ARTHUR *is very sleepy in his small bed.* DORA *plumps down on the floor.* KATHARINA *and* ELISCHEN *raise her up and lay her on one of the beds.*]

FANNY [*impatiently*]: Now wake up, silly boy!

[*Shakes him lightly.*]

KATHARINA: Not so rough, Fanny.

FANNY: Don't you and Elischen take Dora for a walk every morning?

ELISCHEN: Oh, we three wanted a change.

FANNY: I can't hold her. I don't have the muscles.

ELISCHEN: The only one of us sisters with muscles is Katie.

KATHARINA: It takes more love than muscles to take care of Dora.

[DORA *tries to ask something but cannot be understood because of her swollen tongue.*]

ELISCHEN: She says we always get into arguments over her. Our poor Dorchen!

[*Kisses her very kindly and warmly.*]

KATHARINA: We should be ashamed of ourselves.

[DORA *nods agreement.* ARTHUR *opens his eyes wide; they are moist and sad.*]

FANNY: What's wrong with you, then, silly boy?

ALL [*setting him upright against the pillows; abruptly, with curiosity*]: How was it yesterday at the chaplain's? Tell!

FANNY AND ELISCHEN [*together*]: Just look, our bride!

FANNY: What did he say?

ELISCHEN: Well, speak, Arthurchen!

ARTHUR: Nothing!

FANNY [*mimics him*]: Nothing! He must have said something!

ELISCHEN: Well?

KATHARINA [*with common sense*]: The poor boy does have to recollect himself first.

ARTHUR: I got a hobby horse from the Christ child.

ELISCHEN: From the Christ child?

FANNY: Why not, then?

ARTHUR: And a plate of goodies—[*melancholy*] and a lot of other things too—

ELISCHEN: Boy, what is the matter with you?

ARTHUR: Nothing!

FANNY [*picking up the candy frog from a fold of the pillows*]: This must have run over your tongue.

[*She looks at the green animal, smiling to herself.*]

ARTHUR: Leave my frog alone.

[*Tries to smack her.*]

FANNY: Now at least he's awake!

ALL [*urging him on*]: Tell us about it.

ARTHUR: What should I tell?

[DORA *tries to say something and is unable to do so.*]

There was a Christmas tree. Ursula and Narcissa prayed to Jesus, who was bleeding.

FANNY: Who are they?

ARTHUR: Who?

FANNY: Ursula and Narcissa.

ALL: Are they children too?

ARTHUR: Uncle Bernard's nieces. He had the biggest cup, with "Bernard" written on it, and we had anise bread and almond cake and afterward pudding with saffron sauce. And then I galloped home on my hobby horse.

[*Looks around the room for it.*]

FANNY: Do you know what you are?

[ARTHUR *opens his mouth.*]

A little camel.

ARTHUR: He sent greetings to you all.

FANNY: Really?

ALL: Really?

ARTHUR: He wanted to give each one of you a stole with mouse tails—[*noticing the horror in the eyes of his sisters;* DORA *bursts into thick laughter*] with gold fringes, he said, and rosettes for your hair and a Testament by Goethe—rhymed by Jesus's mother.

ALL: What?

ARTHUR: It's darn well true.

ALL: Naa—

[ARTHUR *sinks back into the pillows, melancholy.*]

ELISCHEN: There is something wrong with the boy.

KATHARINA: He's got a stomachache.

[*From outside, the sisters hear the witch song sung maliciously by three voices.*]

VILLAGERS OF GAESECKE:

Maria, Joseph, it's ringing tonight
Bimmel la bammel,
Wash yourself in Christ's blood white,
Bimmel la bammel!
If the Eucharist damns your sin,
Bimmel la bammel!—

DORA [*thickly but intelligibly*]: I'm so afraid—
VILLAGERS OF GAESECKE:

—Pull your witch's tail in
And be damned to hellfire pain,
Hellfire pain, h, h, hellfire pain.
But Jesus our savior, we thank him all
For redeeming our souls from eternal fall.

[ELISCHEN *busies herself with* DORA, *warming her hands*.]

DORA: I won't go into the garden anymore, either.
ELISCHEN: But Dorachen, you must overcome your fear.

[KATHARINA *puts her mink collar around* DORA*'s neck.* KATHARINA *and* ELISCHEN *carry her out of the room. The winter sun shines warm and bright*.]

FANNY: Arthurkin Aronymuskin, I'll give you a new set of blocks.

[*He sits up in the pillows quick as a flash*.]

Tell me exactly, did Bernard speak of me? Fanny? Did he send greetings to everyone or just to me, Miss Fanny? [*Emphasizing*] Fanny, me!

ARTHUR [*pleasant, naive*]: Maybe I'll recall when I have the new set of blocks.

FANNY [*takes her purse and counts into his hands*]: One, two, three, four, five, six, seven, eight, nine, ten coins.

[FERDINAND *and* BERTHOLD *enter, bringing the hobby horse and the other Christmas presents and a large yellow bag of goodies.* LENCHEN *comes tripping into the room with them.*]

BERTHOLD AND FERDINAND [*together, looking at* FANNY]: From the heart-bishop on Catholic Church Square.

FANNY: You silly little rascals, get yourselves out of here.

[*She winks at* ARTHUR.]

Arthur Aronymus must go back to sleep.

[*She pulls the drapes as* LENCHEN *lays her little head next to* ARTHUR'S.]

ARTHUR [*to* LENCHEN]: There's something for you in my jacket, Lenchen. I don't want anything.

[*He turns his face to the wall.* FANNY *leaves, annoyed.* LENCHEN *rummages in his jacket pocket, takes out the wax angel, and lays it next to* ARTHUR *on the pillow. Outside, the Christmas bells ring on without pause.*]

Scene 8

[*Midday. Before* CHAPLAIN MICHALSKI'S *house.* FANNY *stands by the hedge around the little garden, waiting for him. The entrance to the house is on the side. Opposite is Prell's big wine garden at the side of the square.* CHAPLAIN MICHALSKI *is just coming out of the church; his congregation walks piously across the square. Snatches of organ music can be heard.* NATHANAEL BRENNESSEL *comes roaming around* CHAPLAIN MICHALSKI'*s house. Warm winter sunshine.*]

NATHANAEL BRENNESSEL [*speaking loudly enough for* CHAPLAIN MICHALSKI *to hear, with the thought of getting a small handout from the sympathetic chaplain*]: The fox has its hole, the bird has its nest; only the wandering laborer has no pillow to rest his head on. So said Lord Jesus too. [*Sees* FANNY] Yes, yes, yes. [*In flute tone*] Only Nathanael Brennessel has no heavenly little bed where he can snooze sweetly.

CHAPLAIN MICHALSKI [*deliberately ignoring the last words; kindly*]: Only the savior was no wandering laborer but the *savior.*

NATHANAEL BRENNESSEL: Didn't he roam through the land, though, if you please?

CHAPLAIN MICHALSKI [*recognizes* FANNY, *who waits disconcerted, and goes up to her*]: Miss Fanny, [*alarmed*] nothing has happened to my little friend Arthur Aronymus, has it?

FANNY: It's about that that I've taken the liberty of waiting for you, Chaplain.

CHAPLAIN MICHALSKI: For the love of heaven!

NATHANAEL BRENNESSEL: But he was standing in the window just now, happy as a lark, whinnying into the landscape with a toy horse.

FANNY: On the contrary, he's been crying since he came home yesterday evening.

CHAPLAIN MICHALSKI: For the love of heaven.

[*He opens the house door.*]

Won't Miss Fanny tell me more about it in my quarters? Even though my housekeeper is spending the Christmas holidays at her daughter's.

NATHANAEL BRENNESSEL [*to himself*]: On Christmas it would be better not to be a Jew.

CHAPLAIN MICHALSKI [*who has heard him*]: I've been wondering about that, dear Brennessel, since you never come to confession.

[*Puts a gold piece into his hand.*]

NATHANAEL BRENNESSEL: They say the white Jews are worse than our kind!

FANNY: Our grandfather in Paderborn convinced the billy goat [*she hesitates*] that he's Pan. He's got that into his head.

CHAPLAIN MICHALSKI [*respectfully*]: If such a God-pleasing person as the great rabbuni says so, it must be true, Miss Fanny.

[*The two go into the house and are heard speaking through the open window.*]

FANNY: He can get very impudent, believe me, Chaplain.

CHAPLAIN MICHALSKI [*smiling ironically; then in a fairy tale tone, as one tells something to a child*]: That's just what Pan does—particularly when he's aroused.

FANNY: You are divinely good, Chaplain.

[*Tries to kiss his hand.*]

CHAPLAIN MICHALSKI: Miss Fanny, we don't live in the Middle Ages, after all. But we've gotten off the subject. [*Disconcerted*] What's wrong with my dear little friend?

[*They step to the open window.*]

FANNY [*as though speaking a memorized piece*]: Yesterday evening he didn't come bounding up the stairs into the house in his usual mischievous way. He was completely subdued, in fact. Even Mother couldn't comfort him.

[*She acts upset.*]

CHAPLAIN MICHALSKI [*catching on*]: Oh?

FANNY: Now my mother wants me to ask the chaplain most respectfully whether my wild little brother perhaps misbehaved, and to beg pardon if so.

CHAPLAIN MICHALSKI [*keeps understanding the situation more fully and replies in the same conventional tone*]: Miss Fanny, please be so kind as to tell Madame your mother that my little friend behaved himself perfectly, and that it is only in a blunder on my part that the cause of his depression could possibly lie.

FANNY: I'll never believe that of you, [*suddenly with more warmth*] Chaplain Michalski.

CHAPLAIN MICHALSKI [*drawing a chair up to the window*]: May I offer you a chair? For the sun is shining as though it were May.

FANNY: I don't want to take up any more of your lovely Christmastime.

CHAPLAIN MICHALSKI: But first our respected Miss Fanny must have a look at the decorated tree.

FANNY [*turns her face toward the room*]: And how fragrant it is!

CHAPLAIN MICHALSKI [*stepping back from the window, he plucks a little chocolate basket from the tree and offers it to* FANNY]: And the joy of my little guests yesterday evening. Miss Fanny, why didn't you accompany your little brother, whom I love so much?

[*Outside, an organ grinder on the walk by the square begins to play "Maria, Joseph, it's ringing tonight."* CHAPLAIN MICHALSKI *listens, horrified.*]

FANNY [*her emotions touched; half to herself*]: Even today—

CHAPLAIN MICHALSKI: Troublemaker! I'll reprimand him.

[*Rushes out of the room with the speed of an overgrown schoolboy.* FANNY *rises and, leaning far out of the window, looks after him as he rushes off. The organ grinder takes his organ on his back and disappears into a nearby house.* CHAPLAIN MICHALSKI *returns, smiling, to the room.*]

Pardon, Miss Fanny; the trick here is to act both quickly and energetically!

FANNY: The police sergeant gave my father a curt answer when he made a complaint about the illegal song: "Then we'd have to tune a lot of throats to a different key."

CHAPLAIN MICHALSKI [*calming* FANNY]: Hopefully the people who have gone astray will find their way again soon.

FANNY: We're all secretly afraid for our sister who has St Vitus's dance, but none of us dare confess it to the others. And we have to urge Dorachen to get her to walk in the garden. I'm the one who takes her the most often. Yesterday a fellow like that shouted through the hedge, "You're coming along now too, you little witch!"

CHAPLAIN MICHALSKI: These horrible relapses to the religious aberrations of the Middle Ages.

FANNY [*deliberately sentimental*]: Even today, when the lights are burning on the branches.

[*Turns her face toward the Christmas tree*.]

CHAPLAIN MICHALSKI: Do you really enjoy seeing them burn? We'll close the window and pull the curtains so as to see it in full Christmas glory.

FANNY [*overcomes her loving anguish and restrains him from closing the window*]: People will think—you've—gone away—Chaplain.

CHAPLAIN MICHALSKI [*moved by* FANNY'*s reserved maidenliness; striving to answer with self-control*]: We shouldn't give the impression of things that *aren't* true, either! Although my mother [*he points to her picture*] would say, "Bernard will have gone off to dreamland."

[*He lights the candles*. FANNY *trembles with anticipation*. *He returns to her at the first window*.]

Miss Fanny, [*he turns again toward the Christmas tree, as does she*] blessed are they who hang their life on childlike joys.

[FANNY *does not understand what he actually means.*]

Now we stand before the holy light of the world, Miss Fanny—you—Fanny, like a bride of Christ.

[FANNY *is disconcerted.*]

Miss Fanny, [*he touches her hand*] the light unites—[*he falters*] all hearts—[FANNY *trembles from happiness;* CHAPLAIN MICHALSKI *again in control of himself*] as yesterday the throbbing hearts of the children came together with mine.

FANNY: You preached once that Christ is the light of the world.

CHAPLAIN MICHALSKI [*eagerly*]: Have you been to hear me preach, Miss Fanny?

FANNY [*disconcerted*]: For the ending.

CHAPLAIN MICHALSKI: Were you afraid that if someone had seen you, except our savior—

FANNY: Our grandfather was still alive.

CHAPLAIN MICHALSKI [*thinking to convert her*]: I fancy the great rabbi was, after all, a tolerant person. Jesus, our Lord, would have loved him.

FANNY [*after some deliberation, touchingly*]: Chaplain, I don't know how to say it.

[CHAPLAIN MICHALSKI *goes to the second window again and blows out the lights on the tree, then returns to* FANNY.]

CHAPLAIN MICHALSKI [*pointing to the rowan tree in the little garden before the house*]: This is my permanent Christmas tree, that gladdens my heart. There are still clusters of berries hanging on its branches, Miss Fanny. If I were a poet and not a chaplain, I would sing your praises, Miss Fanny; I would praise you above the lovely rowan tree.

FANNY [*surprised*]: There are many, many of them among the pine trees at our house. [*Making use of the opportunity to invite him*] Wouldn't you like to come and see them sometime?

CHAPLAIN MICHALSKI: I have only this one bride. You see, Miss Fanny, this rowan tree is my closest friend—my lover. Under her branches I sit and dream, even late in the fall, [*looking at* FANNY *and playing on her feelings*] of the world that I have renounced.

FANNY: Chaplain—

CHAPLAIN MICHALSKI: Just look at her radiant coral jewelry in October, Miss Fanny.

[FANNY *cries from excitement. He continues to play on her feelings—to save himself from his own.*]

Surely you don't envy the lovely rowan tree her jewelry, do you?

[FANNY *is taken aback.* CHAPLAIN MICHALSKI, *almost tenderly, but controlled*]

And at that, she blooms all alone, has no little sisters and brothers to take care of. When I pass the big mansion garden at eventide in summer and you and all of the children are sitting on the broad lawn or playing blindman's buff, I think to myself, what a fine task for the older children, to take care of the younger ones.

FANNY [*in control again and somewhat annoyed*]: Now you're really talking like my father.

CHAPLAIN MICHALSKI [*laughing at the top of his voice*]: Age protects from foolishness.

FANNY [*cooled down*]: That out of them all, you had to choose that unruly little urchin—that my father will never understand.

CHAPLAIN MICHALSKI: And Madame your mother?

FANNY: She does idolize the boy. I like him very much too. [*Conventionally flirtatious*] If only someone would love me too.

[*Pause.*]

CHAPLAIN MICHALSKI: Ah, I had the idea that Dr. Faust was smitten with Miss Fanny?

[*Looks across into Prell's wine garden.*]

FANNY: Hm—hm, that monkeyish person! Do you know him?

CHAPLAIN MICHALSKI: I can't know all the Dr. Fausts.

[*Pause.*]

Back in October [*pointing to the rowan tree again, dreamily*] my beloved rowan tree wore a dress of fire. She was my chaste goddess, my pious glowing sister, and already I'm waiting for the fall of next year that will adorn her for me again.

FANNY [*rises, bows her head before* CHAPLAIN MICHALSKI, *and says softly, extending her hand*]: Chaplain—

CHAPLAIN MICHALSKI: Fanny!

Scene 9

[*Afternoon, still half light. In the great dining room the members of the Schüler family are gathering, except for* MENACHEM, SIMEON, *and* JULIUS. *A small, festively decked table stands almost in the middle of the room, on it two candelabra. A large mirror on the wall reflects the room with the massive buffet and all of the other furniture.* MRS. SCHÜLER *stands before the little table, laying a green-velvet-bound diary on the small lectern. She straightens the flowered armchair before the table and lights the candles.* FANNY *stands pensively by a curtain.*]

MRS. SCHÜLER: What's the matter with you, Fanny?
FANNY [*mournfully*]: How does my mother mean?
MRS. SCHÜLER: Can it be that you're in love, child?
FANNY: But Mother—[*holding back her tears*].
MRS. SCHÜLER: Haven't you always confided everything else to me? Hasn't your mother been a good friend to you, my child?
FANNY [*changing the subject, in an everyday tone*]: Sometimes I don't understand my mother at all—[*snippily*] the whole day long—Father here, Father there, and the twenty-three children! In your place I would long since have given up.

[*Short pause. She suddenly throws her arms around her mother's neck and bursts into tears.*]

MRS. SCHÜLER [*moved*]: But Fanny, my child—I suspect what it is. I know how painful it is.
FANNY [*abruptly*]: Mother, I want to become a nun.

[*Short pause.*]

I've considered it thoroughly.
MRS. SCHÜLER [*touched*]: And that way you hope to win him, beloved child.

[*Strokes her hair tenderly.*]

FANNY: Whom do you mean, Mother? In heaven's name don't say his name, Mother, in heaven's name!

[MRS. SCHÜLER *remains silent, smiling. A pause.*]

Mother, advise me, what should I do?

MRS. SCHÜLER: I can heartily sympathize with the decision to become a nun, child—in order not to lose him spiritually? But you do know—the Catholic clergy are forbidden to marry. And you're not Catholic, either.

[FANNY *shrugs her shoulders, as though that could be changed.*]

And how strict life is in the convents: have you heard about that too?

FANNY [*mournfully, to herself*]: Yes, yes, I'd never see him again—or at the most in dreams.

MRS. SCHÜLER: You see!

FANNY: Oh, Mother, one really can confide everything to you—you're my very best friend, aren't you?

[*Kisses* MRS. SCHÜLER *tenderly.*]

MRS. SCHÜLER: Do you feel that?

[*Pause.*]

FANNY: Mother, it's the chaplain.

[*Pause.* MRS. SCHÜLER *smiles.*]

I was at his house on Christmas morning, Mother.

MRS. SCHÜLER [*anxiously*]: Did *he* advise you to go into a convent? Tell me the whole truth!

FANNY: Of course not—that's just it. He takes me for just a superficial thing from the mansion garden. The little urchin is a thousand times dearer to him.

MRS. SCHÜLER: That's all we need, for you to be jealous of your eight-year-old brother. Honestly, Fanny!

FANNY: No one ever believes that pretty girls [*glances fleetingly toward the mirror*] have depths.

MRS. SCHÜLER: That's what disappointed young girls say, child.

[*Pauses hesitantly.*]

I too have—

FANNY: Suffered? were you going to say, Mother?

MRS. SCHÜLER: Well—

FANNY [*confidentially*]: Miss Paderstein, the old gusher, once told me in confidence that you really loved Father's brother Uncle Berthold, with his blond hair and his daydreams.

MRS. SCHÜLER [*very disconcerted but not wanting to lose* FANNY'*s trust; girlishly*]: Well, yes, I was in love with him then, but I learned to love your father, my child.

FANNY [*regarding her mother full of love, almost like a suitor*]: Henriettchen, right now you look just like *mon amie* Antoinette from boarding school in Münster.

MRS. SCHÜLER [*holds her hand smilingly in front of* FANNY'*s mouth*]: If someone should hear us.

FANNY [*as though to a friend*]: Mother, I want to impress him! How can I do that?

MRS. SCHÜLER: There must be other ways! But one doesn't change one's faith like changing clothes, even to impress one's beloved.

FANNY: Oh yes; beloved—

MRS. SCHÜLER [*testing her*]: And besides that, to strip off our eternal faith in the one and only God, the soul of your proud heart; could you do that?

FANNY: But we all have just one God! His God is my God!

MRS. SCHÜLER: But do you want to pray to him in a house of worship that is strange to you, among hostile people?

[*From the highway,* VILLAGERS OF GAESECKE *returning home are heard singing the witch song.* MRS. SCHÜLER *points outside.*]

Isn't this confirmation of my words enough to convince you, Fanny?

FANNY [*listens with her mother*]: Up in my room last fall I heard those same harsh voices from the garden, and Clara gave these people hot coffee even so.

MRS. SCHÜLER [*lays her hand on her wounded heart*]: How that amazes me. That these very people—

FANNY: Don't listen. We were having such a good time talking.

MRS. SCHÜLER: The children will be here soon, and Father will begin reading from his diary. Try hard to pay attention, Fannychen, you know how it provokes him when people don't pay attention. And he has such a weakness for his little entries.

FANNY [*nods, then again, mournfully*]: I forgot to tell you how I arranged to visit him in his house.

MRS. SCHÜLER: Yes?

FANNY: I said that you sent me to find out, in your name, if our Arthur Aronymus had misbehaved yesterday—on Christmas Eve—because the boy hadn't opened his mouth since.

MRS. SCHÜLER: You shouldn't have done that, Fanny, for the sake of the innocent boy.

FANNY: But it worked beautifully, Mother. He had me in to look at his tree. He lit the candles. Ah, the scent is still in my nose. Everything smells of fir trees now: our rooms, my dress, my wardrobe, and all the clothes in it [*rapturously*]. Then I had to sit down in a chair facing his tiny garden, at his window. Mother, he loves a rowan tree; he's in love with a rowan tree, most of all in the autumn when it bears its red corals.

[*Short pause.*]

He's charming, Mother!

MRS. SCHÜLER: And then?

FANNY [*mournfully*]: Yes, then I came home.

[MRS. SCHÜLER *gives a sigh of relief.*]

Mother, please, please, bring me a pair of coral earrings from Paderborn, as dark red as can be! You do plan to go—with Arthur Aronymus. Always the urchin! To make up to me you've got to bring me the coral earrings.

MR. SCHÜLER [*enters the dining room with the children; to* MRS. SCHÜLER]: Is no one missing?

MRS. SCHÜLER [*counts*]: Even Titichen is here!

[*She takes the smallest one,* TITI, *onto her lap. The twin* METAS *sit in* KATHARINA'S *lap.* MEYERCHEN *stands in front of* KATHARINA. ELISCHEN *holds her arm around* DORA; *she unobtrusively places a book,* Goethe's Correspondence with Lessing, *on the chair.* MAX *takes a seat on a little stool next to his father.* ALEX *sits in his wheelchair by the fireplace.* ARTHUR *and* LENCHEN *sit pressed close together on a chair. The remaining children are on chairs along the wall, at a large table. As* MR. SCHÜLER *is taking his place,* MAMSELL, *the old cook, hurries into the room.*]

MR. SCHÜLER [*raising his voice*]: It's a shame that Simeon and Julius and Menachem and his family aren't here.

MRS. SCHÜLER: How anxious they must be during their examinations in Paderborn—

[FERDINAND *gives* BERTHOLD *a nudge. They bite back their laughter.*]

MAMSELL: The flour hasn't come yet from the miller. [*Importantly*] Should Clara run over there quickly, Madame Schüler?

MR. SCHÜLER [*watching, astonished*]: And who might this be?

MRS. SCHÜLER [*letting* MAMSELL *know not to interrupt with any more questions*]: Doesn't Father recognize our cook, then, who has lived under one roof with us these twenty years?

MAMSELL: Naw, the squire doesn't know me, seems like. Like his own children this morning! Ha, ha, ha! He almost drove them out of the Garden of Eden, by durn, like the Almighty did Eva and Adam after the fall.

[*All laugh.*]

MR. SCHÜLER [*smiling benevolently*]: Most respected Cook, with this swarm of children, such things can happen now and then, can't they? And now you may vanish!

[*Outside, the witch song is being sung in the distance.*]

DORA [*with thick tongue*]: They'll come and get me soon; I'm so afraid!

[*She gives a violent shake. It takes all* ELISCHEN'*s efforts to hold her.* ELISCHEN *kisses her very kindly and soothingly.*]

FERDINAND [*to parents*]: They say she's a witch—and bewitched seven children in the village!

MR. SCHÜLER [*beckons* KATHARINA *to him; quietly in her ear*]: Your mother doesn't suspect anything about the anonymous letter, does she?

[KATHARINA *raises her hands negatively.*]

MRS. SCHÜLER [*to* FERDINAND]: Who has taken you in with that nonsense?

[*He hesitantly points to* ARTHUR. MRS. SCHÜLER, *forcing herself*]

Stand in the corner and don't move until I call you.

[LENCHEN *accompanies* ARTHUR *to the corner.*]

MAX: Hahahaha!

MR. SCHÜLER: This time Mother has beat me to it. Which reminds me of another matter.

[*Calls* FANNY, *who is leaning against the curtain in the window niche, apathetically awaiting the reading.*]

Fanny! [*She is abruptly conscience stricken*] The mayor informed me at our domino game yesterday evening that my daughter, Miss Fanny, goes out walking late every evening alone—?

FANNY [*half to herself*]: Only that stupid billy goat Brennessel could have tattled to the mayor.

MR. SCHÜLER: What an inappropriate expression for a young lady: "billy goat"! Shame on you!

MRS. SCHÜLER [*fibbing on* FANNY*'s behalf*]: The day before yesterday I went with Fanny on her harmless little excursion.

FANNY [*boldly*]: The evening air does me good—[*glances quickly at the mirror*]. It preserves the complexion.

[ELISCHEN *and* KATHARINA *exchange glances.*]

MRS. SCHÜLER [*prudently and lovingly*]: Why does Father keep us waiting so long for the thrilling conclusion of his diary, as he put it yesterday? Moritz!

MR. SCHÜLER [*opens the diary, smiling*]: Observe the example of your mother, with what love she has once again kept our little table in order. [*Chivalrously*] So, as my consort demands.

[*He clears his throat and bows as though at court.*]

Listen attentively now to the closing chord of my youthful days. [*Reads*] "I take pen in hand in order to dedicate the last pages of my modest diary to you, Gotthold Ephraim Lessing. Accept them from your most humble servant. In parentheses: That night they were giving his *Nathan* at the ducal Goethe theater in Weimar."

[ARTHUR *looks around at* DORA *and says something to her in sign language.* DORA *laughs convulsively.*]

MRS. SCHÜLER [*to* MR. SCHÜLER]: Please, please, don't stretch our impatience to the point of torture, Moritz!

[FANNY *shrugs her shoulders, looking at her mother.*]

MR. SCHÜLER [*absorbed in himself*]: "Paderborn. Thursday, the 25th of September 1810. I, Moritz Schüler, the firstborn of my parents, and my younger brother Berthold arose from our beds at eight o'clock in the morning. Not awakened as usual by the harmonious striking of the wall clock [*he points to the wall clock*]. Its mute hand confessed many an occurrence to us. Suspecting that our good and honorable parents still rested in the arms of Morpheus, we were mightily startled to find neither Father nor Mother, neither in their bedchamber nor in the living room. We two brothers were ashamed, even though we were tired from studying, to have slept the sleep of the just. And so to have missed the terrifying cries for help that must have issued from our respected parents!"

MRS. SCHÜLER [*sympathetically*]: Oh!

MR. SCHÜLER: "For the first time we two young men, we brothers, got into a quarrel with each other."

[FANNY *notices disagreement in* MRS. SCHÜLER'*s expression. Their glances meet uncertainly.*]

LENCHEN [*raising her finger from the corner, as in school*]: Mother, may Arthur Aronymus sit down again?

[MRS. SCHÜLER *nods quietly, and the two sit down to the right and left of* ALEX'*s wheelchair.*]

MR. SCHÜLER [*absorbed*]: "From the street roared the rage of the goaded Christians, and we two youths rushed reconciled and united, in nightgown and cap—that is, practically naked—

out onto the streets of Paderborn. And there! What presented itself to our gaze?

[*He looks at each member of the audience. Short pause.*]

Whom did we catch sight of?

[*Short pause.*]

My brother Berthold: 'Moritz, do you hear our parents calling from high up in the cathedral?' I looked up, tears came into my eyes, and I answered: 'No doubt about it, my brother, it is our parents.' So we pushed our way through the staring masses of Paderborn, bounded like warhorses up the spiral stairs of the Catholic house of worship, ever higher, ever higher, until we stood before the small iron gates that cruelly separated us brave sons from our tormented parents."

MRS. SCHÜLER [*in suspense*]: And?

MR. SCHÜLER [*himself deeply moved*]: "Never shall I get over the sight, dear reader, that offered itself to our bewildered eyes. Squeezed into the bell tower with the other honorable Jewish families of Paderborn, our respected parents suffered the torments of hell. And not only the aroused Christians did we subdue, I and Berthold, but in the end the police as well, who got in our way. Without bragging about my manliness, I did fight like a man until, the last abused Jew freed, my brother Berthold's strength—to report it all accurately—failed him."

[FANNY *winks roguishly at her mother.*]

ARTHUR [*almost in tears*]: Always so sad.

MR. SCHÜLER [*praising him warmly*]: Yes, yes, my son! [*Reads on*] "But as the evening came with its stars, the streets shone once again, cleansed of the outrage of the rebellious mob, and Father and Mother sat in fond embrace on the sofa, we brothers at their feet. And peace entered into the great city Paderborn, into every room, into the tiniest chamber. [*Pompously*] And everyone's bosom swelled, and the heart began to beat *lovingly*. The End!"

[*He takes a deep breath.*]

ELISCHEN [*to herself*]: Influenced by Goethe.
MR. SCHÜLER: Do you think so, Elischen?
MRS. SCHÜLER [*cutting her off*]: A Lessing was lost in Father.
MR. SCHÜLER: Thank you, Henrietta.
MRS. SCHÜLER [*gestures to the children to go outside*]: That certainly was an afternoon!

[MR. SCHÜLER *is flattered.*]

Will you grant me a request?
MR. SCHÜLER [*like a king*]: Even to the half of my kingdom, Esther Henrietta!
MRS. SCHÜLER: I'd like to go to Paderborn tomorrow. To visit my father's grave.

[MR. SCHÜLER, *with a kingly gesture, nods in agreement.*]

And Moritz, I'd like to take Arthur Aronymus along. Let him come, for me.
MR. SCHÜLER [*still blissfully in higher spheres*]: His favorite grandson.

[*Nods in agreement.*]

FILIGRAN [*entering the room; somewhat nasally*]: Mr. Squire, two of the checkered cows are calving. Pardon, Madame. [*Bows to* MRS. SCHÜLER.]

[MR. SCHÜLER *hurries into the garden with* FILIGRAN. MRS. SCHÜLER *dries her brow with a small handkerchief. She is tired out, as after an operation. She leans back in her armchair and closes her eyes.*]

Scene 10

[*In the old Jewish cemetery in Paderborn. Snow is falling; it is early January.*]

MRS. SCHÜLER [*coming up to the gate, holding* ARTHUR *by the hand*]: Now be good, my child, [*pointing upward*] so that you make your dear grandpa happy.

ARTHUR: Is he up there in heaven, then?

MRS. SCHÜLER: Indeed he is. An angel escorted him.

ARTHUR: Oh, Grandpa laughed so, when I and Lenchen did somersaults on his Persian rug. Ephraim combed its fringes every morning.

[*Sees that his mother is crying. A cuckoo calls.*]

Listen, Mother! [*Counting*] One, two, three, four, five, six, seven, eight! [*Mimicking Westphalian farmers*] Just as old as I am, that's how old Grandpa got. A fine age, eh Mother?

MRS. SCHÜLER [*cannot help laughing*]: Rascal! Sometimes people really did believe your dear grandpa was as old as this rascal here. But then [*admonishing*] it seemed to me that he was as old as God.

ARTHUR: Because he talked so much about the dear God?

MRS. SCHÜLER: For that too, my child, but also because he shone with light, and he spread eternal peace, and—all who looked on him were comforted.

ARTHUR [*in the same sad tone*]: Everywhere.

MRS. SCHÜLER [*making a turn into a row of gravestones, smiling*]: And you must always be a good person, my child, in honor of Grandpa.

[*Suddenly* ARTHUR *jumps several times.* MRS. SCHÜLER, *startled*]

But boy, you were going to be good, weren't you?

ARTHUR: Because you keep on crying, Mother.

MRS. SCHÜLER [*stops before a grave whose stone is engraved with two praying hands and the inscription of her father*]: There lies our beloved, unforgettable grandpa, [*emphasizes*] the renowned rabbuni of the Rhineland and Westphalia, my child.

[*She meditates, absorbed, then lifts* ARTHUR *up.*]

Now get out your little stones from your pouch and lay them out on the big stone tablet in a pattern, as you do your blocks.

ARTHUR [*removing stones very precisely*]: And this stone, with ore in it, in the middle. Mother, why should I lay the stones on the monument? Caspar always takes his father an old wreath made of straw flowers on Sundays.

MRS. SCHÜLER: I'll explain it to you when you're older, my child; then [*laying stones on top of* ARTHUR'S, *not so carefully as he.* ARTHUR *ponders, shaking his head at his mother's lack of talent*] we'll build Grandpa a residence as high as heaven. In any event, my little Arthur Aronymus, this was your first serious building project, my boy.

ARTHUR: Now you're talking just like Grandpa-rabbi, Mother.

MRS. SCHÜLER: Now fold your hands and pray.

[*He folds his hands like those on the gravestone and starts to say his evening prayer. But he suddenly begins to cry, and* MRS. SCHÜLER *begins to pray inaudibly. She puts her arm around* ARTHUR. *They stand together very moved and still before the grave. From a side path voices drift over to them.* MRS. SCHÜLER *dries* ARTHUR'S *wet little face.*]

Now, my darling, we'll go and see Ephraim again, in Grandpapa's little house. Good old Ephraim will soon light the Sabbath candles in his room.

[*They walk along the quiet path, hearing the voices of the* JEWISH GARDENER *and the* CHRISTIAN GARDENER, *who are busy binding the tree trunks against the winter frost.*]

JEWISH GARDENER: Say it again if you're brave enough. Come on now!

CHRISTIAN GARDENER: I just meant it like—but if you're determined to hear it again, I'll say it again and spell it out for you. I said, the thing to do is come down this way so the last thing y' do is wrap the necks of the Jewish trees behind the Jewish graves.

JEWISH GARDENER: So, I just wanted to hear it again.

CHRISTIAN GARDENER: Put in a louder complaint, at your Semitic legal office. It's just a pity [*watches him keenly*] they don't burn the Jewish brothers for witches too.

JEWISH GARDENER: My mother is buried here, God rest her soul, but in another minute I'm going to lose control of myself.

CHRISTIAN GARDENER: Come on and attack me, you cowardly Jew!

[*The* JEWISH GARDENER *is about to rush at him.*]

MRS. SCHÜLER [*to* ARTHUR]: Stay right there and don't move. [*Turning toward the* gardeners] But you men, here in the holy garden—

CHRISTIAN GARDENER: He always starts leading me on.

JEWISH GARDENER [*panting*]: He said—

MRS. SCHÜLER: Yes, yes, I heard it, what he said. [*Turning toward the* CHRISTIAN GARDENER] You should go and work at one of your own churchyards, if you can't even cherish love after people are dead.

CHRISTIAN GARDENER: At our churchyard? That doesn't pay, Madame; the Jews pay much better.

JEWISH GARDENER: We're good for that.

MRS. SCHÜLER: But don't you know, man, that above us dwells one and the same God?

ARTHUR [*afraid for his mother; to draw her away from the men*]: Mother, the lights will be lit already for sure.

JEWISH GARDENER: It's still light, boy.

ARTHUR: Precisely—

CHRISTIAN GARDENER [*obliging*]: Only about four o'clock, young gentleman.

ARTHUR: Mother, in a minute he'll sock you.

MRS. SCHÜLER [*to* JEWISH GARDENER]: How long has your colleague been working at our cemetery?

JEWISH GARDENER: Since they brought back the witch superstition. To smooth things over they're also putting Christians into this holy job.

CHRISTIAN GARDENER: How can I help it, by thunder, that they're hunting your witches again? My grandmother, my father's mother, was a cantor herself.

MRS. SCHÜLER: So? You're Jewish from your father's side? And aren't you ashamed, man, to attack your own blood like that?

JEWISH GARDENER: You holy barrel organ!

CHRISTIAN GARDENER: See there, all made up again. If you're Christian, even only half, you don't think anything about it.

MRS. SCHÜLER: Now make peace with each other, for we are all God's children.

CHRISTIAN GARDENER [*offers the* JEWISH GARDENER *his hand*]: Shake.

[JEWISH GARDENER *hesitates*.]

See, Madame, he doesn't know anything about loving thy neighbor.

[MRS. SCHÜLER *encourages the* JEWISH GARDENER *to shake hands. She takes a ducat from the little pouch* ARTHUR *wears at his side*.]

MRS. SCHÜLER: Go and refresh yourselves together in memory of the holy rabbuni Uriel, whose body rests in this consecrated ground.

JEWISH GARDENER: Excuse, excuse, Madame Schüler. Now I recognize Madame again, the saintly Rabbi Uriel's daughter Henriettchen.

[*Kisses the flounce of her cloak. Meanwhile the* CHRISTIAN GARDENER *breaks off a sprig from a small arbor vitae and attaches it to* ARTHUR'S *cap.* JEWISH GARDENER *murmurs to himself.*]

His heart was a vessel of bronze. Into it the Almighty poured his will.

[*Twilight begins to fall. The men place their spades against the tree trunks and stroll out of the pious garden behind* MRS. SCHÜLER *and* ARTHUR. *Nothing is heard but the sound of the gate latching behind them. A star comes out and shines directly over* RABBI URIEL'S *grave mound.*]

Scene 11

[*In the large living room of the Schüler mansion. Conferring together are* MR. *and* MRS. SCHÜLER; *the three eldest sons,* MENACHEM, SIMEON, *and* JULIUS; KATHARINA; MR. *and* MRS. PADERSTEIN. FANNY, ELISCHEN, *and* DORA *enter, followed by* HUGO PADERSTEIN.]

DR. VOGELSANG: [*to* MRS. SCHÜLER, *taking his leave*]: Chin up, *chére* Madame Schüler, your Dorachen will be recovered very soon. Baldrian, baldrian, [*to* KATHARINA] keep up the baldrian!

MRS. SCHÜLER: And there won't be any aftereffects?

DR. VOGELSANG: She'll be the cheery and graceful little maid she was before.

SIMEON: The superstition of the village people seems to me to be more threatening in its effects.

DR. VOGELSANG [*stepping back into the center of the room once more*]: Yes, no healing herb grows that we medical people could use against this epidemic. But young squires Simeon and Julius are just home from the university in the provincial capital. What do they think there about this medieval mischief?

JULIUS: It's from there that all the other cities and villages of Westphalia have been infected.

DR. VOGELSANG: An evil seed indeed—

MRS. SCHÜLER: —strewn over our peaceful village.

[DR. VOGELSANG *exits*.]

MR. SCHÜLER: In my opinion it was strewn especially to take revenge on us, and by one of our fellow citizens.

MRS. SCHÜLER: Yes, people only do such vicious things for some strong reason.

MRS. PADERSTEIN [*cajoling*]: And you surely haven't given them any, Henriettchen.

SIMEON [*to parents*]: I warned you about letting every Tom, Dick, and Harry come into the garden.

MENACHEM [*to* SIMEON]: Naturally my brother would rather have seen the windfall fruit rot in the meadow.

SIMEON [*hard*]: Reserve keeps people at a distance.

MRS. SCHÜLER: How little you resemble my sweet father, Simeon.

MR. PADERSTEIN [*crows*]: That God-fearing man!

[ARTHUR *and* LENCHEN *sit bent over behind the side of the fireplace facing the door.* ARTHUR *points to* MR. PADERSTEIN.]

ARTHUR AND LENCHEN: He's a crow!

SIMEON: He was a rabbi and no landowner—period.

MR. SCHÜLER: We are here not to quarrel in the presence of our friends [*indicates* MR. *and* MRS. PADERSTEIN] but to save a child, my child, from the hands of the anti-Semites.

MRS. PADERSTEIN: Mr. Schüler is right.

MR. PADERSTEIN [*crows*]: I should say so.

[*His head thrown back like a bird, he drinks the spilled coffee from his saucer, then rises to go and sit next to his wife on the sofa.*]

Move over a bit, little woman.

ARTHUR [*to* LENCHEN]: Caw, caw, caw.

MR. SCHÜLER: What was that?

MRS. SCHÜLER [*suspecting* ARTHUR; *indifferently*]: The logs in the fireplace are crackling.

SIMEON: What in general is Father thinking of proposing to the chaplain?

MENACHEM [*to* MR. *and* MRS. PADERSTEIN]: My Elfrieda no longer dares to go out with Oskar in Erwitte.

JULIUS: At seven o'clock, that is, in a quarter of an hour, Michalski is supposed to come.

[*The big wall clock in the neighboring dining room strikes twice.*]

SIMEON [*to* MR. SCHÜLER]: If Father were perhaps to offer him a sum of money—for benevolent purposes?

MRS. SCHÜLER [*with a pleased sigh*]: That is a generous thought, Simeon, and from *you*, Simeon. It was on the tip of my tongue.

[SIMEON *politely kisses his mother's hand; they sit next to each other.*]

SIMEON: Naturally we'll take up a collection [MRS. SCHÜLER *is disappointed*] among the Jews of Westphalia, since they are all involved.

[*Short pause.*]

JULIUS: Watch out. The walls have ears.

MRS. SCHÜLER [*rises, walks to fireplace; to the children behind it*]: Get yourselves out this door at once.

[*They exit; she secures the door.*]

SIMEON: Our children have become immune in this blessed family.

[*Everyone is suddenly cheerful.*]

MR. PADERSTEIN [*crows*]: Common sense he does have, even if he *is* tightfisted.

MR. SCHÜLER [*to* SIMEON]: I'm thinking about your suggestion; it's not bad.

SIMEON [*industriously writing in his notebook*]: In Münster at least twenty Jewish families will participate, as well as the rich Jewish merchants in Paderborn, Dortmund, Bochum, Lippstadt—and incidentally, Health Commissioner Greenbaum's wife has her two brothers from California staying with her at the moment.

[MRS. PADERSTEIN *waves at* HUGO, *who, without knocking, has opened the doors and waits in the doorway.*]

HUGO: They've found white gold there—it said so in the local paper. [*Pushing himself with rude familiarity between his parents on the sofa*] And now they're busy driving out the Indians.

MRS. PADERSTEIN [*terribly proud of him*]: Go on—

HUGO: Under the Portuguese commander—what is his name, anyway, the monsieur—the Indians believed he was the white savior. [*Fanatically*] A devil he is, a nasty devil!

MRS. PADERSTEIN: He's studying the Incas and their leader. [*Aside to* HUGO] What's he called? Shief?

HUGO [*shouts into her ear*]: Chief Big White-Horse Eagle! How often do I have to tell you?

MR. SCHÜLER: Well, have we come together for private purposes?

[*Frowns darkly.*]

MRS. PADERSTEIN [*blindly favoring her child*]: He'd always like to fight with the Incas against our side.

HUGO [*with a ridiculous commanding gesture*]: I'd like to lead them on against the palefaces, by thunder.

MRS. PADERSTEIN [*proud of him*]: Ha, ha, ha, ha, ha.

SIMEON: To business!

JULIUS: In a few minutes he'll be here.

MR. SCHÜLER: Those in favor of the collection, raise your hand.

HUGO [*believes the collection is for arming against the Indians*]: I'm not raising my hand.

SIMEON: Shut up.

[MRS. PADERSTEIN *is insulted.*]

MRS. SCHÜLER [*admonishing*]: Simeon!

[*All raise their hands.* CHAPLAIN MICHALSKI *is heard outside speaking with* FANNY *and* ELISCHEN. KATHARINA, *sitting next to* SIMEON *in the living room, blushes.* CHAPLAIN MICHALSKI'*s words are heard as he speaks to* DORA.]

CHAPLAIN MICHALSKI: Young Miss Dora seems to be all well again.

ELISCHEN [*opens the door for him and announces*]: Chaplain Michalski.

[CHAPLAIN MICHALSKI, *who has lifted* ARTHUR *up in the air, is seen setting him down on the hall floor. He enters. All rise uneasily.* MR. SCHÜLER *is in full self-control; the sunny, grave beauty of* CHAPLAIN MICHALSKI *impresses him favorably.*]

MR. SCHÜLER [*with a polished gesture*]: May I present, Chaplain Michalski, my wife Madame Henrietta; my eldest daughter, Katharina; Menachem, Simeon, and Julius, my three eldest sons; and our friends Mr. and Mrs. Paderstein. My wife and I are deeply pained, Chaplain, not to be welcoming you into our house for a happier reason.

[MRS. SCHÜLER *offers him her hand and makes as though to kiss his, but he kisses her hand.* FANNY, ELISCHEN, *and* DORA *come timidly into the room and sit down on chairs along the wall.*]

CHAPLAIN MICHALSKI: We clergymen, Madame Schüler, by no means exchange chivalry for the cassock.

[*Even* SIMEON *cannot keep from admiring* CHAPLAIN MICHALSKI'S *beauty and noble bearing.*]

MRS. SCHÜLER: I've just become convinced of that, Chaplain.

[*He sits down in the armchair offered him between the parents.*]

JULIUS: I've already had the honor of seeing you in Paderborn, in your own great house, the cathedral, Chaplain.

CHAPLAIN MICHALSKI [*interested*]: Did you attend our divine services, Mr. Schüler?

JULIUS: Without giving you a stock answer—we *are* speaking honestly man to man—I'm interested in the religious relics in the Catholic houses of God.

SIMEON: Even if the mummy of the devil incarnate were waiting for him in a reliquary.

CHAPLAIN MICHALSKI: If only the devil, the evil element, weren't *eternally young*.

MRS. SCHÜLER: *You* say that, Chaplain?

CHAPLAIN MICHALSKI: As a horrible example to the human race, Madame.

MR. PADERSTEIN [*crows*]: My opinion exactly. That's right!

[MRS. PADERSTEIN *nods agreement.*]

CHAPLAIN MICHALSKI: The strangleholds that Beelzebub gets on us ever and again—I admit, we are often beaten—offer our Catholic Christians the opportunity for penitent atonement.

MR. SCHÜLER [*intent*]: Please go ahead and speak freely, Chaplain.

CHAPLAIN MICHALSKI: The church in its quality as shepherd stresses the loving acceptance of that very black sheep who has gone astray. Didn't the Lord sit at the same table with publicans and sinners and eat with them? When the Church, following in the Lord's footsteps, practices patience toward its souls who have gone astray in dark pathways, they are given time to understand and to turn over a new leaf. Only this principle leads to the complete redemption of erring emotions in the human breast.

SIMEON: If you please, Your Reverence—

CHAPLAIN MICHALSKI [*correcting him*]: Chaplain!

SIMEON: I stand corrected, Chaplain! And won't the principles of the respected Catholic Church suffer a fiasco in case the threats [*with slight sarcasm*] of the erring souls transform themselves into action?

[MRS. SCHÜLER *admonishes him with a look.*]

CHAPLAIN MICHALSKI [*noticing; politely*]: I love every clear question, no matter how sharp it tastes.

MR. PADERSTEIN [*listening intently and with utmost good will*]: Caw! Caw!

CHAPLAIN MICHALSKI: In the thousands of divisions in the Vatican an answer waits for every question, and the Vatican also has a gauge capable of measuring the aberrations of its faithful Catholics down to the last degree.

JULIUS: And it didn't stop the bloody pogroms a hundred years ago in Spain and here in this country, Chaplain? Have you read what Lessing wrote to Goethe?

ELISCHEN [*unassuming but confident in her knowledge*]: I can recommend it to you, Chaplain.

CHAPLAIN MICHALSKI [*bows, smiling politely*]: Lessing and Goethe are two authors that I prize highly. The Holy Father in Rome, in his infallibility, is beyond judgment.

[MRS. SCHÜLER *sighs very deeply.* CHAPLAIN MICHALSKI *speaks to her with an infinitely loving, comforting look.*]

Like Our Dear Lady. I know how to appreciate it.

SIMEON [*looking at* CHAPLAIN MICHALSKI; *softly to himself*]: This isn't getting us anywhere.

ARTHUR [*rushes abruptly into the room*]: I've just been *so naughty* again, I've got to go to the corner.

[*All laugh.* MRS. SCHÜLER *motions him to leave the room at once.*]

MR. SCHÜLER [*pours wine for* CHAPLAIN MICHALSKI]: Well, how do you explain to yourself, Chaplain, the sudden hatefulness of your congregation, directed especially toward my house?

CHAPLAIN MICHALSKI [*wisely*]: Did not also a Caiphus once sit as high priest in Judah, who let the noblest Jew, the savior, be crucified—

[*Deep silence.*]

SIMEON: One could conclude from that that a single person is capable of overturning the divine principle.

CHAPLAIN MICHALSKI [*wisely, devoutly*]: Only of veiling it—through the darkness of sin.

[SIMEON *falls silent, feeling himself superior.*]

MR. SCHÜLER: We've gotten off the track, it seems to me.

MRS. SCHÜLER: May I take the liberty of interrupting this interesting discussion with a private question? Are you really convinced, Chaplain, that the dark superstition threatening Gaesecke will soon dissolve into good will?

[MR. SCHÜLER *takes from his wallet the letter which he earlier opened in the garden, the anonymous message, and holds it out to him.*]

CHAPLAIN MICHALSKI: Absolutely, like a cloud.

MRS. SCHÜLER [*to* MR. SCHÜLER, *indicating the letter in surprise*]: But I don't know anything about this.

CHAPLAIN MICHALSKI [*reading the letter; smiles*]: I've even been informed [*lovingly ironic*] that your little witch has hexed children in our village.

[*The others exchange looks, shocked at how lightly and banteringly* CHAPLAIN MICHALSKI *regards the letter.*]

The market woman came, then came a day laborer, an idler, and who knows how many more, all bringing me the news of the little witch in the village.

[FANNY's *rapturous gaze does not leave* CHAPLAIN MICHALSKI's *face.*]

ELISCHEN: If you please, Chaplain, was it the market woman from the Wednesday market [*quietly*] who gathered the windfalls in our garden last fall?

MRS. PADERSTEIN [*clicks her tongue*]: Ingratitude is the only reward in this world.

CHAPLAIN MICHALSKI: Probably. [*After a pause, straightening his upper body solemnly*] I take the liberty—of making a suggestion to you, Mr. and Mrs. Squire Schüler, for the primary purpose of eliminating this *evil* here in our village and [*with emphasis*] any *danger* threatening your little daughter Dora. [*Clearing his throat*] Namely—to have one of your children raised in the Catholic faith.

MRS. SCHÜLER [*thinking of* FANNY]: In heaven's name.

CHAPLAIN MICHALSKI [*looks up, perceiving her thought*]: But no, Madame Schüler, I was thinking of my little friend Arthur Aronymus, your son, who is as dear to me as a little brother. [*Almost with rapture*] Yes, I love him with my whole heart. [*Tears come to his eyes*] He is the dearest little person in this wide world to me. He is the most priceless little fellow I've ever met.

[MRS. SCHÜLER *weeps softly.*]

With this humble gesture to our one and only beatific Church you will blunt once and for all any danger threatening your daughter Dora.

[*Long pause. Those present are variously moved, disconcerted, horrified.*]

MR. SCHÜLER [*rising with a nobility for the first time truly human*]: Reverend Chaplain, allow me, in the name of us all, to thank you for your suggestion, as sensible as it is well meant. Unfortunately the following circumstances oblige me to reject it with all due respect. I, as well as my blessed father and his blessed father and the grandfathers of his fathers, and the ancestors of Madame Henrietta's father, who rests in God, have always come to God by *direct* ways; and I should have my son, still a child, led to *His son*—by *roundabout* ways? The Lord protect us from all evil! *ADONAI YISHMERENU MIKOL RAR*—

[MR. *and* MRS. PADERSTEIN *burst into tears.* HUGO *looks at a paleface with respect for the first time.* MR. SCHÜLER *caresses his weeping wife. The children gaze at their father in admiration; only* FANNY *sits bent over in her chair, as though mourning.* CHAPLAIN MICHALSKI *rises, defeated, then regains control of himself. He bows, stirred to his innermost being. No one notices as he leaves the room.*]

ARTHUR [*bounds suddenly into the room from the hall*]: I gave Bernard my tweeter on the green ribbon for a present.
KATHARINA [*to parents*]: His flute.
ALL [*to* ARTHUR, *eagerly*]: What did he say?
ARTHUR: Nothing!
MRS. SCHÜLER: Nothing, Arthurchen?

ARTHUR: He just kissed me here and here [*points to his right and left cheeks*]. But he didn't take Fanny's bouquet.

[*Only* ELISCHEN *and* MRS. PADERSTEIN *hear these last words.*]

ELISCHEN [*softly to* KATHARINA]: That will do her good.

MRS. PADERSTEIN [*to* MRS. SCHÜLER, *hypocritical but kind*]: She's so romantic, our lovely little Fanny.

JULIUS [*lost in thought*]: Already a pope in dignity.

SIMEON [*dispassionate, pitiable*]: Father should send scouts into the enemy camp to find out what the enemy is planning in his tent.

MR. SCHÜLER: That goes against our grain, your mother's and mine.

FANNY: I refuse to spy.

MRS. PADERSTEIN [*babbling*]: What is your mother to do, my friend Henrietta, worry herself to death?

MR. PADERSTEIN [*crows*]: How you spoke, Moritz! Give me your hand, my friend!

MENACHEM, SIMEON, AND JULIUS: And we must agree with Mr. Paderstein, Father.

MRS. PADERSTEIN [*in a very high voice*]: Like a god!

MRS. SCHÜLER [*lovingly*]: This time you truly remind me of my blessed father.

ARTHUR [*hurries to* FANNY, *whispers into her ear*]: I'm not going along *either*, but I'll tell Bernard!

[FANNY *leaves the room.*]

MR. SCHÜLER [*like a biblical patriarch*]: Make ready then, my children!

MRS. PADERSTEIN: Our little Hugo will go along, since he's the tallest. He can peer into every window, no matter how high.

HUGO: Should I run quick and get my battle-axe?

MR. SCHÜLER: Go forth, then, with God, and bring me information: Heinrich Menachem! Simeon Mordechai! Julius Ahasuerus!

[BERTHOLD *and* FERDINAND *come into the room.*]

And you, my sons Berthold and Ferdinand Samson! And you, my daughters Katharina Deborah! Elise Naomi! [*Looks in vain for* FANNY. *Unprofessionally, imitating* RABBI URIEL] My blessing goes with you!

ARTHUR [*softly to his mother, somewhat jealous for his grandfather*]: That's what Grandpa always said to you and Father.

[*The children all exit,* HUGO *slinking behind like an Indian.* MR. *and* MRS. PADERSTEIN *leave for home.* MR. SCHÜLER *escorts them to the gate.*]

Mother, I want to ask you something. Are there two guardian angels for children?

MRS. SCHÜLER: How so, Arthurchen Aronymus?

ARTHUR: One with *black* wings stood by Grandpa and laughed very softly with him while Lenchen and I did somersaults on the carpet, and then said good night to him.

[MRS. SCHÜLER *is amazed.*]

And Bernard had all *white* wings just now. Tell me about the guardian angel with the funny wings!

MRS. SCHÜLER: How the heaviness leaves my heart! [*Trembling*] Dear boy—come, I'll tell you about the guardian angel that watches over children!

Scene 12

[*Before* CHAPLAIN MICHALSKI'S *little house. Full moon to one side. Soft light in one of the windows and one of the small attic dormers. An oil lamp stands on* CHAPLAIN MICHALSKI'S *table. He sits writing on a large sheet of official stationery, in the raised part of the room. On the table a glass pitcher of milk and some white bread on a plate. Climbing over the low fence and whispering to one another are seven of the Schülers*—MENACHEM, SIMEON, JULIUS, BERTHOLD, FERDINAND, KATHARINA, ELISCHEN—*and* HUGO.]

HUGO [*slinking*]: I'll climb up and sneak up to the window.

[*All stand beneath the window.*]

FERDINAND AND BERTHOLD [*together*]: Get up on our shoulders, Hugo. You'll already be halfway up.

[*The others calculate in muted words how best to climb up.*]

HUGO [*to the two*]: Don't tell me what to do, you two palefaces.

SIMEON [*whispering to younger brothers*]: Go get the ladder over there! Don't you see it?

[*They very carefully place the ladder against the wall.* HUGO *climbs up and, at the top, holds onto the stucco of the wall.*]

HUGO: It's the chimney sweep's.

JULIUS: The hour bears caution.

HUGO [*hissing down spiritedly*]: What's your book learning to me, you old paleface!

SIMEON [*with the idea of getting* HUGO's *cooperation*]: Oh, let him alone.

ELISCHEN: Just don't fall, Hugo.

[HUGO *keeps climbing higher, holding onto the window sill.*]

KATHARINA: Hold on tight; think of your good mother.

HUGO [*spiritedly*]: All of you quit preaching, will you!

[*Pause.*]

Simeon, I can see him. He's sitting at the table by a lamp with a green shade.

ELISCHEN: What else?

JULIUS: Shh—

ELISCHEN: I'm going to sit down on the bench for a little while; I'm so tired from taking care of Dorachen.

SIMEON: Too dangerous. Better I support you, sister.

JULIUS [*looking upward*]: Go on.

HUGO: Keep cool, the way they do in the tribe.

MENACHEM [*to* KATHARINA]: What is he saying about the family tree?

KATHARINA: He's imagining things about his Indian tribe.

HUGO: Now he's picking up the quill again—now he's stopping to think—I think he's humming, but I don't hear anything!

SIMEON: Can you read what he's written?

HUGO: I won't let myself be ordered around! Otherwise I'll come down.

[*Makes as though to climb down.*]

SIMEON [*skillfully*]: The bold lion, the chief, ordered around?

HUGO [*squinting frightfully downward in his fervor*]: On the table stands a jug of milk. And next to it, on a plate, pretzels to stuff him with like a baby in a nursery. And now he's writing again.

MENACHEM: What is he writing, boy?

HUGO: Just a minute.

ALL: What? What?

HUGO: "I take pen in hand"—he's making a fancy *P* on "pen."

JULIUS: Should I hand you up my lorgnon, Hugo?

HUGO: What for? For the eyes or for the ears? Above he's written—wait a minute—"To His Face."

SIMEON: "To His Grace?"
HUGO: That's it!
KATHARINA: Try to figure out some more, Hugo.
ELISCHEN: Our mother, I'm supposed to tell you, will give you a few ducats for your savings bank.
HUGO: Now, proceed with caution. Shh—now he's folding the letter.

[*Pause.*]

He's sealing it. He's burned his finger.
JULIUS: Shh!
HUGO: It's impossible to be any quieter! Now he's licking his thumb and now his middle finger.
SIMEON: Come down, Hugo, that's enough.
MENACHEM: At least we know that our conference is bearing fruit.
HUGO [*peeks once more through the window, curious*]: His bed is blocked off, and the chamber pot—
SIMEON AND JULIUS: Shh—shh—
ELISCHEN AND KATHARINA: But—Hugo—

[*The first blast on the horn signaling the departure of the mail coach.*]

HUGO: He's getting his cloak. Oh, oh—down quick.

[*Climbs down the stucco of the house front and then, held by* FERDINAND *and* BERTHOLD, *jumps into the garden.*]

KATHARINA [*proud*]: Father's speech has borne fruit.
HUGO [*back on the ground; impatiently*]: Where are the ducats?
KATHARINA AND ELISCHEN: Mother will give them to you herself.
HUGO [*insolently*]: Listen, I'm telling you all: if I don't get them, I'll tip him off to what's been going on, and his chaplain nose will turn as white as his milk bottle.

SIMEON [*superior*]: Among the Indians, or so I believed till now, there aren't any blackmailers.

JULIUS: His parents can congratulate themselves.

KATHARINA [*gesturing toward* HUGO]: After all, he's only half grown.

HUGO [*crestfallen*]: He's already taken his cloak from the wall—quick!

[*They all sneak away from the house on tiptoe and clamber back over the fence.* FERDINAND *and* BERTHOLD *jump over it.* HUGO *like an Indian.* SIMEON *and* JULIUS *help* KATHARINA. ELISCHEN, *driven by a sudden fear that* CHAPLAIN MICHALSKI *might come, leaps like a wild mare over the thorny wattle fence. Her pantalets with their long fringe of lace catch in the thorns. All hide behind the church. They hear* CHAPLAIN MICHALSKI *open his door and see him hurry across the square to the mail coach. Of the coach, only the tiny red lantern lights are visible through the foliage of the trees lining the walks. The horn blows for the second time.*]

SIMEON: Now all of you go home and comfort the parents. I'll wait for him.

MENACHEM: As a farmer I have acquired considerable cunning, and I advise you against this step.

KATHARINA: I'll wait with you, Simeon.

ELISCHEN [*teasing*]: Aha, dear sister, if your Engelbrecht suspected!

SIMEON: Leave off the stupidities.

MENACHEM: To be honorable, one ought to go up to his rooms.

SIMEON [*ignoring* MENACHEM*'s second remark*]: Brother, you're right; it would be undiplomatic to press him further.

JULIUS: I think so too.

ELISCHEN: Then he'll think we're afraid.

MENACHEM: But of course we're afraid. We have every right to be afraid—and the parents too—of what's going to happen.

KATHARINA: If the two of you do go to him, I'll gladly go with you.

ELISCHEN [*commandingly*]: Or I!

SIMEON: Or the whole herd.

[*The horn blows for the third time. Sound of harnesses. All suddenly rush across the marketplace toward home. They have escaped.*]

ALTMANN [*comes partway across the square and stops in the middle to wait for* CHAPLAIN MICHALSKI]: I wish Your Reverence a blessed evening.

[*Points toward the mail coach.*]

Now it's galloped off. [*Touching his legs*] That's not the coach wheels but my old legs creaking.

[CHAPLAIN MICHALSKI *smiles distractedly.* ALTMANN *looks at the moon.*]

How it comes down right over Hexengaesecke like that every four weeks! And I always have a hard time then, blowing all the children to sleep.

[*Clears his throat; spits a long jet.*]

CHAPLAIN MICHALSKI [*distractedly*]: I won't be able to sleep either, old friend. Come, dear Altmann, drink a schnapps with me up in my parlor.

ALTMANN [*trotting after* CHAPLAIN MICHALSKI]: If the dear Lord wants to raise me up.

CHAPLAIN MICHALSKI: Aren't you satisfied with your job, then?

ALTMANN: That glaring red bagpipe up there—[*stopping and looking upward again; angrily*] I'd damn well like to slit open its belly. When the clock strikes from the church tower.

[*They go into the house, and only the dull light in* CHAPLAIN MICHALSKI'*s parlor is to be seen.*]

Scene 13

[*In the background stands the Catholic church on the marketplace. Assembled is the entire population of Gaesecke and environs, including* ALTMANN, *the peddler* LEMMLE TSILINSKY, *and* NATHANAEL BRENNESSEL, *who peers out from behind a large fruit basket left standing there from the market season. The schoolchildren are lined up one behind the other as for a procession and are accompanied by their two teachers. The elegant* ALFONSO KISSINGEN (DR. FAUST) *in lilac trousers;* MR. *and* MRS. SCHÜLER; *their twenty-three children;* MENACHEM'S *wife and son* OSKAR; *the maids and male servants from the whole village, including Schülers' servants:* MAMSELL, *the cook;* CLARA *and the other* MAIDS; GARDENER, MILKMAIDS, BEEKEEPER, *and* HENRY FILIGRAN. *Everyone is under extreme tension.*]

ARTHUR [*comes running last of all, holding* LENCHEN *by the hand*]: Holy strawsack, Lenchen, I was so afraid we'd be late.

LENCHEN: Catch your breath or Father will notice.

ARTHUR: Do you see them?

LENCHEN: They're right here—all together. Mother's looking, Aronymus!

[ARTHUR *nods to* MRS. SCHÜLER *and stamps his feet a few times. She lays her finger warningly on her lips.* ARTHUR *draws* LENCHEN *nearer to himself and begs* MRS. SCHÜLER *in sign language not to tell on them.*]

ARTHUR [*to* LENCHEN]: When is Bernard coming, anyway?

FANATICAL MAN [*to bystanders*]: The nasty little Jewboy is getting beyond himself.

[*Makes as though to slap him.* ARTHUR *stands up to him.*]

I'll teach you to call our chaplain "Bernard."

LENCHEN [*defending him*]: But Bernard is his friend.

FANATICAL WOMAN: Don't you two come from Moses's mansion with the garden?

ARTHUR: Naa, you old golden calf.

[*Bystanders laugh.*]

FANATICAL MAN: I don't believe the Moses from the Old Testament piled up that much dishonest money.

[MRS. SCHÜLER *notices the episode and beckons the children to her.*]

ARTHUR [*to* LENCHEN]: It's better if we don't stand near this bunch, Lenchen. But when Bernard comes, we'll run up to the steps quick.

[*The crowd grows impatient and restless. Murmuring is heard; friction begins to occur. The ringing of the bells stops. The sky becomes overcast in the west, black as pitch.*]

ELISCHEN [*to* KATHARINA *and* FANNY]: Dr. Faust.

[ALFONSO KISSINGEN *approaches the family, distinguished and very elegantly dressed. He stops a short distance from them, behind the four young ladies:* KATHARINA, ELISCHEN, FANNY, *and* DORA. CHAPLAIN MICHALSKI *emerges from the church door, a great scroll in his hand, and stands at the top of the stone steps. The four daughters put their arms around one another,* JULIUS *behind them.* FANNY *trembles with excitement.*]

JULIUS: In truth, the future pope.

KATHARINA [*to her sisters, inadvertently solemn*]: *Our* chaplain—

DORA: Don't the people see me?

[MR. SCHÜLER *raises his head, warning the four to be careful.* MRS. SCHÜLER *puts her arm through his. Their sons raise their hats,* MR.

SCHÜLER *his gray top hat. The other children, well-behaved, are lined up next to one another. The whole Schüler family is dressed in its best.* CHAPLAIN MICHALSKI *points to the threatening cloud growing ever larger and darker on the western horizon.*]

CHAPLAIN MICHALSKI [*as though to himself, but keeping an eye on the crowd*]: The heavens have allied themselves with His Grace the Bishop. [*To the crowd*] I greet you, my dear congregation in Christ, in the name of His Grace, Bishop Matthias of Paderborn.

[*A tremendous thunder clap rolls, like an evil miracle, through Gaesecke. It is February. The people are terrified.*]

SIMEON [*to* JULIUS]: Monumental, his appearance!

CHAPLAIN MICHALSKI [*breaks the seal calmly and firmly, unrolls the document, and reads*]: "I greet you with troubled heart, my strayed sheep, and admonish you to adopt reason, not to persist defiantly in your sin of dark superstition! There is yet time for repentance and atonement, my poor little children, for the salvation of whose souls [*raising his finger, grave and menacing*] I carry the unremitting burden and responsibility in my heart. [*Looking out sternly over the countless heads*] Woe unto you, to still your evil lust, even if only in the hell of your desires, with the fiery death of our good sisters from the ancient house of Israel. Forget not, in your black hatred, that our savior Jesus Christ himself was a Jew, sprung from David's blood. With a thousand tongues will I announce to heaven the sin of each transgressor, that his soul may roast until the Day of Judgment! Therefore, my poor wayward children, look into your hearts; wash yourselves in the innocent spring of repentance. Desist, ye sheep who have become black! And for the third time: desist from your wickedness for the sake of Jesus Christ our Lord!"

[*Short pause.* CHAPLAIN MICHALSKI *folds his hands; with trembling voice*]

"Even if you dwell now in sadness, I shall see you again, your heart will rejoice, and your joy shall no one take from you. '*Et vos igitur nunc quidem tristitiam habetis, iterum autem videbo vos, et gaudebit cor vestrum: et gaudium vestrum nemo tollet a vobis!*'"

[*It suddenly grows so bright that the entire square is as though illuminated with flares. The people sink to their knees, ecstatic, weeping and wailing.* MRS. SCHÜLER *weeps.* MR. SCHÜLER *mops his brow, overwhelmed. The children are all crying.*]

ARTHUR [*to* LENCHEN]: Aw, stop it. Bernard was right; they wanted to roast Dora.

LENCHEN: You're bawling too.

[*Tears run down his cheeks.* CHAPLAIN MICHALSKI *calmly rolls up the scroll, walks gravely back to the door, without looking around, and into the church. There is a triple echo as he shuts the door. The bells ring again. A few make vain attempts to follow him. The square gradually empties. A whirlwind whistles as the storm comes with snow and hail, but the people head home, orderly and pious. The Schüler family is seen briefly behind the marketplace, walking home.*]

Scene 14

[*In the Schülers' garden.* FANNY *and* DORA *sit in the jasmine arbor. Standing together in a group at the bottom of the broad steps leading up to the house are the children, giggling:* ARTHUR, LENCHEN, ELEONORA, ALBERT, BETTINA, MARGARETA, KARL, MAX, MEYERCHEN, OSKAR (MENACHEM'*s son*), *and some of* ARTHUR'*s schoolmates, including* WILLY HIMMEL *and* CASPAR.]

FANNY: Tell the truth: did the chaplain really tell you, before he moved to Paderborn, that you should give warm greetings especially to your sister, Miss Fanny?

DORA [*confused*]: The way I said before—that's right. You should ask him yourself the next time you go to Paderborn.
FANNY [*with emphasis*]: So you were supposed to give Miss Elisa his warm greetings—look at me!

[DORA *nods anxiously*.]

I would have given you my coral earrings—you like them so much—don't you?

[*Pause. The children form a large circle.*]

LENCHEN [*counts off*]: Ikka bikka soda cracker, ikka bikka boo, ikka bikka soda cracker, out goes you!

[*Counts until one child is left: it is* ARTHUR.]

ALL [*shout*]: He can play it the wildest of all!
FANNY: Well?

[*Embraces* DORA.]

Maybe you misspoke, Dora?
DORA: But what would Katharina and Elischen say then?
FANNY: They won't ever find out!

[*Raises her hand as for an oath.*]

DORA [*encouraged*]: Katharina gave me her fan, the one with the cupids painted on it. I don't care anything about Elischen's books—
FANNY [*rather severely but forcing herself to be diplomatic*]: So both of them are behind it [*gently*] and said to little sister Dora, "Dear Dorachen, we took care of you day and night and were always so good to you."

DORA: It was just like that.

[*A few of the children run after* ARTHUR *through the side door into the house, the others gather leaves and twigs*.]

"Since you're our favorite sister, Dorachen—" [*Suddenly afraid*] But if you tell on me to Kathy and Elischen— [*Abruptly*] Here comes the chimney sweep.

[*He goes up the side path to the house*.]

FANNY: He's here to help with the sweeping. [*Swearing to* DORA] I swear it!

[DORA *gazes enraptured at her earrings*. FANNY *reconsiders*.]

Dorachen, the jewelry box from the charming wine salesman: you can take that from my dresser. You know, with the candied fruits.

[DORA *remains silent*.]

We'll agree on something, but tell the *strict* truth!

DORA: Kathy and Elischen told me, besides the fan I could buy a clasp from Lemmle for when I'm old enough to wear my hair up, but I'd have to tell you that Chaplain Michalski sent specially warm greetings to Miss Elisa.

FANNY: And that she shouldn't forget him.

DORA [*miserable over her lie, nods*]: Oh, dear Fanny, it's not my fault.

[FANNY, *almost apathetic from the intrigue, is sunk into herself with unseeing eyes*.]

What's wrong with you, Fanny? Fanny! You're dying! Say something, please, please, please— I'll call Mother!

[ARTHUR *comes staggering down the steps in the clothes* DORA *wore during her illness, the skirt hitched up comically. On his head he wears her former summer hat with its wreath of buttercups and long, dangling velvet ribbons. Several children follow him, representing his sisters and brothers.* MAX *plays their father,* LENCHEN *their mother,* MEYERCHEN *(five years old) his oldest brother,* MENACHEM.]

ARTHUR [*as* DORA; *to* LENCHEN, *theatrically*]: Farewell, Mother! [*Bawls loudly, to* MAX] Farewell, Father!

[*Sticks his tongue out at* MAX, *then gives a kiss to each sister.*]

Today is the day I shall be burned. [*Embraces* MEYERCHEN.] Menachem, my firstborn brother, good-bye!

[*It is beginning to get dark. Two figures step through the garden gate and remain standing by the hedge.*]

LENCHEN [*pretends to weep mournfully*]: Dorachen, my Sweetie-Dorachen!

[*The other children are still busy getting into costume, turning their skirts and jackets around. They make sabers out of branches.* WILLY *has brought his drum and* CASPAR *his helmet.* OSKAR *waits glumly to be costumed.* ARTHUR *hands his mother's large scissors to* MARGARETA, *who attempts to tie them, on a band of rickrack, around the brown cloth that she has put over* OSKAR*'s clothes like a monk's cowl.*]

OSKAR [*tearing the scissors morosely from his side*]: That's wicked!
ARTHUR: Chicken.
LENCHEN [*to* OSKAR, *speaking in dialect for the first time*]: I'm all ready to believe that's what you are.
DORA: At last you're awake again!

[FANNY *begins to weep unnervingly.*]

Should I call Mother?

FANNY [*mournfully*]: Ah, love, all will soon be over.

[DORA *keeps throwing her arms around* FANNY'*s neck.*]

That's what it means to be beautiful.

[*Lifts her head like a queen, takes a tiny mirror from the pocket under her hoopskirt, and looks at herself.*]

DORA: Naaa, no one can do anything about it. [*Suddenly hesitates*] Is the jewelry box still full of fruit?

FANNY: How can you think of the jewelry box at a time like this, Dora, when I'm languishing my heart away?

[DORA *is ashamed.*]

So you really and truly lied?

DORA [*raises her hand to swear*]: Really and truly!

ALL [*to* OSKAR]: What are you standing there so fierce for, you fake saint?

[*One of the boys strips the bark from a rose bush branch on which a squashed rose hip still hangs. It clings to the stripped branch like blood. They make a cross from it and hang it around* OSKAR'*s hips instead of the scissors.*]

CASPAR: Now you look just as poisonous as Uncle Padre.

BISHOP MATTHIAS [*to* CHAPLAIN MICHALSKI]: Shh, my son—!

LENCHEN: Is your uncle in the monastery, Caspar?

CASPAR: Father always says, there he sits and there he should stay.

WILLY [*his honor touched, since his parents are Catholic*]: His father was a heretic.

[CASPAR *gives* WILLY *a clout.* WILLY *slugs back.*]

DORA [*infinitely loving, to* FANNY]: But in the mail coach he looked his eyes out at your window, Fannychen. Honestly, I'm telling the pure truth! I could look Grandfather-rabbi in the eye if he were still alive.

[FANNY *smiles, happy now. The children begin to build the pyre with fallen leaves, dry grass, and twigs.*]

FANNY: But how would he know where my room is?
DORA: Don't take me for stupid, Fanny.
FANNY: How so?
DORA: Katharina and Elischen used to spy on you half the night from our window. Sometimes your window flew open and then snapped shut again, then open, then shut— "She threw him a rose," Katharina called out one time late in the evening—and she was really mad.
FANNY: But you were sick and were asleep, weren't you?
DORA: At the end I only pretended and kept dancing a little more polka than I had to. I hated *so* to go to school, Fanny.

[FANNY *smiles again, over her joy.*]

How you understand me, Fanny.

[*They go into the house.*]

MAX [*to the children, bawling*]: My figures that I made in the sand, you trampled them.
LENCHEN [*in her mother's tone*]: Tomorrow Maxchen will make new ones.

ALL: Maxikin! Maxikin! Maxikin!

[MAX *continues playing with the children. The game begins.* ARTHUR *as the witch* DORA *staggers along the fence, all the children following after, playing the people of Gaesecke and shouting the witch song.*]

WILLY [*with drum*] AND CASPAR [*with helmet; both stepping up to* OSKAR, *the monk*]: Patience, we're bringing her to you right away, Holy Padre, and then she shall burn as in purgatory!

[ARTHUR *climbs a plum tree.*]

ALL [*playing the villagers, shouting*]: Witchling, witchling, come down from the plum tree!

[*They shake the tree and sing the witch song again.* BISHOP MATTHIAS *and* CHAPLAIN MICHALSKI *sneak deeper into the garden and hide behind the long hair of a big willow tree.*]

CHAPLAIN MICHALSKI: The Witch Mysterium acted out by innocent children.

BISHOP MATTHIAS [*crosses himself;* CHAPLAIN MICHALSKI *does likewise*]: Indeed, a shocking echo of the witch superstition.

CHAPLAIN MICHALSKI: His Grace's immediate energetic intervention is urgently necessary.

ARTHUR [*suddenly hearkens; all children do likewise*]: Father is coming.

CHAPLAIN MICHALSKI [*to* BISHOP MATTHIAS]: Of him he's afraid.

[BISHOP MATTHIAS, *continuing to listen, holds his hand gently before* CHAPLAIN MICHALSKI'*s lips. The children, wrong about* MR. SCHÜLER, *continue playing. Wild confusion begins among them.* LENCHEN *as* MRS. SCHÜLER *and* MAX *as* MR. SCHÜLER *lament, and the children playing the sisters and brothers flee to those playing the people of Gaesecke.*]

LENCHEN: Oh, our child! Oh, our Dorachen!

[*The family members draw back, lamenting, to the steps as the Gaeseckeans take hold of the witch, bind her, and drag her before the monk,* OSKAR.]

OSKAR [*ominously*]: Now we've got the devilish villain; confess, witch, and repent your sorceries, you Satan's wench!

BISHOP MATTHIAS [*astonished at the boy's sadism*]: See there!

ARTHUR [*falsetto*]: I'm not a witch, I'm not a witch!

CHAPLAIN MICHALSKI [*to* BISHOP MATTHIAS]: That's the priceless boy.

ARTHUR [*almost squeaking*]: I'm Schülers' Dora!

OSKAR: That's nothing to us; but I ask her, the devilish villain, will she repent her misdeeds and cleanse herself in the blood of Jesus? In that case she won't be roasted on the pyre, the devil's offspring!

ALL: The pyre! The pyre! The pyre!

[*They sing the witch song.*]

CHAPLAIN MICHALSKI [*to* BISHOP MATTHIAS]: The wayward times have taught them this language.

[*All leap around like little devils.* ARTHUR *bites the monk in the hand.*]

OSKAR [*hard and vengeful*]: Drag her to hell!

[*Singing the witch song, they drag* ARTHUR *to the pyre. The family members rush suddenly down from the steps after the monk.* LENCHEN *as* MRS. SCHÜLER *embraces his hips; the others fall at his feet.*]

FAMILY: Mercy! Mercy! Mercy for our Dorachen!

[BISHOP MATTHIAS *crosses himself again, deeply moved.* ARTHUR *stands bent over on the pyre, the children dancing around him. Suddenly he springs down from the pyre in one bound, losing* DORA'*s skirt and knocking the monk over. The ravening mob chases after. The words are no longer discernible.*]

BISHOP MATTHIAS: Should one laugh or cry?

[*And he begins to laugh so hard that the children, in their chasing around, abruptly stop and listen.* CHAPLAIN MICHALSKI *is disconcerted by his laughter in this deadly serious matter.*]

Well, well, my dear son in Christ, don't reproach your old spiritual brother and uncle—[*grabbing* CHAPLAIN MICHALSKI'S *arm to keep from falling over with laughter*] ha, haha, ha, ha—that he's not a spoilsport, for out of the hearts of children bubbles the spring of laughter—and how bitter it often tastes.

[CHAPLAIN MICHALSKI *is about to reply understandingly. A* MAID *approaches them.*]

MAID: I'm supposed to see who the two figures behind the willow tree are—?

[MRS. SCHÜLER *follows the* MAID. *Her step is light; she swings her body youthfully. The children try to hide as they see the* MAID. BISHOP MATTHIAS *still cannot control himself.*]

MRS. SCHÜLER: Can I believe my eyes—our most respected Chaplain Michalski?

BISHOP MATTHIAS: And his old bishop.

CHAPLAIN MICHALSKI: His Grace Matthias of Paderborn, Madame Schüler.

[*Kisses her hand.* BISHOP MATTHIAS *automatically extends his hand to be kissed.*]

MRS. SCHÜLER [*simply and kindly*]: What a pleasure for me and my husband and for my children and—[*looks around for* ARTHUR] Where is he?

CHAPLAIN MICHALSKI: He's got him!

[*Picks* ARTHUR *up and carries him to* BISHOP MATTHIAS.]

Live right here!

MRS. SCHÜLER [*to* CHAPLAIN MICHALSKI, *indicating* ARTHUR]: He's gotten so wild again since his idolized Chaplain Bernard no longer lives here in Gaesecke.

BISHOP MATTHIAS: And we, his bishop, Madame, carry the guilt for that.

MAID [*as though driving a herd, with a little switch in her hand*]: Now quick into the bath tubs. Passover is already here! And you other urchins, take off home!

[BISHOP MATTHIAS *looks after the children. Cannot stop laughing.*]

MRS. SCHÜLER: Tonight our Easter celebration begins, and it would be the greatest honor and joy for my husband and me if Your Grace and our unforgettable chaplain would celebrate the seder evening with us.

BISHOP MATTHIAS [*gallantly, turning to* CHAPLAIN MICHALSKI]: His bishop is no spoilsport, you may tell the hospitable Madame Schüler, my dear son.

CHAPLAIN MICHALSKI: His Grace and my humble self accept with pleasure the kind invitation of Madame Schüler.

BISHOP MATTHIAS: Yes, we two intruders would like very much to celebrate the pious Easter tradition with the husband and the charming wife and the—[*to* CHAPLAIN MICHALSKI] how many is it?

CHAPLAIN MICHALSKI [*laughing*]: Twenty-three!

BISHOP MATTHIAS: The twenty-three children.

MRS. SCHÜLER: And the additions. [*Turning to* CHAPLAIN MICHALSKI] Katharina has married, our second daughter, and has been visiting in our house with her doctor since yesterday. Heinrich Menachem and his wife have come to celebrate too, with their little son [*points to the little monk,* OSKAR]. He is two years older than his uncle, our Arthur Aronymus.

[BISHOP MATTHIAS *makes a sinister face at him, mimicking* OSKAR'S *expression.*]

ARTHUR [*blissful over the return of his friend*]: Bernardchen, you won't ever go away again, will you?!

[*The* MAID *herds the children through the back gate into the house. It is suddenly illuminated with the glow of candles.* MRS. SCHÜLER *escorts the two clergymen up the steps. It has grown dark. A lantern is lit before the house. Through the gate steps the very elegant wine merchant,* ALFONSO KISSINGEN (DR. FAUST), *followed by seven* POOR JEWS *invited from the community. After them, dressed alike,* ALEXANDER *and* SIEGFRIED OSTERMORGEN. *Last of all* MR. SCHÜLER *in his gray top hat, highly distinguished, comes through the gate and up the steps into the house. Stillness reigns in the garden.*]

Scene 15

[*In the great dining room of the Schüler mansion. Order of seating at the seder table:* MR. SCHÜLER *at the head with* BISHOP MATTHIAS *opposite; along the left side* FANNY, ALFONSO KISSINGEN, DORA, ARTHUR, LENCHEN, MAX, META, LOUISA, BERTHOLD, KARL, SIEGFRIED OSTERMORGEN, BETTINA, ALEXANDER OSTERMORGEN, ELISCHEN, TITI, *and* MRS. SCHÜLER; *along the right side* ALEX, ELEONORA, JULIUS, MEYERCHEN, MENACHEM, OSKAR, ELFRIEDA, FERDINAND, ALBERT, MARGARETA, HENRY FILIGRAN, AUGUST, KATHARINA, ENGELBRECHT, SIMEON, *and* CHAPLAIN MICHALSKI.

At the small table sit seven POOR JEWS: ALTMANN, LEMMLE, NATHANAEL BRENNESSEL, *and the* THREE PERLMUTTERS, *junk dealers, with their little nephew,* JOSEFCHEN. *The board is festively decked with a snow-white cloth. The daughters, grown-up and small, wear velvet dresses and the younger sons, velvet jackets. Two Jewish candelabra stand on the table before* MR. SCHÜLER, *the candles lighted. Before him are also a large platter with three loaves of unleavened bread wrapped in a napkin and several small plates with radishes, bitter herbs, parsley, and hard-boiled eggs in salt water.*]

MR. SCHÜLER [*with polished gesture*]: Before I begin the ceremony, allow me, Your Grace and Chaplain Michalski—

MRS. SCHÜLER: The guardian angel of our house—

CHAPLAIN MICHALSKI: He only leant me his robe.

MR. SCHÜLER [*pointing to* ALEX *in his wheelchair*]: This dearest youth, my son Alex, caught a bad infection some years ago, from which we hope to see him cured in the near future.

[BISHOP MATTHIAS *smiles lovingly at the sick boy.*]

To my left [FANNY *casts a quick glance into the wall mirror*] my eldest daughter Fanny, who expanded her vocabulary this past year in a French boarding school in Münster.

[FANNY'S *and* CHAPLAIN MICHALSKI'S *eyes meet. He notices her coral earrings, with obvious joy.*]

Next to my dear eldest daughter, Mr. Kissingen from Kissingen in Bavarialand. A tried and tested wine connoisseur.

[BISHOP MATTHIAS *gazes at* ALFONSO KISSINGEN, *pondering.*]

CHAPLAIN MICHALSKI [*as though to himself, but* FANNY *reads it from his lips*]: Dr. Faust—

MR. SCHÜLER: Here our Dora, her cheery self again! She turned sixteen yesterday.

[*Thanks* BISHOP MATTHIAS, *then* CHAPLAIN MICHALSKI, *with a polished gesture.*]

Our Lenchen, Arthur Aronymus's faithful little sister.

BISHOP MATTHIAS: She reminds me unmistakably of your good, gentle little mother, Bernard, this charming child.

MR. SCHÜLER: My Max, our prospective sculptor. Meta and Louisa, our little twins.

BISHOP MATTHIAS: To a hair—

MRS. SCHÜLER: That's why we simply call both of them Meta.

MR. SCHÜLER: Karl, my promising son. Mr. Siegfried Ostermorgen. Our Bettina; Mr. Alexander Ostermorgen, Siegfried's brother, the sons of my school friend Ostermorgen from Bochum. My third eldest daughter, Elisa-the-well-read. [*Indicating* MRS. SCHÜLER *with a courtly gesture*] My dear wife, Madame Henrietta, already known to Your Grace.

MRS. SCHÜLER [*lifting* TITI]: Our youngest.

MR. SCHÜLER: Next to Alex, Eleonora. After Goethe's Eleonora who drove at break of day!

BISHOP MATTHIAS [*to* CHAPLAIN MICHALSKI]: The priests count ten Eleonoras out of every twenty maidens being confirmed.

MR. SCHÜLER: Our third son, Julius. Versed in the works of Goethe. Our little Meyerlein, who wants to be a farmer! [*With sweeping gesture*] Augustus.

BISHOP MATTHIAS: With the imposing brow of the Roman.

MR. SCHÜLER: Menachem, my firstborn, his faithful wife Elfrieda, and their promising son, Oskar.

[BISHOP MATTHIAS *knits his brow ominously into furrows, imitating* OSKAR.]

Dear Berthold, named for my only brother. Our Margareta. Monsieur de Filigran, my overseer. My beloved second-eldest daughter, Katharina, and her husband, the apothecary Dr. Engelbrecht Vogelsang from the Wupper Valley; the poor fellow lost both of his parents on the same day last month. Next to him my second son, Simeon, my moral support. And now we've come to our highly respected chaplain.

BISHOP MATTHIAS [*to* CHAPLAIN MICHALSKI, *pointing to the little side table, also festively decked*]: And who are they?

MR. SCHÜLER [*whispers*]: Seven poor Jews of our community, as is customary with us Jews on the seder evening. [*He introduces them, then points to* ALTMANN] The solicitous father of our village, Altmann! He blows Gaesecke's children to sleep every evening with his horn. [*Indicating* NATHANAEL BRENNESSEL] Our globetrotter, Nathanael Brennessel! A tireless traveler.

[NATHANAEL BRENNESSEL *giggles*.]

The renowned father of my wife, Henrietta, called him Pan. [*Pointing to* LEMMLE] Lemmle Tsilinsky from Lemberg, our wholesale merchant. I can recommend his wares with good conscience.

[*In his bashfulness* LEMMLE *almost tears the buttons off his caftan*. MR. SCHÜLER, *graciously*]

My three good friends the Perlmutters. They collect the village's antiques! Their little nephew, Joseph.

ONE OF THE PERLMUTTERS: Josefche, stand up!

BISHOP MATTHIAS [*to* CHAPLAIN MICHALSKI]: Antiques?

CHAPLAIN MICHALSKI [*smiling*]: Three junk dealers.

BISHOP MATTHIAS [*inspired by the humbleness of the master of the house*]: In truth we are dining with a prince.

MR. SCHÜLER [*puts his prayer shawl over his shoulders and prays*]: *Boruch ata adonai elohenu melech haolum hamozi lechan min haarez. (King of the world, who brings forth bread from the earth.) He reads a short passage from the Haggada aloud, from the little Paschal book. He unwraps the unleavened bread from the napkin and breaks it into small pieces. He dips the first piece in salt, lays bitter herbs on it, rises, and himself offers it to* BISHOP MATTHIAS. *The second piece is for* ARTHUR *to take to* CHAPLAIN MICHALSKI. ARTHUR *is very dejected.*]

BISHOP MATTHIAS: I think Bernard's little friend doesn't really want to join in this evening—?

MRS. SCHÜLER: He wanted to sit next to his dear chaplain, Your Grace.

BISHOP MATTHIAS [*Automatically assuming command of the table*]: And he's right! Let him change places quickly with his elder brother, so that we shelter no unsatisfied guest among us at the table.

[BISHOP MATTHIAS *routinely offers* CHAPLAIN MICHALSKI *his hand to kiss.* SIMEON, *not very willingly but with well-bred control, rises and sits down in* ARTHUR'S *place between* DORA *and* LENCHEN. ARTHUR *beams at his mother; from then on he and* CHAPLAIN MICHALSKI *sit hand in hand. To each of the children and guests, the two brothers* BERTHOLD *and* FERDINAND *must offer pieces of the unleavened bread dipped in salt, with bitter herbs.* SIMEON *and* JULIUS *have begun to fill the glasses with Mosel wine.*]

MRS. SCHÜLER [*softly to* ELISCHEN]: If only the carp doesn't get cold.

[*On the table stand great covered platters, and the gravy boats hold raisin sauce.*]

BISHOP MATTHIAS: I beg our kind host not to forget a single word or God-ancient syllable of the ceremony of the holy seder evening. We, Our Grace the Bishop Matthias, would reproach Ourselves and even imagine that We were disturbing the peace of the ceremony, whereas [*turning to* MRS. SCHÜLER] We would like to feel Ourselves completely at home.

MRS. SCHÜLER: Your Grace, my husband and I would never have dreamed that the bishop and the chaplain, whom we are so happy to see again, would celebrate this holy festival with our family.

BISHOP MATTHIAS [*laughing broadly*]: But the charming and youthfully fresh Madame Schüler has not imagined Us, Bishop Matthias of Paderborn, to be a hypocrite!

[BISHOP MATTHIAS *gestures, meaning "By no means."* MR. SCHÜLER *speaks a few more words of blessing, then rises and himself refills* BISHOP MATTHIAS's *glass with* Mosel. *Hands the bottle to* SIMEON. *Little* OSKAR *stares at* BISHOP MATTHIAS *unblinkingly, almost ambitiously, but darkly.*]

ARTHUR [*to* CHAPLAIN MICHALSKI]: Just look, Bernard, how Oskar is looking at *your* bishop; I don't like it at all.

[MAMSELL *and* CLARA, *waiting in the dining room, begin to serve the carp upon a signal from* MRS. SCHÜLER. *They offer the platter to* BISHOP MATTHIAS *first.*]

BISHOP MATTHIAS [*digs in; to* CHAPLAIN MICHALSKI]: this will taste mighty good to your uncle. [*Enjoys himself like a child.* CHAPLAIN MICHALSKI *somewhat embarrassed.* BISHOP MATTHIAS *speaks like a child, winking at the* children] He always has to fret over his bishop uncle—who has already given him an opportunity in the garden—

[*The children laugh gaily.*]

CHAPLAIN MICHALSKI: But Your Grace!

BISHOP MATTHIAS: —an hour ago, when the mischievous little Matthias [*to the children, as one of them*] was amusing himself so heartily in the garden over these rascals here. [*Indicates the children at the table, then suddenly bursts into uproarious laughter and can hardly get control of himself.*] But from now on, no more witchburning!

CHAPLAIN MICHALSKI [*humbly*]: It was a happy hour for your spiritual son, to hear Your Grace laugh so heartily.

[BISHOP MATTHIAS *again routinely extends his hand for* CHAPLAIN MICHALSKI *to kiss. Calm is restored. All eat the fish and trimmings with good appetite. Noticing that* MR. SCHÜLER *wants to continue with the ceremony,* BISHOP MATTHIAS *lays down his knife and fork, folds his hands before him on the table, and attentively raises his large head with the laughing round eyes.*]

BISHOP MATTHIAS: Let the master of the house speak. [*Admonishing the small* children *with his finger*] We reverently await his word.

MR. SCHÜLER: Your Grace was pleased to direct an unspoken question to my humble self regarding the bitter herbs. They symbolize the bitterness of the servitude suffered by our people in foreign lands, while the unleavened bread symbolizes the hurried departure from Egypt to freedom.

[*All resume eating, including the* POOR JEWS *at the little table, who murmur piously together.*]

ONE OF THE PERLMUTTERS: Two goyim at *his* seder evening?

LEMMLE [*timidly*]: The one next to the bishop is a half Jew.

NATHANAEL BRENNESSEL: Now when I go to Paderborn, I'll know where to stay!

ALL: Well, where?

NATHANAEL BRENNESSEL: In the cathedral with His Magnificence. With Him!

[*Indicates* BISHOP MATTHIAS *with his eyes.*]

ALTMANN [*philosophically*]: Don't talk nonsense. A new world history is beginning!

A PERLMUTTER [*to the other two*]: We'll pick the old one up from the houses with our dogcart.

BISHOP MATTHIAS [*dunking another piece of unleavened bread in his Mosel, to* CHAPLAIN MICHALSKI]: Excellent! [*Helping himself to the pudding being offered to him*] Just dunk a little piece of the holy unleavened bread in your Mosel too, Bernardchen.

[*Motions to the children to do likewise.*]

MR. SCHÜLER [*diplomatically to the* POOR JEWS, *whom he has temporarily forgotten*]: Now have you, my dear guests, not been forgotten in any way either?

LEMMLE [*unwraps a little white fur collar from an old scrap of newspaper and gesticulates until* ARTHUR *notices and goes over to his table*]: Didn't he bring me his goodies on the Christian Christmas morning, with tears in his eyes.

[*Smiling shyly, he lays the little collar around* ARTHUR'*s neck.* ARTHUR *bows first to* CHAPLAIN MICHALSKI *and then to the whole company.*]

CHAPLAIN MICHALSKI [*with lowered head, to* ARTHUR]: Didn't you want to take them from me?

ARTHUR: I don't know, Bernardchen!

MRS. SCHÜLER: Mr. Lemmle Tsilinsky, that is very touching of you! Father, just look at the elegant present!

[MAMSELL *offers the food to* BISHOP MATTHIAS *once more, then to all at the table.*]

BISHOP MATTHIAS: Splendid, splendid. The bishop is not one to disdain good food, respected Cook!

OSKAR [*suddenly hard and sinister*]: I'm going to be a monk.

BISHOP MATTHIAS [*turning to* CHAPLAIN MICHALSKI]: What does he say?

MENACHEM: Ssh!

BISHOP MATTHIAS: How often we and the great rabbuni of the Rhineland and Westphalia discussed deep religious problems late into the night.

MRS. SCHÜLER: And now my poor father rests alone in the earth—

BISHOP MATTHIAS: The ways of God are inscrutable, his acts an eternal riddle to us.

ARTHUR [*loudly, in* RABBI URIEL'S *voice, as though through a medium*]: The rabbuni is not alone—*he is gathered to his ancestors.*

[*All very deeply shaken, including* MR. SCHÜLER. *Pause.* ARTHUR, *coming to, runs bewildered from the dining room.*]

BISHOP MATTHIAS: To manifest itself, this truth sought the pure heart of a child.

[MRS. SCHÜLER *has tears in her eyes.* CHAPLAIN MICHALSKI *hurries after* ARTHUR.]

CHAPLAIN MICHALSKI: I'll bring him back.

BISHOP MATTHIAS: Our dear Chaplain Bernard loves the boy. I can understand it.

[FANNY *leaves the room.* KATHARINA *and* ELISA *exchange meaningful glances. To* SIMEON, *who is filling his glass again*]

If you please, mister cup bearer. Such a drop of "flowing golden sunshine"—in the words of our immortal Westphalian poet Peter Hille. He should be made a saint.

[*Pause.* BISHOP MATTHIAS *notices* FANNY'S *empty place; with a father's concern*]

Hm, hm, what drove the lovely maiden from the table?

[*Pause.*]

She would have provided our Bernard with a wealth of material for a little volume of graceful poems.

ELISCHEN: I *thought* the chaplain wrote poetry.

BISHOP MATTHIAS [*rather gravely*]: Religious poems now and then—within the high dignity of his requiem services. He shall recite one for us at once.

[CHAPLAIN MICHALSKI *and* ARTHUR *come back into the dining room,* CHAPLAIN MICHALSKI *holding a large set of building blocks under his arm. Hidden behind* CHAPLAIN MICHALSKI, ARTHUR *builds an elaborate cathedral on the floor.* BISHOP MATTHIAS *has not noticed that the two have returned. He is thinking about* ALFONSO KISSINGEN.]

BISHOP MATTHIAS: Now it dawns on Us! How is the old Señor Giacomo, your Papa, and your loveliest little sister, the Señorita Jeannetta?

ALFONSO KISSINGEN [*bows with Spanish* grandezza]: My old Señor and I, his son, remember your distinguished visit with special contentment.

BISHOP MATTHIAS [*his eyes meet* MR. SCHÜLER'S *significantly*]: A wine grower as rich as Solomon, the young señor's father—

ALFONSO KISSINGEN: The old nobleman rooted himself resignedly in Bavaria's soil.

BISHOP MATTHIAS [*kindly*]: But he still had the arrogance of the Spanish Jew, Pappa Giacomo! Isn't that so, my young friend?

[FANNY *returns and stands behind her mother's chair. Voices are heard outside, before the house.*]

MRS. SCHÜLER [*to* FANNY]: You're so restless.

CHAPLAIN MICHALSKI [*comes up to the table and says to* BISHOP MATTHIAS]: The little rascal has built me a cathedral, sir.

BISHOP MATTHIAS [*admires the grandiosity of the childish structure*]: My goodness! [*Motioning to* ARTHUR] Come to Bishop Matthias. We'd like to shake the great builder's hand.

[ARTHUR'S *parents are very flattered.* BISHOP MATTHIAS, *in raised voice.*]

I bless the ancient nation Israel! Each of the children represents a little Torah in velvet carrying case, but one of the little Torahim wears silver bells around its neck. I think [*stroking* ARTHUR'S *hair*] it's this one!

[*Embraces* ARTHUR. *All are deeply touched.*]

Yes, yes, charming Madame Mother, the old gray bishop [*looks about for denials*] knows about Judaism's reliquary too. [*Routinely offers her his hand to kiss.*]

[ARTHUR *bounds back to* CHAPLAIN MICHALSKI, *who is admiring the little church with solemn delight. In high spirits,* ARTHUR *suddenly jumps on it, sending the blocks flying.* CHAPLAIN MICHALSKI *is pale and disconcerted.* BISHOP MATTHIAS *notices what has happened.*]

BISHOP MATTHIAS: Now he has indeed escaped from you, poor Bernardchen! But take comfort, my good son-in-Christ, the ancient God of Israel does not leave the souls of his children to fend for themselves!

MRS. SCHÜLER [*nodding her head in appreciative agreement*]: And with a little love, Jew and Christian *can* break their bread together in harmony, even if the bread is unleavened.

VILLAGERS OF GAESECKE [*making a terrific noise outside*]: We want to see our bishop!

THREE MAIDS [*rushing into the dining room, speaking at the same time as the* VILLAGERS OF GAESECKE]: They want to see their bishop! They're everywhere!

[BISHOP MATTHIAS *rises forcefully.* KATHARINA *opens the door to the terrace. All rise to follow him; only* FANNY *holds her mother back; near them* ALFONSO KISSINGEN *waits chivalrously.*]

FANNY: Mother, just think, he called me poor girl! Me, beautiful Fanny—poor girl?

ALFONSO KISSINGEN: The flower of Westphalia? [*Suspects and is jealous.*]

FANNY [*made even angrier by his remark*]: Poor girl, I? [*Laughing scornfully*] The sill—the chaplain calls *me* poor girl?

MRS. SCHÜLER [*shrugs her shoulders*]: How much heart's blood do you suppose that cost him! But Fanny!

[*Hurries out onto the terrace.*]

ALFONSO KISSINGEN [*goes to* FANNY, *now silent and deep in thought; enthusiastically*]: Should I challenge him with Spanish sabers, Miss Fanny?

[*Leads her out onto the terrace on his arm.*]

VILLAGERS OF GAESECKE [*all assembled outside, cheering* BISHOP MATTHIAS *and then singing*]: Now thank we all our God!

[*Village band joins in with trumpets, French horns, drums, flutes, accordion, and other appropriate instruments.*]

Appendix: Scene 15

as performed in Zurich in 1936 with Lasker-Schüler's participation

[*In the great dining room of the Schüler mansion the seder evening is being celebrated by* MR. *and* MRS. SCHÜLER; *their twenty-three children, as well as* MENACHEM'*s wife and ten-year-old son and* KATHARINA'*s husband,* DR. ENGELBRECHT VOGELSANG; BISHOP MATTHIAS; CHAPLAIN MICHALSKI; HENRY FILIGRAN; ALFONSO KISSINGEN; ALEXANDER *and* SIEGFRIED OSTERMORGEN; *and seven* POOR JEWS *from Gaesecke:* ALTMANN; LEMMLE TSILINSKY; NATHANAEL BRENNESSEL; *and the* THREE PERLMUTTERS, *junk dealers, with their little nephew,* JOSEFCHEN. *The board is festively decked with a snow-white cloth. The daughters, grown-up and small, wear velvet dresses and the younger sons velvet jackets. Two Jewish candelabra stand on the table before* MR. SCHÜLER, *the candles lighted. Before him are also a large platter with three loaves of unleavened bread wrapped in a napkin and several small plates with radishes, bitter herbs, parsley, and hardboiled eggs in salt water. The celebration begins with all singing together or with the ceremony of the bitter herbs and the breaking of the matzoth. At the end of the ceremony,* MR. SCHÜLER *turns to* BISHOP MATTHIAS.]

MR. SCHÜLER: Your Grace was pleased to direct an unspoken question to my humble self regarding the bitter herbs. They symbolize the bitterness of the servitude suffered by our people in foreign lands; the unleavened bread—the hurried departure from Egypt to freedom.

[*If the ceremony of the ten plagues has been performed earlier, he also speaks the following sentence.*]

And from the cup of joy we took ten drops, as a sign of sorrow for the ten plagues which the Lord our God laid upon the Egyptians.

[*The* POOR JEWS *at the little table murmur piously together.*]

ONE OF THE PERLMUTTERS: Two goyim at his seder evening?

NATHANAEL BRENNESSEL: Now when I go to Paderborn, I'll know where to stay!

ALL: Well where?

NATHANAEL BRENNESSEL: In the cathedral with His Magnificence. With Him!

[*Indicates* BISHOP MATTHIAS *with his eyes.*]

ALTMANN [*philosophically*]: Don't talk nonsense. A new world history is beginning!

ONE OF THE PERLMUTTERS: We'll pick the old one up from the houses with our dogcart.

BISHOP MATTHIAS [*to* CHAPLAIN MICHALSKI]: Who are they?

MR. SCHÜLER [*whispers*]: Seven poor Jews of our community, as is customary with us Jews on the seder evening. [*Pointing to* ALTMANN] The solicitous father of our village, Altmann. He blows Gaesecke's children to sleep every evening with his horn. [*Indicating* NATHANAEL BRENNESSEL] Our globe-trotter, Nathanael Brennessel, a tireless traveler.

[NATHANAEL BRENNESSEL *giggles.*]

The renowned father of my wife, Henrietta, called him Pan. [*Pointing to* LEMMLE] Lemmle Tsilinsky from Lemberg, our wholesale merchant. I can recommend his wares with good conscience.

[*In his bashfulness* LEMMLE *almost tears the buttons off his caftan.* MR. SCHÜLER, *graciously*]

My three good friends the Perlmutters. They collect the village's antiques! Their little nephew, Joseph.

ONE OF THE PERLMUTTERS: Josefche, stand up!

BISHOP MATTHIAS [*to* CHAPLAIN MICHALSKI]: Antiques?

CHAPLAIN MICHALSKI [*smiling*]: Three junk dealers.

BISHOP MATTHIAS [*inspired by the humbleness of the master of the house*]: In truth we are dining with a prince.

[LEMMLE *unwraps a little white fur collar from an old scrap of newspaper and gesticulates until* ARTHUR *notices and goes over to his table.*]

LEMMLE: Didn't he bring me his goodies on the Christian Christmas morning, with tears in his eyes.

[*Smiling shyly, he lays the little collar around* ARTHUR'*s neck.* ARTHUR *bows first to* CHAPLAIN MICHALSKI *and then to the whole company.*]

MRS. SCHÜLER: Mr. Lemmle Tsilinsky, that is very touching of you. Father, just look at the elegant present!

CHAPLAIN MICHALSKI [*with lowered head, to* ARTHUR]: Didn't you want to take them from me?

ARTHUR: I don't know, Bernardchen.

MRS. SCHÜLER: Your Grace, my husband and I would never have dreamed that the bishop and the chaplain, whom we are so happy to see again, would celebrate this holy festival with our family.

BISHOP MATTHIAS [*laughing broadly*]: But the charming and youthfully fresh Madame Mother has not imagined us, Bishop Matthias of Paderborn, to be a hypocrite? How often we and the great rabbuni of the Rhineland and Westphalia discussed deep religious problems late into the night.

MRS. SCHÜLER: And now my poor father rests alone in the earth—

BISHOP MATTHIAS: The ways of God are inscrutable, his acts an eternal riddle to us.

ARTHUR [*loudly, in* RABBI URIEL'*s voice, as though through a medium*]: The rabbuni is not alone. *He is gathered to his ancestors.*

[*All very deeply shaken, including* MR. SCHÜLER. *Pause.* ARTHUR, *coming to, runs bewildered into a corner of the room.*]

BISHOP MATTHIAS: To manifest itself, this truth sought the pure heart of a child.

[MRS. SCHÜLER *has tears in her eyes.* CHAPLAIN MICHALSKI *hurries to* ARTHUR *and brings him slowly back to the table.* BISHOP MATTHIAS *embraces him.*]

I bless the ancient nation Israel! Our Lord Jesus said in Capernaum, "Many will come from East and from West and will dine with Abraham, Isaac, and Jacob in the kingdom of heaven." Every one of the Children of Israel represents a little Torah in its velvet carrying case, but one of the little Toroth wears silver bells around its neck. I think [*strokes* ARTHUR'*s hair*] it's this one!

[*All are deeply touched. To* CHAPLAIN MICHALSKI]

He has indeed escaped from you, poor Bernardchen. But take comfort, my good son in Christ, the ancient God of Israel does not leave the souls of his children to fend for themselves!

MRS. SCHÜLER [*nodding her head in appreciative agreement*]: And with a little love, Jew and Christian *can* break their bread together in harmony, even if the bread is unleavened.

ARTHUR [*softly, to* CHAPLAIN MICHALSKI]: Just look, Bernard, how Oskar's looking at your bishop.

OSKAR [*hard and sinister*]: I'm going to be a monk!

BISHOP MATTIAS [*bursts suddenly into uproarious laughter and can hardly get control of himself*]: But from now on no more witch burning!

[*All laugh, the children's laughter outringing all.* MR. SCHÜLER *joins heartily in the laughter. The sons add their voices to the singing: two verses of "Lecho Ulecho." After the second verse the tumultuous noise of the crowd is heard outside.*]

VILLAGERS OF GAESECKE: We want to see our bishop!

THREE MAIDS [*hurrying into the room, speaking together*]: They want to see their bishop!

[BISHOP MATTHIAS *rises forcefully. All rise.* BISHOP MATTHIAS *and* CHAPLAIN MICHALSKI, *leading* ARTHUR *between them, walk to the terrace door, which is opened for them. The parents and older children follow. Only the* POOR JEWS *and a few of the smaller children remain in the room.*]

BISHOP MATTHIAS [*on terrace, to the crowd*]: My beloved brothers and sisters in Christ! My heart is moved by deep joy. In this hour, in which I stand as mediator between those of you *before* this house and those *inside* this house, the word of our holy apostle Peter is fulfilled for me: "God does not look at people according to what they are in human society; rather do all those, in every nation, who fear him and live righteously, find favor in his sight."

[*All sing "Great God, We Praise Thee." Village band, with trumpets, French horn, drums, flutes, accordion. As the anthem is sung and the lights in the large room gradually dim, the curtain falls.*]

I AND I

A Tragedy for the Theater

in Six Acts

with Prelude and Postlude

CHARACTERS

Baal
King Saul
King David
King Solomon
Else Lasker-Schüler, *the poet*
Faust (Aribert Wäscher, *the actor*)
Mephisto (Karl Hannemann, *the actor*)
Marthe Schwerdtlein
Scarecrow
Three Ritz Brothers [referred to throughout the original in English]
Max Reinhardt, *director*
Stage Director
Theater Doctor
Critics
Finance Director
Gershon Swet, *chief editor*
Spectator
Learned Scholar
Audience
Marinus van der Lubbe
Adolf Hitler
Hermann Göring

Josef Goebbels
Joachim von Ribbentrop
Heinrich Himmler
Alfred Rosenberg
Baldur von Schirach
Rudolf Hess
Robert Ley
Nazi Soldiers
Devil's Servants
Dancing Devils of Both Sexes

The prelude, postlude, and act 6 take place in Jerusalem in the early 1940s, the prelude and postlude in a theater in the Hell Ground[1] by the Tower of David, act 6 in the garden of an eye doctor. Within this framework, acts 1 through 5 represent a play within a play that takes place in Hell.

The unpublished manuscript of this play was edited for posthumous publication by Margarete Kupper.

PRELUDE

[*Behind the curtain the poet* ELSE LASKER-SCHÜLER *is heard speaking to her companion on the way to the theater.*]

ELSE LASKER-SCHÜLER: It was ten and a half years ago in the godforsaken Nazi city—
I flew, invisible, a lightly suspended golden ball,
Headlong through the murderous howling, over the vassals on the Spree.
Since that time I regard myself according to a higher view of life,
And not as you, overclever citizen, assess me.
My plumage and the vulture quill—(beware of feather thieves!)—
I use to write here in my blood on rusty papyrus leather.
I would rather write my manuscript on the yellowed page of my heart—
But then I would be held, bought and paid for, in every hand.
I do care somewhat about their opinion—
That is, whether they were charmed with my book on their bookstand.
We would eventually become book-related.
Ah, I'm tired, dear guests, ladies and gentlemen in the parquet, the first balcony, and the boxes,
And you impecunious guests in Olympus.
I know, we can't dwell our whole life (now and then, I suppose)
In the nest on a steep cliff,
Recklessly chased to and fro by blustery November storms,

Arbitrarily torn to pieces by the amorous spring games of a faunish rogue,
Ultimately exposed to the daggers of July's torrid days.
. . . My destiny upraised me to the clouds . . .[2]
You wonder that, after drinking the silver drink,
I have come back to your earthly bonds.
For a poet's unbounded dream
There is truly no room in your constructed world.
Pardon the presumption, my companion,
You see, I lead a higher life—
Lightless nights ignite themselves from my happiness!
The stars rise in my glance—
Star years ago already I tarried on Earth!
And only my poems were no illusion!
Stay with me, on through the streets to the theater.
We'll leave the open city early as on a workday.
The tower clock, like mine, runs slow!
The billboard dreams are already sparking off houses
From right to left and forth and back
Exchanging their light like spoonerisms.
A witches' sabbath sprays me full in the face,
Just as I'm looking at an image, setting it mystically in a poem.
So follow me, *my dearest friend,*[3] first into the lobby—
And listen to my Hell play in the parquet before my heart's stage.

[ELSE LASKER-SCHÜLER *whistles and sings the ending of the song "Muss i denn," softly and with lively spirit: "Muss i denn, muss i denn zum Städtli hinaus, Städtli hinaus—und du, mein Schatz, bleibst hier." The curtain opens slowly. At first a small pause. In the orchestra a simple barrel organ plays the ending stanza: "Muss i denn, muss i denn zum Städtli hinaus, und du, mein Schatz, bleibst hier."*]

ACT 1

[*Near the Tower of David, called the Hell Ground by longtime residents of Palestine. In the royal box of crumbling old stone, in elegant armchairs, sit* KING SAUL, KING DAVID, *and* KING SOLOMON, *eerily motionless, painted with gold and many colors like the figures in a wax museum. In the director's box* MAX REINHARDT, *brought by request from Hollywood to Jerusalem as general director. Opposite him the* THREE RITZ BROTHERS, *comics. The* THEATER DOCTOR, *arriving early, is just taking his seat. The* CRITICS *with crossed arms. They greet one another before the play.* ELSE LASKER-SCHÜLER, *poet, author of the visionary tragedy, steps before the audience.*]

ELSE LASKER-SCHÜLER: From silent Eternity, which cannot be incarnated in word and deed,
I come today into the world created by you, *at home for the weekend,*
Into your earthly world, a world spoiled for me, honored people;
From the star-flashing lip into the slack maw of tepidity—secretly home;
A drenched poodle and once again from—humane feelings.
However, not for this reason alone, Audience—
For God's reasons, the human soul
(Indeed, any soul still incarcerated in the body)
Can find no peace in Heaven,
(Though it isn't so far from Earth),
But still the poet's inspiration keeps longing to rise back again from the realm of the cold word into the blue cloud.

[*In the orchestra several barrel organs are suddenly heard playing.*]

Hear, Audience, the murder tale
That I wrote for myself in darkest night!
And since the tale I tell is true,
Banish every doubt:
What you see is not an apparition,
For I divided myself into two halves shortly before dawn,
Into two parts: I and I!

A LADY FROM THE AUDIENCE: Sleepwalker—

ELSE LASKER-SCHÜLER: Where the profile meets its *en face*,
And the *en face* meets its profile.
I'm bleeding from it still, all by myself.
For I called out to myself all my life and heard myself at last,
And now am freed from infinite solitude!
Though I and I never came together in life,
My two halves have now achieved this bold rendezvous in an
instant.
We have, as my public will learn,
A monstrous genius for mimicry,
And though never mixed in the dark narrow body,
We'll find ourself united on the wide stage,
Between virtues and sins,
Enlightened, I and I finally joined together!
As surely was unspokenly intended
According to the higher testament's will!

[*Short pause.*]

Attention!
To my mother, these lines,
The devotee of Goethe: she is
The godmother of my two halves.
Honored Audience, you yawn as out of one mouth—

Why the overture embellished with poetry?
Here's the announcement direct from me:
Satan, devil of all devils, has—capitulated!

[AUDIENCE *reaction, babble of voices.* ELSE LASKER-SCHÜLER *tries in vain to continue.*]

GERSHON SWET: I would have published the fact long since!

[ELSE LASKER-SCHÜLER *tries in vain to continue.*]

GERSHON SWET: The report is a hoax!

VOICE FROM THE AUDIENCE: For the birds!

ELSE LASKER-SCHÜLER: Gershon Swet, you have interrupted me twice!

YOUNG WOMAN FROM THE AUDIENCE: The so-and-so!

ELSE LASKER-SCHÜLER: In my lifetime—and from the edge of the stage—I spoke the truth more naked than naked! In prose as well as in verse!

LEARNED SCHOLAR: Verse . . . If I might ask . . .

VOICES FROM THE AUDIENCE: Holland lost! Belgium *perdu*, France, Denmark, Norway . . .

GERSHON SWET [*calming the audience*]: *Ha'aretz* would have published the fact long since!

ELSE LASKER-SCHÜLER: Gershon Swet, you've made a mistake, because of what I haven't yet said: Satan, devil of all devils, has capitulated! Yes! However: before the Lord God in act 4!

KING DAVID [*rising, unmoved*]: Blessed art thou, Eternal One—king of the world—*Baruch atta adonai melech haolom* . . .

[*The curtain falls but immediately rises again. The play begins.* MEPHISTO *leans on the red grapevines of the terrace of his palace in Hell.*]

MEPHISTO: Even if I haven't written out my ideas in iambs and trochees, I'm still the one who put them into action.

[FAUST *is indifferent.*]

MEPHISTO: Was it that I made a fool of you in front of the bourgeois citizens back then, Doctor Faust? Speak up: what was it, Heinrich, that displeased you? Perhaps the overdone style of the Devil's interior decoration? Sit down, my friend. I'm nervous, and it's high time that I knew the reasons for your anger.

FAUST: Devils that you sent into the world report that my drama, the first part and the second as well, has been booed and burned once and for all in the marketplace in Weimar.

[*Short pause.*]

MEPHISTO: I smelled it, poor friend. I like to smell charred book pages, and those with your poetry I enjoyed even from far away.

[*Short pause.*]

No reason to brood about it, Doctor Faust; the Testament written by *God* was also burned, the first part of the Bible and the second part as well.

FAUST: Yes, late into the night I ask in prayer—forgive me—whether Earth and Heaven and Hell were really created by God, whether they didn't somehow form themselves according to some model—

MEPHISTO [*cynical*]: Extremely long-lasting—

FAUST: If they don't just exist in the human mind, I mean, the world—What does the Public think? That it was a fantasy, in the human imagination? In the human imagination?

MEPHISTO: The homeless children of Adam, driven out of their Eden world, already lived in the illusion of a world!

FAUST: And you, Mephisto, benighted man?

MEPHISTO: *Myself* you're asking—As the Eternal One planned, I crept into the darkness of my homeland. [*Bragging*] And God's earthly kingdom died from my serpent's bite.

FAUST: I'm not following you, my prince.

MEPHISTO: Billions of humans like you are going around in circles, because they don't know the way.

FAUST: And sits the Eternal One still upon his throne?

MEPHISTO: I don't know for certain.

[*Short pause.*]

But now I ask you, Doctor Faust, most politely and humbly, why He created the Devil, me, out of mud and scorn, and to last a lifetime?

FAUST: I'm sorry for you, Mephisto . . .

MEPHISTO: But humankind certainly didn't turn out to be any tastier, even though they're baked from better dough. When I look at them I want to throw up, my best Heinrich! You as well as I, we all have to bite the sour apple.

[*Short pause.*]

It tasted good to Adam Cadmon and still today after the Flood, death, and destruction—

FAUST: And everywhere nothing but darkness, nowhere growing light—

MEPHISTO: Nowhere! And I sought it, like you—for I am, Herr Faust, a human being, like you!

FAUST [*astounded*]: "And even if you come at the last hour" says the Lord, Lord—

[*Takes a deep breath.*]

MEPHISTO: The idea of going home was thought up by the world before it even came to the world.

FAUST: Audacious mocker from the First Creation, who—

MEPHISTO: Stayed faithful—

FAUST: In his godforsaken nature.

MEPHISTO: According to God's decree, faithless images of God like you, my friend, fall under my horse's hoof.

FAUST: Why do evil, Mephisto, Devil's man?

MEPHISTO: Do you regret your banishment?

FAUST: I'm not equal to it—

MEPHISTO: Compliments to God! Every citizen would like to buy a trusty house of cement, for shelter against the eternal element! For the element creates hate within the little pygmies! That is: overwhelming force worries them.

FAUST: How your speech, Princely One, shames me . . .

MEPHISTO: I strongly hope that the confused remnants of Creation are paralyzing you only temporarily.

FAUST: I am ashamed—

MEPHISTO: I feel your heart's distress and blush with you on the cheek of your heart, [*cajoling*] like the young virgin from Anno 80, I'm starting to blush for shame with you, Heinrich . . .

FAUST: Is Satan alluding somewhat indelicately to Margarete?

MEPHISTO [*dissembling*]: Your error, Faust, embarrasses me—

FAUST [*aside, to himself*]: My God, I didn't resist temptation.

[MARTHE SCHWERDTLEIN *enters*.]

MEPHISTO [*turns his back to* FAUST]: I'd like to spit into his holy face! Frau Marthe Schwerdtlein, read us my entry under F.

MAX REINHARDT: *Attention!* Mephisto, repeat the last lines again with much more contempt: I'd like to spit in his holy face! etc.

MEPHISTO: I'd like to spit in his holy face!—Well, old lady, are we getting there?

MARTHE SCHWERDTLEIN [*muttering to herself as is her habit*]: Otherwise the broth will get cold. Patience, Herr Satan, I can't find it so fast—Herr Satan knows that Marthe Schwerdtlein is going blind.

MEPHISTO: By the way, Margarete makes up her little mouth sweetly every evening with romantic red, as the fashion is these days. And since she put on fat as she grew older, she now squeezes her body—still seductively milk-white—into a corset.

MARTHE SCHWERDTLEIN: Herr Satan knows I'm going blind—[*Reading from the great folio book, like a little girl who has just learned to read*] The maiden—Faust lost his reason when he met her, he asked Lord Satan how he could get her.

[MARTHE SCHWERDTLEIN *exits*.]

FAUST: My Gretchen . . . [*To* MEPHISTO, *furious*] You're digging a trap in my mind!

MEPHISTO: You blossomed forth much statelier than I—

[MARTHE SCHWERDTLEIN *enters again and curtseys incessantly, practicing*.]

FAUST [*melancholy*]: A brooklet smiled from out her chin—[MEPHISTO *laughs scornfully*.] Devil!

MEPHISTO: You forget, my friend, that I am *your own* devil.

FAUST: What material are you made of? Surely not human salt, and not the earthly dust of long-lost kingdoms.

MEPHISTO: Herr Doctor Faust is mistaken; the few angel-like creatures that differ in appearance from my archperson are not enough for the noble spices of humanity.

[FAUST *falls to his knees*.]

What's troubling him, the great poet man?

FAUST: I beg the Lord, I, his child, implore him—for light.
There is a weeping in the world,[4]
As though the Dear God had passed away,
And the leaden gray shadow that falls unfurled
Weighs like graveyard clay.
Come, we'll hide ourselves close to each other;
Within all hearts as though in coffins
Life lies smothered.
Love! We'll kiss deep, you and I—
A longing is knocking at the world
Of which we soon must die.

MEPHISTO: He doesn't hear you . . . for even the Hell where you find yourself, my boy, is a modernized Hell, not God's. A monk made up Purgatory as punishment for poor sinners.

FAUST: That's not anywhere in the Bible, is it? Do you have some kind of fragment? something lost?

[*Short pause.*]

Otherwise He would come and help me and I would bow before Him . . . [*Singing in organ tones*] And I would bow before Him . . .

MEPHISTO: I am His witness—God is *here!* It was He who cursed me ruthlessly in Paradise! And not a single grain went unrecorded! The first woman plucked me with the fruit from the branch!

[*Short pause.*]

Soothe your torture further in song, Heinrich, go ahead and sing, sing the chorale more piously—I'll just keep in practice stirring up my flames!

[MARTHE SCHWERDTLEIN *comes onto the terrace again.*]

MARTHE SCHWERDTLEIN: Herr, if I may venture to come forward again: dinner is served. The tender angel wings are burning. [*Counting the number of guests on her fingers*] What is it? One, two, three guests? There are four guests awaiting Herr Satan in the dining room.

[MEPHISTO *gets up noisily.*]

MAX REINHARDT: If I may ask, Mephisto, get up with less noise, more royally!

MEPHISTO: It doesn't seem right to me to parody Goethe without exaggerating.

MAX REINHARDT: I respect your refusal, Mr. Devil.

[MAX REINHARDT *notices the actor* KARL HANNEMANN *in the wings.*]

Karl Hannemann, you take over this bombshell of a role. Your late father, before he became a general director, made himself a name playing Mephisto at home and abroad.

ELSE LASKER-SCHÜLER: . . . Juniper Karl! . . .

[MEPHISTO, *regretful but controlled, hands his devil's beard to his colleague* KARL HANNEMANN.]

KARL HANNEMANN: The devil's beard is already sticking fast to my chin. [*Turning toward* MAX REINHARDT] I fear it's old, with thin hair?

MAX REINHARDT [*roguishly*]: You can't grow a new one before the premiere day after tomorrow.

[MAX REINHARDT *gives the sign to begin again from the top.*]

ELSE LASKER-SCHÜLER [*forgetting theater, stage, and players*]: Juniper Karl, sing me the aria by Grieg: "*Ich liebe dich, ich liebe dich! . . .*"[5]

MEPHISTO: "*Ich liebe dich! Ich liebe dich . . .*"

WHOLE CAST: "*Ich liebe dich! Ich liebe dich . . .*"

MAX REINHARDT: Mr. Hannemann, you are an operetta star!

WHOLE CAST: *Bravissimo, bravissimo!*

[*They applaud wildly.*]

MAX REINHARDT: But now, before we continue rehearsing, I assume that it is clear to you, ladies and gentlemen, that Mephisto and Faust are a pair of twins! They're essentially *one* person and always were.

FIRST RITZ BROTHER: Clear!

SECOND RITZ BROTHER: Clearer!

THIRD RITZ BROTHER: Clarissa!

MAX REINHARDT: And also known to you, in any case, that Herr Faust came toward himself on a black-and-white checked stallion. And further, ladies and gentlemen, that in the end, Good usually conquers every person's evil urge! But unfortunately, gentlemen and ladies, Good seldom holds its ground . . .

THREE RITZ BROTHERS: In its foxhole!

[MEPHISTO *and* FAUST *rise, bow to the audience.* FAUST *yields the curtain to* MEPHISTO, *and they stride off center stage. The curtain falls in the form of a heart.*]

ACT 2

[*In the dining room of the Hell palace.* HERMANN GÖRING, JOSEF GOEBBELS, RUDOLF HESS, *and* BALDUR VON SCHIRACH *rise at the appearance of* MEPHISTO *and* FAUST. *They recognize* MEPHISTO *as Satan only when he turns fully toward them.* FAUST *at first remains standing in the middle of the room.*]

MEPHISTO: What brings me the honor, gentlemen? [*Without waiting for their reply*] Take some refreshment, gentlemen, after your journey here to the underworld!

[MEPHISTO *invites the guests to sit down at the table, which has been laid for dinner.* DEVIL'S SERVANTS *are busy with table arrangements, show the guests their places. The smallest* DEVIL'S SERVANT *dries the sweat from* GÖRING'*s brow and cheeks with his little tail.*]

MEPHISTO [*emphatically to* FAUST]: Opposite me, noble friend.

SCHIRACH [*brashly and with curiosity to one of the* DEVIL'S SERVANTS]: What is the name of the pale man he calls "noble friend"?

GOEBBELS: You dreamed it, man! Just hold your kettledrum cheeks!

SCHIRACH: He looks as pale as the marble bust of Rosalinda we brought with us in the crate.

GOEBBELS: The Tragedy, part 3—

GÖRING [*reprimanding*]: Thunderation!

[MEPHISTO *signals* MARTHE SCHWERDTLEIN *to begin serving.*]

MEPHISTO: It is the custom at my court that every guest, invited or not, discuss his *business* with me over a glass of wine at dinnertime. I assume you are here about customs duties, gentlemen?

GOEBBELS [*softly to* GÖRING]: What customs duties is the Hell swine talking about?

GÖRING: Bastard, shh!

MEPHISTO: I ask you since my time is limited—time comes across very sparingly into my Hell. I assume that your business concerns delivering petroleum fresh from our source here, gentlemen.

GÖRING, GOEBBELS, HESS, AND SCHIRACH: Heil Hitler! For Germania and for Rome, your Excellency.

FAUST [*correcting them*]: Your Highness!

GÖRING, GOEBBELS, HESS, AND SCHIRACH: Your Highness!

[DEVIL'S SERVANTS *fill the diners' beakers.* MEPHISTO, *laughing satanically, fills* GÖRING'*s beaker himself. Flames shoot out from the wine with a hissing sound, and the heavy vapor surrounds him. In the reflection of the bewitched fire-wine,* GÖRING *recognizes the burning Reichstag, showing palely on the broad wall of the dining room. (To be shown by means of a film.)*]

MEPHISTO [*raising his goblet in kingly style*]: Honored guests from Germania's provinces, I thank your Führer Adolf for the honor of his trust—

GÖRING, GOEBBELS, HESS, AND SCHIRACH: Heil Hitler!

MEPHISTO: For his trust and the honor of sending me the marshal himself and the bravest of his army—

[GÖRING *rises, staggering, and bows to* MEPHISTO.]

MEPHISTO: The German trio from his sphere. In the near future, gentlemen, his powerful army will stand against England in the field. I played three houses of cards—Belgium, Poland, the

Netherlands—into Herr Adolf's hand. La France taken in a trance—however, joining it with the German province, I judge to be a—*mésalliance*, gentlemen.

FAUST [*shaken by his satanic friend's manner*]: Satan—! [*No longer in control of himself*] Dark one from Original Creation, why do you politely restrain the howling jackal in your wild nature?

MEPHISTO: That is yet to come; I do not stem from some lowly cult.
My blood is old!
Yes, my noble *haute volée*[6] is to blame.
Heinrich, because you are so closely grown together with my heart,[7]
I disdained to consume the succulent stag for my *lunch* in Eden;
And the blue blood of the first human pair:
Your jackal refused to use it to quell the glowing fire.
Make me fly into a passion over the liquid in rotten arteries?
My hatred—a noble hatred—demands better wine!

[MEPHISTO *turns back toward the Nazis*.]

Most of our sinners have come to us from Paris—into the flaming dungeon. [*Ironically*] Let the Führer not drive his gallant army blindly into that very murky source. Rotten blood dripped its first drop from a Jewish cell!

GÖRING, GOEBBELS, HESS, AND SCHIRACH: Heil Hitler!

MEPHISTO: From the highest summit to the Seine, one single Madeleine! [*Exchanging a glance with* FAUST] The old lady with the beard, who was standing on my desk: our grandma on both sides, gentlemen! I'm a blood relative of Herr Adolf.

[*Short pause*.]

We two, he and, gentlemen, *myself*, inherited intrigue from the Hell lady . . . only against England did it not lead to victory! But you pushed trustingly against us two devils. I warn my cousin against battles across the ocean. Yes, gentlemen, I'm afraid of too much pushing for victory; at the end your Führer will lose the stolen world in war.

GÖRING, GOEBBELS, HESS, AND SCHIRACH [*automatically*]: Heil Hitler—

MEPHISTO: Assure him that I'm quite at his disposal, even if my Hell is fairly burnt out at the moment. I could lend him the purgatory oven, where the sinners roast, for little Cohn.

[DEVIL'S SERVANTS *look up astonished from their steaming dishes. They wear long yellow tailcoats, napkins between their arms and sides.* MARTHE SCHWERDTLEIN *helps them serve.*]

MARTHE SCHWERDTLEIN [*bustling around, sticky-sweet*]: Fallen angel wings plump and tender . . .

MEPHISTO: That's what she calls the fleshly question marks—please forgive the lady for her chatty manner! She's over one hundred and ninety-five years old by Christian reckoning.

SCHIRACH [*brashly*]: My old master already cold at fifty! They're ahead of us here in Hell: human beings are advanced to devils, their flame of life stirred up anew—they go right on breathing forever.

GÖRING [*satiated*]: Absurd!

[*He snorts like a tiger.*]

Is it allowed—sewed up in these damn clothes—to let out my belt? [*Dead drunk, to* MEPHISTO] And humbly ask for oil!

HESS [*sober, interrupting* GÖRING]: And the monopoly for delivering oil to Germany, Your Satanic Majesty, and to Rome.

MEPHISTO: As thanks for the pact, I'll take that musical little city in the Eifel. What is it called in your poetry, Heinrich?

GOEBBELS [*affectedly*]: Whatever it's called—and no doubt, complete with cat and mouse, my Führer will gladly sweep it out of his land as a return favor to Your Majesty.

SCHIRACH: Generous as the Führer is, Goethe was basically too much of a Christian for him. He said that Prometheus was created on order, too.

MEPHISTO [*to* FAUST]: I'll dig up Hermann and Dorothea for you before you see another morning.

GOEBBELS: Those two long dead misbaptized Jews? [*Completely drunk*] And let them graze with the lambs in the pasture . . . Woe to the Germanic race who pollute their German blood with Jewish seed, woe to all Jewry!

SCHIRACH: Rise up, Germany! Death to the Jews!

GÖRING, GOEBBELS, HESS, AND SCHIRACH: Woe to all Jewry! Heil Hitler!

[MARTHE SCHWERDTLEIN *comes back into the dining room.*]

MARTHE SCHWERDTLEIN: Pardon, Herr Satan and the gentlemen in the dining room, a young lad, his name is Grynspan, ah, I'm sorry for him, and so are the rest of the Hell personnel. He comes with his poor shaved head on his arm and hopes that Satan will take pity on him.[8]

GOEBBELS: Drag the crooked little Moses son before the throne of Hell, my little madame; I like to watch Jews being accused.

FAUST [*taken aback*]: God gave him the strength to do the courageous deed, the same holy strength that he gave to the great prophets in Egypt land.

GOEBBELS: You chalk-face!

MEPHISTO: Don't insult the noble poet!

GOEBBELS: Is there no wall in the Underworld, then?

SCHIRACH: Himmler would have pulled his tongue out of its frame!

GÖRING [*totally drunk*]: To the wall, to the wall, to the wall!

ONE OF THE DEVIL'S SERVANTS [*accusing*]: And bury him, as Mosche did me, in the sand.

MEPHISTO: He ran penitently to me, a rabbit nicely dipped in egg and breadcrumbs.

FAUST: The slave whip still in his hand.

[*The guests laugh diabolically. Flames shoot from the beakers up to the ceiling.*]

GÖRING [*pointing to* MEPHISTO]: Devilish fellow!
GOEBBELS: He's painting, he's painting the Devil on the wall to amuse us! [*In his local dialect*] I like it here in the Hell state, what do you think, Baldur, old scoundrel; I'll get away from that rubbish at our place and help Satan as his viceroy, dagger in sleeve, and run the thing with him!
SCHIRACH [*in strong local dialect*]: According to Adolf's plan, as soon as he has our world in hand he'll go hell-steam-ahead after Hell!

[MEPHISTO *laughs interestedly.*]

HESS: What is the clod betraying?
GÖRING [*waking up*]: Hold your breath, or the two of you will be lying under the moss before this day is out!
GOEBBELS: Five times a hundred thousand devils came into the world back then!
SCHIRACH: Jeez, the poor devils didn't have a cent of money.
GÖRING [*coming to again*]: So spoke Pipifax the Small—

[*Points to* GOEBBELS.]

GOEBBELS: You're dumb as bean straw! I alone, I alone am a devil comme il faut!

[MEPHISTO *rises aristocratically, disgusted, and after him* FAUST. *They lean against one of the pillars in the room. From all nooks and corners flames lick wildly. From all sides* MEPHISTO *conjures* DANCING DEVILS OF BOTH SEXES.]

MEPHISTO: Your Satan has devilish fun with the Nazi race!

FAUST [*bitterly*]: As in the year 1800, Devil—measure beyond all measures!

MEPHISTO: Thus it looked in the days of the young Heinrich—like that! Ah, if he could ask the Frau Counselor, for the young writer forgot because of this pretty little goose—Frau Mother lay on the neck of her mama's boy, or at least on his Schiller collar. They were already calling him the favorite son, the favorite son of the teenage muse, who was also guilty of her son's being high strung! And I, my Heinrich, naturally fanned the flames! Mother Goethe played right into my hands! She had nothing at all, upon my soul, against a short affair! Against a one-day marriage for my sake. But, Heinrich, experience shows that a short marriage with bourgeois blood is not good for any writer. I refused my blessing! I have no more to say!

MARTHE SCHWERDTLEIN [*daring to go up to* FAUST]: Handsome sir, may I dare?

FAUST [*listening closely to* MEPHISTO]: I just now thought I heard Margarete's virginal blond voice coming as though from heavenly realms . . .

MEPHISTO [*to himself*]: The young lady won't destroy anything in my Faust, now that he has ripened . . . [*To* FAUST] Take her hand for the minuet! Sober up, dear Heinrich, don't go all a-quiver at the grandmotherly *fichu* and crocheted lace of her bosom. In any case, go earlier to bed and sip chamomile tea and a bit of nice comforting gruel before you go!

[*The flames die away. It slowly grows dark. Curtain falls. The barrel organs play the tune "Freut euch des Lebens, wenn noch ein Lämpchen glüht," etc., brutally accompanied by the hoarse, uncontrolled voices of the Nazis: "Five times a hundred thousand devils," etc.*]

ACT 3

[*On a terrace overlooking the Hell park,* MEPHISTO *and* FAUST *are playing chess. In the space under the terrace* MARTHE SCHWERDTLEIN *is spinning at her spinning wheel. Near her, a fountain surrounded with cupids, who pour water from jars into the basin of the fountain. In the middle of the fountain is Psyche.* GOEBBELS, *who has remained in Hell, slinks in spying mode through the park areas, draws near to the bench, to* MARTHE SCHWERDTLEIN; GOEBBELS; MEPHISTO; FAUST; *the idol* BAAL *(a mighty block of stone to the right of the fountain); the weak-minded young devil* MARINUS VAN DER LUBBE.][9]

GOEBBELS: It seems that you find it pleasant, little madame, to sit by the fountain in the morning hour. The cupids are sweating from drawing water—just look there. The Psyche, whose feet they water, is, I believe, somewhat too thin.

MARTHE SCHWERDTLEIN: Love brought her and her little friends to Hell. Just look at the little heart up there in the fountain—and the even smaller one in her chin.

[*Short pause.*]

Last evening keeps dancing around in my mind. I never saw so many jewels sparkling—

GOEBBELS [*pointing to the dreadful idol in the bushes*]: And who is this monster and the little monsters supporting the clubfoot?

MARTHE SCHWERDTLEIN [*nervously*]: Hohoho! . . . His name is of noble old stud and he possesses world soul, says Doctor Faust, Herr Nazi! [*Stroking* GOEBBELS*'s club foot*] As a matter of fact, he's something like you, Herr Nazi, if our Baal were of flesh and blood. Patience, I'll name his name in a minute—

GOEBBELS: The crumbling idol is reflected unbrokenly in the pond.

MARTHE SCHWERDTLEIN: In every bright surface in Hell Valley the Hell god Baal is reflected, Herr Nazi, you get quite used to it in time.

GOEBBELS: In any case, that interests me very much, little madame, but it would interest me more if instead of him our Führer, Germania's god, were brought here![10]

MARTHE SCHWERDTLEIN: The savior? [*Looking shyly up at the terrace*] Our—Jesus—Christ?

GOEBBELS: As though the little madame were born yesterday—[*in dialect*] the old Jew doesn't count anymore!

[MARTHE SCHWERDTLEIN *is surprised.*]

The Führer sent him back to Bethlehem with his New Testament, where the Jewish priest was born—by return mail via the poor-sinners-trolley and then a pleasant water journey in an apple boat—

MARTHE SCHWERDTLEIN: That's hard for me to believe.

GOEBBELS: He should leave us Aryans alone. Heil Hitler!

MARTHE SCHWERDTLEIN: What is the name of your god, then?

GOEBBELS [*sarcastically*]: Adolf Hitler!

MARTHE SCHWERDTLEIN: And the Madonna, who bore god?

GOEBBELS: She resembles you, Marthe Schwerdtlein, to a hair.

[*He moves insolently close to her.*]

MARTHE SCHWERDTLEIN: That all seems so odd to me—You know? I haven't heard anyone speak of him till this very day—but then I'm not experienced in these matters.

GOEBBELS [*pulling a little picture from his wallet*]: I carry him with me always, our Aryan god. He was called Lord Wotan by the old Germans. Little madame, just have a look at Wotan.

MARTHE SCHWERDTLEIN [*her hearing growing worse*]: Chicken?

GOEBBELS: Chicken—Heissassa!

MARTHE SCHWERDTLEIN: A handsome man—

GOEBBELS: A handsome man—[*sarcastically*] a noble profile! Heil Hitler!

MARTHE SCHWERDTLEIN: What was he earlier, dear sir, before he took up being a god?

GOEBBELS: Heissassa! A chicken!

MARTHE SCHWERDTLEIN: By my troth, Herr Nazi, he just walked past me, his body puffed up, his feathers spread out—

GOEBBELS: The rooster in the basket!

MARTHE SCHWERDTLEIN: He looked a little irritated to me.

GOEBBELS: Der Führer.

[GOEBBELS *laughs resoundingly. The two chess players look up a moment from the chess board.*]

Chicken! Chicken! The little madame is hard of hearing?

MARTHE SCHWERDTLEIN: And still so young. The water splashing all the time makes it a little hard to converse.

GOEBBELS: Very hard! Very hard!

MARTHE SCHWERDTLEIN [*affectedly*]: Come sir, it's all right, sit a little closer to me, I—I—I'll gladly accept your proposal.

GOEBBELS: Alluring Madame . . .

MARTHE SCHWERDTLEIN [*flirting*]: Just don't break my tortoise shell comb . . .

GOEBBELS: I'm gentle as a lamb, sweetest love.

MARTHE SCHWERDTLEIN: My little boy . . .

GOEBBELS: The reddening of your cheeks becomes you deliciously—

MARTHE SCHWERDTLEIN: My beloved, we can chat—et cetera—undisturbed over there, little boy, in that tiny room in the bay window with the jasmine growing above it.

[*She points to a little window in a small house deeper in the park.*]

GOEBBELS: So early in the morning, dear girl, that would be a sin even in Hell.

[*She pouts like a teenager over the rebuff. The feeble-minded devil* VAN DER LUBBE *dances over the lawn repeating the same song over and over, accompanying himself on a wooden beam in the form of a fiddle, working at it with a narrow saw: "In Cutta, Calcutta, the Rajah Maharajah . . ."*]

GOEBBELS: Who's that coming there?
MARTHE SCHWERDTLEIN: Our feeble-minded little devil—
VAN DER LUBBE: "The Rijah, Rujah, Rajah, the rajah grandpapa!"
GOEBBELS: But haven't I seen the fellow?—
MARTHE SCHWERDTLEIN [*straining to hear*]: Whom?
GOEBBELS: Him.
MARTHE SCHWERDTLEIN: The prince from Netherlands India. If he weren't here in the Kingdom of Hell, he would be sitting, says Doctor Faust, in Vampur near Calcutta on the soft throne of his fathers.
GOEBBELS: It seems to me that he finds it here sort of—
MARTHE SCHWERDTLEIN: If he didn't climb into the flame bath every day, the crazy boy who hasn't a shred of skin left on his body—doing penance for his murders, ach, he's stewing like a chicken in the soup pot.
BAAL: For your soul, carrion!
GOEBBELS: Who said that?
MARTHE SCHWERDTLEIN: The idol with the horse hoof over there.

[GOEBBELS *regards his foot with embarrassment.*]

GOEBBELS: You idolatrous sow, stout and swollen, you must have dropsy! Just like a Jew—offending a high official, Satan's honored guest! Damn!
VAN DER LUBBE: "In Cutta, Calcutta, the Rijah, Rujah, Rajah, the rajah grandpapa . . ."

[VAN DER LUBBE *disappears on a side path, but the melody can be heard for a long time.*]

GOEBBELS: I hope, Frau Marthe, that I haven't understood you correctly—

MARTHE SCHWERDTLEIN: How would it be if you were to lodge a protest with Satan?

GOEBBELS: Let's disappear through the garden door.

MARTHE SCHWERDTLEIN: This disturbance really embarrasses me. Follow me, sweetheart, don't be shy. In a trice we'll be past the monument. [*Affectedly*] Heil Hitler . . .

GOEBBELS: Together to the fountain and Baal, divine woman, with you through life into death. Thou my soul and refuge!

MARTHE SCHWERDTLEIN: How did it all happen?

GOEBBELS [*lying*]: Here on the grounds of Hell—I don't comprehend it— [*Lays his hand over his eyes in order to see better into the distance*] There our Nazi Earth already in view . . .

MARTHE SCHWERDTLEIN [*caught on a thorn bush*]: O my pantaloons!

GOEBBELS [*continuing*]: . . . A poem . . . Come, come!

MARTHE SCHWERDTLEIN: I don't have time to go very far, sweetheart, at most as far as the barracks.

GOEBBELS: If it's not taking too much of your time away from cooking and housekeeping, I make so bold as to ask my sweetheart to show me around here. Including the abbey!

MARTHE SCHWERDTLEIN: Abbey? What do you mean by that?

GOEBBELS: I'd like to get a look at the deviltry.

[*Both hear again the melody of* VAN DER LUBBE*'s little song: "In Cutta, Calcutta, the Rijah, Rujah, Rajah."*]

MARTHE SCHWERDTLEIN: Here above, my beloved friend, a paradise in comparison. [*Points to the way that leads downward toward the legion*] This slope leads down into raging fires, where father devils and their devil sons practice with fire forces and in their eagerness often blaze like wood shavings—ever since the Nazi has been mobilizing and, as the Devil's friend Faust tells us, disfiguring the face of humanity and its world.

GOEBBELS: Oh, to see this magic of Hell excites me, most gracious lady, you fairy of all fairies!

[*The two disappear, descending the slope. Flaming red and glowing, the sun rises glaringly and spreads its light over all Hell.* MEPHISTO, *illuminated scarlet red, leans far out over the terrace railing.*]

BAAL: On my honest thumb sit ye down, little lark; rejoice me with your young songs.

ACT 4

[*Two of the* DEVIL'S SERVANTS *are raising the blinds on the terrace. Through the growing light of dawn,* MEPHISTO *and* FAUST *are seen playing chess. From far away, the ceaseless muffled sound of marching, later growing louder in an enormous crescendo.* MEPHISTO, *distracted, raises his head and leans far back in his elegant armchair.*]

FAUST: You're not with it today, Satan. Yesterday's wine, new from the cask, beclouds the mind.

MEPHISTO: The berries breathed poison gas instead of sunshine when they were growing. But in Hell—life exists even in the smoky cask.

FAUST [*listening*]: Is this muffled noise coming from the roof?

MEPHISTO: The sound is decreasing already. It's soldiers, by trade or by force: tin soldiers, barbarians, enslaved Belgians, Netherlanders, Poles, French, from the stolen countries, all on the march.

FAUST [*forgetting where he is*]: The devil take the rowdy from Braunau once and for all!—Pardon, Satan; you could actually take him, couldn't you?

MEPHISTO [*laughing*]: Already doing it! They are *already* halfway to the State of Hell in two and a half days. Things are going wrong for them down here.

FAUST: This dry, tireless noise, methinks, resounds through all Creation.

MEPHISTO: God is on watch, friend, and [*boasting*] Satan is awake! We won't let ourselves be bothered [*ironically*] by Cousin Adolf here in our chess game.

FAUST: That, Your Highness, you have now from this son of Earth!

MEPHISTO: He speculates on my throne. But my hand's in the game, just my one passion here in exile.

FAUST: Your Hell exile for you?

MEPHISTO: Only eternity is no exile. To find your way to it, Heinrich, you roamed—not always virtuously, but always unsullied—through the vale of Earth: the land of—sins.

FAUST: The wind is silent today in the lindens, the violet has wilted away in my glass, and you, my friend—I *may* call you friend—why so pale?

MEPHISTO: Heinrich, your lyric talent amuses me, Satan, and—moves me anew.

Kiwitt, kiwitt, kiwitt—over all the summits is peace—
In all treetops
You feel—
Hardly a breath . . .
Kiwitt, kiwitt—the little birds are silent in the forest . . .
Just wait, soon—
You too will be at rest—[11]

FAUST [*after a pause*]: Your talent for reciting, Satan, is surprisingly fine. Hardly nibbling at the word, yet its breath penetrates into the heart. But this aging commentary? And not a poem from my youth, bubbling over with life?

MEPHISTO: Still so vain after a hundred and fifty years, my Faust? But woe to the poet whose verses no longer charm him. From the youth, you became the man, tam, tam, tam! Envied me for my wisdom tooth. [*Spoken like drum beats*] Tam tamm, tam tamm!

FAUST: Tam, tam, tam! Tam, tam, tam!

MEPHISTO: *C'est un homme!* That's what Napoléon said about you. Madame Counselor joyfully awaited her son, distinguished by the Emperor—*at home*.

ELSE LASKER-SCHÜLER [*softly to* MEPHISTO]: Juniper Karl, pardon, pronounce the *m* in "at home" like *n*, so that it rhymes properly with Napoléon.

MAX REINHARDT: Ssh ssh . . .

MEPHISTO [*acknowledging* ELSE LASKER-SCHÜLER]: *Eh bien*, that's what Napoléon said about you; Madame Counselor, your mother, joyfully awaited her son, distinguished by the emperor.

[MAX REINHARDT, *script in hand, shrugs his shoulders, surprised.*]

FAUST [*singing*]: "*Mein Kaiser, mein Kaiser gefangen!* . . ."[12]

MAX REINHARDT: Mr. Wäscher, more shocked anger: "*Mein Kaiser, mein Kaiser gefangen!*"

MEPHISTO: I sparkled long ago from the Mosel wine when the noble Jew, Heinrich Heine, author of this song, sang it so sadly with his friends.

FAUST: A falcon, Bonaparte clove the sea of clouds and swooped to Earth, proud Basileus. Single-handedly he led his army!

MEPHISTO: And shared the soldiers' oath with them. [*Leaning over the chess board*] But, friend, let's not lose ourselves going backward in time. From a man you became an old man, went daffy over that silly young thing, Heinrich. I lent you my magic wand, my devil's member—but since abstinence, alas, it's been all downhill for me.

THREE RITZ BROTHERS: *Shocking* . . .

FAUST: Downhill?

MEPHISTO: For my heart's old recklessness I dug the grave myself. But you, bitten by the tarantula of materiality, stripped the dusty caterpillar skin away from soul and body, and grabbed greedily for idle possessions. And now you've laid the holy grave of your cowl around me, which couldn't fail to have a corrective effect on my transformation.

FAUST: I wouldn't venture to correct. And also my prayer would be caught on the thorn of my heart.

[*Pause.*]

MEPHISTO: Doctor Faust is right; I'm not with it. The national bank in the Upper World throws my world into difficulties, too. I fear that I'll soon be bankrupt. But the Devil has withstood worse misfortune, because he plays white and black in the course of time—at the same time.

[*He absentmindedly seizes a chess piece.*]

And what makes me ever more fearful: how state and star lie behind these matters of war and economics. After all, we did hear the good angel Gabriel sing—it was on the Lord's day of rest.

[FAUST *is moved.*]

Angel tones that offended me sorely.

FAUST: Offended?

MEPHISTO: No matter how hard I wrestle with it, the satanic element presses toward divine morality.

[*The last pieces disappear from the chessboard.*]

FAUST: O Satan, and even if you come at the last hour—

MEPHISTO: Humankind is falling! A new round is beginning. And yet it's always the same princely personages that are playing! As long as the moon is still shining, populate the board for another round of chess, my friend! [*Reaching quickly over the chessboard, seizes his king*] Check to the Eternal One! . . .

[*A heavenly white light surrounds the chess players.*]

FAUST [*shaken*]: Who was that?—

MEPHISTO: Rouah!—A fire went out from the Eternal—

FAUST [*passionately*]: Don't play around with the Great Flood, Satan! O God, forgive him—

[MEPHISTO *is defiant.*]

O God, forgive him, who grew dearer to me every day, for the sinful defiance that his life in Hell built up in him his whole life long.

[*It thunders softly following a flash of lightning—light rain, a rainbow visible.*]

Look at the peace arch, Satan, there on the horizon—the father reaches you his father hand.

MEPHISTO: I could throw the colored lassos better in my younger years!
Measure and moderation for the good old Earth heart,
As it believed itself to be suffering and was indeed suffering.
It deviates not from the chosen pace,
Falls not into dark courses.

FAUST: And never loses its balance.

MEPHISTO: But I foam over in the watering places
And ignore the commandments of the congregations.
I spit devilish arbitrariness into life's face,
Give birth to death and extinguish the light of life,
I like to paralyze and weaken the elements
And spur them on to kill time with storms.
—It strikes noon, do you hear it, friend, from the tower?
Who will tell you that it hasn't just struck—midnight?
Already timeless time—

FAUST: Eternity?

MEPHISTO: Long ago I heard the first cuckoo calling
In the young morning of Creation's first day,
The original cuckoo, just hatched, calling.

FAUST [*eagerly*]: And did it go on, Satan, on and on?

MEPHISTO [*considering*]: *Remember*, Heinrich, countless thousands of years later, when I took you out of the bourgeoisie—[*contemptuously*] that woman came along just in time for my purposes—I grabbed you! Satan knew what he was doing.
Where I found you, your hand entwined with her hand,
There the Devil rustled with his poison through the foliage of the arbor.
Heinrich, I love you . . . you are my faith . . .
On pathways along which you rapturously walked,
A sweet butterfly, and captured the maiden's heart,
Shouting for joy as when you caught butterflies as a child—
For you I committed sins more unforgivable by far,
I crept after you into the holiest chorale of the house of prayer,
And—as I worshipped you—the bells trickled the silver day into the valley.

FAUST [*after a short pause*]: My laughter tore itself out of me,
My laughter with the child's eyes,
My singing, springing laughter
Sings in the daylight to the dark night before your door.
It tore itself out of me—just for fun
To kindle the gloomiest inside you.
Now it smiles like the laughter of old age
And suffers—the calamity of youth.

MEPHISTO: I did recognize the beginning in your drunken boy song, the inspiration and meaning,
You come, as do I, the Devil—from out of pre-memory!
I know that when you speak, it is I myself from out of childhood.
From a distance you impatiently saw the wild clouds draw near,
And tamed the storm, the weather steer in its rage,
And wandered nevertheless between eternity and bourgeois morals,
Eventually laid yourself down in the middle of them.
I shook mightily on your door, brother mine!
As thanks for it you call me Devil,

As every human and every human brute
Welcomes me after their own fashion.

FAUST: No one has ever spoken to me this way, Satan. My mother, if I sometimes slept too late for her, still did not dare to knock on my door to let a friend in, not even Bettinchen, who liked so much to wish me good morning.

MEPHISTO [*imitating* MARTHE SCHWERDTLEIN]: Hohohohoho! She did like Mynher the glasses grinder of Amsterdam; and even if he didn't kiss the ladies' hand, still he did all kinds of other things! The storm bell rang early from the tower: Old affair . . . old affair!—puffed up folly.

[FAUST *smiles embarrassedly.*]

The good clever woman, she starched the collar of your doublet herself, and full of sensual happiness (I seem to see it still), she looped the velvet band around the cue of your silver wig. Once there fell a rumbling thunder rain, but her wild fellow was not to be persuaded to stay at home, and he bestrode his black-and-white piebald stallion. Then—I approached him—the Devil incarnate—approached you, heart's comrade. With strong reins we held the black-and-white horse.

MARTHE SCHWERDTLEIN: The Devil incarnate—approached our Heinrich?—In trouble—Herr Direktor Reinhardt.

MEPHISTO: Anxious and troubled by the excess of mysticism in the encounter, you longed for marriage, parental joy, and hearth. Only at the last minute, boldly resolved, did you raise your gray bird's-eye gaze to unrestrained spheres and thrust behind you the barque of matrimonial galleys.

[MEPHISTO *rises majestically. Imitating the creator, he traces a wheel through the wide hot airs of Hell. It hisses and bubbles. The ground in the park begins to smoke, to melt into a mass of lava. The* NAZI SOLDIERS, *marching in with their leaders, sink in up to the head. They scream.*]

NAZI SOLDIERS: Heil Hitler!

GÖRING [*coming through the door and irretrievably seized by the flood*]: Devil's work!

BAAL: That humans actually push their evil deeds off onto the Devil—to rest virtuously in the arms of their neighbor . . .

[*The brightening morning illuminates the action.* FAUST *sees the situation more clearly.*]

FAUST [*exhorting* MEPHISTO]: Eternal life to those who can speak much of love—a loving person can only end in resurrection! . . .

MEPHISTO [*sarcastically*]: No matter how high the torch may flame, hate comes into play . . . [*Pointing sarcastically to the lava morass*] I'm only sorry about the tasty clover my herds used to enjoy on summer days.

FAUST: The wailing of the soldiers, Satan—my heart, it can't stand it—

MEPHISTO: I did bet that their murderous doings would pass away, even though an unsolvable problem for Doctor Faust. The problem's solution—their well-deserved destruction—pains his German heart.

FAUST: Like the Great Flood, the lake steams and bleeds ghastly . . .

MEPHISTO: The course of the worlds is not stopped even by *myself*, Satan. Therefore, let Doctor Faust put up with his slightly scratched turtle-dove heart.

FAUST [*urgently*]: And since the world was, after all, good—"and it was good!"—

MEPHISTO: How comes it that such a spawn could overwhelm the rest of humanity?

FAUST: It was, after all, created in his image.

BAAL: The face of Earth, saturated with God, turned away from its creator and fell into decay!

MEPHISTO [*pointing to* BAAL]: Eternal Eternity speaks, my Heinrich, from this petrified time.

BAAL: What is humanity then, without God? If it does not follow his divine commands?

KING DAVID [*rising*]: Living it is dead! . . .

BAAL: If it is no longer moved by God's laughter, its balance will be destroyed.

MEPHISTO: Like Cain, and commit murder on its brother!

FAUST [*to himself*]: And sweep the Earth away with itself!

MEPHISTO: Listen how the ancient stone rages in the grim avalanche.

FAUST: I thought it was the voice of God.

[*Pause.*]

You *are* related to Cain, aren't you? Were you joking?

MEPHISTO: I did indeed write that down, a flaming *menetekel* on the Hell wall of my house, and assumed that Doctor Faust understood the joke. But—I, God's little devil, related to *him?* God's little devil, that He, the Lord, built with his own hands, when the world was still brewing in holy voluptuousness, related to him?

[MEPHISTO *laughs, inflamed by his anger.*]

FAUST: You mythical embryo, you—human trickster and thinking reptile, lurking in the pools of the dark tree, lying in wait for the love-play.

MEPHISTO: Behind the blind disk of the moon, the Eden world [*reciting like a child*] unsuspectingly carried the little Satan in its womb. Meanwhile a people bore the wayward son of Earth in rape and murder on a platform in the back room.

FAUST: Satan, set my pulse back . . . I cannot stand my country's fate.

MEPHISTO: Close your eyes as in the gray dawn when you finally stretched out in bed after a night of student carousing. And dream sweetly of Lottie and Friederike—the Present is already beginning to nod. Madam innkeeper, bring us your golden drink; merry song wants out of our throats!

[FAUST *and* MEPHISTO *sing.* MEPHISTO *asks the* AUDIENCE *to sing along.*]

FAUST *and* MEPHISTO:

> *Çaça* carousing, let's not go out of our mind!
> Those who don't come along get left behind!
> *Edite, bibite, collegiales,*
> *Post multa saecula, pocula nulla—*
> *Post multa saecula, pocula nulla—*
> *Post multa saecula, pocula nulla!*[13]

MEPHISTO: I carried on pretty wildly in His Earth world, my friend.

FAUST: Tell, Devil, what you did!

MEPHISTO: I stole from the Lord—I, a rascal made from unfermented element, to play pranks on His day of rest. One drop was enough for the chemistry—the gracious winds, dear God, how they stormed in an instant—and sin didn't exist back in those days—they tore at His golden portal and I stood laughing over my prank in the sugar cane. So young and so rascally!—Father God held it against me for disturbing his rest. I was just seven years old, and when it got cold in the fall I wore long, green leaf-pants and lined the seat with mosses for any eventuality. My favorite was to sit in the calyx of the waterlillies with the frogs, and now and then I broke me off a juicy little thigh, quick, if the dear Father happened to be looking at His first human pair and His animals. But in the apple blossom, in which I hid after the naughty deed, voracious Eva discovered me and didn't leave even me. And plucked me, poor devil child, naked as a poodle, from the branch. It cracked so loudly,

I was just having a midday rest in the seed core, a *weekend* nap! After this episode the sly woman tattled on me secretly to Michael and Gabriel and their two brother angels—

FAUST: And for fear the Father could find out about the little devil son's—

MEPHISTO: Exactly so, for fear that He could find out about my naughtiness, I slunk off and away with the, alas, expelled human couple.

[FAUST, *excited by* MEPHISTO'*s report, embraces him stormily*.]

Hung on a golden spring cloud,
When the world was still a child—
And God still a young father.
Swinging—hi!
Up in the sky,
And my wool hair fluttered roundabout,
Teased the tottering Granddaddy Moon,
Noshed sunshine from Gold Mama Sun,
—I locked God the Father up in heaven,
And the world in His halo.
—And God rumbled: Klummbumm, klummbumm!
And the whipping winds whistled.
But later Father laughed two thunders
With the angels over my—mortal sin . . .
I'd give ten thousand Earth joys
To live again so born-of-God
Amidst His band of angels.
Ah, when I was still God's little devil!

[*Pause*.]

FAUST [*rapturous*]: Whether this godly event ever happened or never happened under God's roof, God tells it Himself on holidays in his heavenly blue robes. A true gold ruby in the dark chamber of your forehead, Satan, till the Last Judgment.

MEPHISTO: And yet they flee the Devil and drag him up out of the dung, where only a human heart is suited for doing evil. Lay my fragile hair, that used to be a curly ring of ringlets, in an envelope—

You awoke, brother mine, my heart, my arteries, my veins,
And were my eyes not turned to stone—they have never been red from weeping!—
I, Satan, would be weeping tears—

FAUST: Give me a little drop of time
To praise our unity,
Intimately wrapped in chaste love.
I would gladly sacrifice my life for—you, my precious companion.

[*The thundering march of the Nazi host drives all the* DANCING DEVILS OF BOTH SEXES *into the upper sphere of Hell.* MEPHISTO *bends over the terrace railing, and, at his sign, the* DANCING DEVILS OF BOTH SEXES *form into an orderly procession that proceeds uphill along the paths of the Hell park, an endless procession that later disappears into a cloud formation. Bringing up the rear,* VAN DER LUBBE *plays his song like a psalm on his wooden fiddle.*]

MEPHISTO [*to* FAUST]: And who looked after that poor boy? I or your God? And let him eat of bread and fish at his own table?

[MEPHISTO *regards* FAUST *inquiringly.*]

FAUST [*hiding his head in his hands*]: It's not proper to spy on the Eternal One.

MEPHISTO: Your schoolboy wisdom certainly wouldn't impress Sabaoth, the Lord of the Stars, Faust.

FAUST: One day the father of all life just couldn't forgive you anymore—I have bound my life to yours—to end together in peace some day, with you to flow melodically into heaven's spring.

MEPHISTO: Your belief in God's love, Heinrich, stands on weak feet. Many times, dear boy, you let yourself be put off by me, I who was never expelled by God the Lord in His own mind. God is here—God is here! But I can't rightly love—the Invisible Man. Tell me, friend, who took you in when you fell into sin?

FAUST: It's not for us to understand God in all details.

MEPHISTO: You parson, you! Your answer would arouse great aversion in God the father—I knew Him.

FAUST [*listening*]: O God, the murderous marching is louder now.

MEPHISTO: They too renounced God and His heavenly reaches.

FAUST: Scorned Him—

MEPHISTO [*testing* FAUST *and inquiring*]: Facts could induce me to accompany Herr Adolf, hellishly armed, to Columbia, before his black star begins to sink.

[*Short pause.*]

What does Doctor Faust think?

FAUST: Satan, Devil, forgive the son of Earth, but Your Highness has never spoken in a more flippant tone.

MEPHISTO [*seizing* FAUST's *hand*]: Would you even today offer the Kingdom of Heaven—to the Evil One as a reward?

[*Short pause.*]

You are immortal, Heinrich, preserved by the world in marble clay, and I—cannot die. How do you picture the situation—the Devil on high in the cathedral of Heaven?

[FAUST *is silent, perplexed.*]

A dove with a singed leaf in its beak. The devil is already wilting—for him there is no pardon from the Creator. Separated from star and star, my Hell revolves, a dark spot in the universe. And neither person nor prophet brought it darkening to its fall. It lives even today—for theatrical purposes only in the illusion of worlds!

ACT 5

[*Two* DEVIL'S SERVANTS *open the blinds*. MEPHISTO *and* FAUST *come back onto the veranda*. MARTHE SCHWERDTLEIN *enters the veranda at* GOEBBELS'*s instigation*. GOEBBELS *stays hidden in the entrance hall at the entrance to the veranda, behind* FAUST'*s marble statue*.]

MARTHE SCHWERDTLEIN: Pardon, Herr Satan, when the Nazi heroes entered our Hell garden, they—[*puts her hand behind her ear in order to catch* GOEBBELS'*s prompting words better, which he repeats impatiently*]

GOEBBELS: Got into a morass—

MARTHE SCHWERDTLEIN: Got into molasses.

GOEBBELS: In the heat of Your chess session, Highness—

MARTHE SCHWERDTLEIN: In the heat of Your chess obsession, Highness, it escaped you that—what?

GOEBBELS: Stupid cow!

MARTHE SCHWERDTLEIN: Stupid cow—what?

FAUST: What?

MARTHE SCHWERDTLEIN: Help, help, Herr Satan, or else . . .

GOEBBELS: Drown her!

MARTHE SCHWERDTLEIN: Browner! Browner![14]

MEPHISTO [*amused*]: Where were you early this morning?

MARTHE SCHWERDTLEIN [*pretending not to hear*]: What?

MEPHISTO: Madam matchmaker, today is not May!

MARTHE SCHWERDTLEIN: But the god of the Aryans did lay an egg!

FAUST: By my troth, the woman is not so blind.

MARTHE SCHWERDTLEIN: And what I wanted to say, gentlemen,

[*turning toward where* GOEBBELS *is hidden*] the other Nazi gentlemen called him Hermann—What?—Sun, moon, and stars shone from his front—What?—façade and—too bad, too bad, too bad, so sad, so sad, so sad, hoho ho!

MEPHISTO: He's drowning right in front of Hell Baal. Enough, Madame, he has evaporated happily. What is the rotted hoof doing, still running around in the Hell valley? His intelligence is limping behind today, and if the gossiping vassal doesn't break his neck, let his horse foot be his Valhalla.

[*A bone-shattering cry sounds from the entrance hall of the veranda.* GÖRING *calls to* MEPHISTO *from the lava mass before his head sinks into the hissing flood.*]

GÖRING: Him up there on the steps of Hell—let him go croak; he was always in my way, at every turn.

MARTHE SCHWERDTLEIN: Help, Satan, hurry over here! Otherwise it's all over for my poor little sweetheart!

GOEBBELS [*angrily, raising his upper body with difficulty*]: Heil Hitler! My faith, my trust—

[GÖRING'*s head pops up once more.*]

GÖRING: Heads up, Madame, what are you cackling like that for?

MARTHE SCHWERDTLEIN: Hoho ho!

[*More* NAZI SOLDIERS *are heard approaching.*]

SCHIRACH: Adolf, Adolf, why hast thou forsaken me?

ROBERT LEY: As true as I'm Ley, he'll have his turn after us!

[MEPHISTO *holds* FAUST *back as he starts to rise impetuously to meet and warn the approaching* NAZI SOLDIERS *to the left of the Hell park.*]

MARTHE SCHWERDTLEIN: No one takes pity on my need—

FAUST: I would gladly sink into death there with the host!

[*He throws the chess pieces violently together on the board.*]

My heart, my brain, and all of my vitals are collapsing. I beg, Prince, stir up the flames of Hell yet wilder and let me die—me, the poet son of Germany, together with the son of my German Fatherland, together with my people!

MEPHISTO: O this world of humankind! If God weren't God, He would have lost his mind! [*To* FAUST] You put up with much worse—the world always gave you a problem to solve. [*To two of the* DEVIL'S SERVANTS] Get rid of the biting stallion from the veranda steps! Throw him to the rest of the heroes in the dark cesspool. [*To* FAUST] You know I love all the horses and the nags, though when such a monster of a horse's foot crosses my path now and then, I look upon my own well-formed little cloven foot with great joy!

FAUST [*sinking into his very successful poetic meter*]: I would hardly believe even my friend Friedrich capable of such a well-resolved rhythm—with grace, Prince, and with new poetic meter, with gold patent-leather shoe and with elegant greeting, you arise out of our gouty iambic, the omnibus of the old poet's traveling coach.

MEPHISTO [*obviously flattered*]: As a child I used to grind out lovely little verses, but I left the real writing to you. If the price of writing paper should fall again, it would be of special satisfaction to me to be recognized and sung about by you. And with the knowledge of all the religious authorities. When your feelings sing, my blood dances—

FAUST: Satan, don't play blindman's buff with me any longer—

MEPHISTO: And Satan is blinder, even blinder than you. If death should actually befall me, I could give you an answer: that a Whitsun-purified afterlife, behung with wreaths of light, is handed out only to those who are pardoned by God. The moon, Heinrich, and its stars are the poet's prize! You are immortal, Heinrich, and I cannot die. No heirs are waiting for assiduous bookselling. And yet your kingdom is not of this world. And today you're still living dreamily, where it pleases you, here in Hell in seventh Heaven—in the blue.

FAUST: The university reproached me with it long ago, and the professors.

MEPHISTO: I scorn the professors for their erudition. The time for playing is lost to the gentlemen. But we, how playfully, rhyme plays with the two of us. The professors, on the other hand, teach dryly about ways they have mostly never trod themselves. But every student fills his little can for his little water sprite with soup stars and antediluvian ooze for the midday dinner at home.

FINANCE DIRECTOR [*to* MAX REINHARDT *only*]: Five percent of the subscribers are professors, and other complimentary tickets—

MAX REINHARDT: I request that you shout more melodiously, colleague; we are rehearsing, as you see, in the outdoors. [*To* ELSE LASKER-SCHÜLER] Honored Poet, will you allow me to strike out these last lines?

ELSE LASKER-SCHÜLER: You're asking the stars—ask the devil; he gladly answers questions like that.

FIRST RITZ BROTHER [*to his brothers*]: Heads or tails? [*Pulling a silver dollar out of his jacket pocket*] I bet he says no!

MEPHISTO: No! As an expert in the field I say: No!

FIRST RITZ BROTHER: Okay!

MEPHISTO [*continuing to rehearse*]: You are immortal, I repeat, my friend, while I cannot die. They use me all the time in puppet shows! The smallest child tosses me into the gutter, broken, in a puppet's body. But advanced to the status of big shot, I grew anew on the day your heirs got together. Disgustedly kicking me out, the hand pulling the Faust strings disappeared into the dark afterlife of my fragments. From the assembled circle of your heirs, gathered together by the notary (they drank chocolate from Mother Counselor's Sunday cups), there arose one of your favorite sons, Faust: August—the very one who always defied you and showed the most intensive boredom while listening to your writings. Affectedly, in stiff ruff and cuff, his great father's gold lorgnette in his hand, he rose and in your posture, aristocratically restrained, as his father had often appeared at court in the radiance of a thousand candles, recited your noble death lament to a dignified reception by the aunts and uncles:

> Over all the summits is peace—
> In all treetops
> You feel—
> Hardly a breath . . .
> The little birds sing in the forest, kiwitt, kiwitt,
> Just wait, soon—
> You too will be at rest . . .

[FAUST *weeps*.]

MEPHISTO: And now that I begin to confess, Doctor Faust starts to weep? On our first day risen from the dead.

FAUST [*deeply shaken, buries his head in* MEPHISTO*'s hands*]: I cannot find myself again
In an eternal blessedness that is foreign to me—
It seems to me that I lie worlds away from myself—
In between the first night of total anguish.
I wish that a great pain would rise up—
And fling me cruelly down!
And rip me suddenly unto myself!
And that an urge to create would lay me
Once again in my homeland
Under my mother's breast.[15]

MEPHISTO: Your motherland home is without a soul . . .
Roses bloom there no more in the warm spring.

FAUST: Would like to have a sweetheart . . .

MEPHISTO: And bury myself in her flesh.

FAUST [*looking painfully out over Earth and Hell*]: Satan, lift my face far and farther away from the past.

MEPHISTO: Yes, I learned this art from God—

To lift the gaze from time that has flowed past.

But once again, brother, we are totally in the flow!

Happy in the student choir on Syrius!

Call Susanna, fill us our tankard with foaming hops drink!

Two thirsty throats we, we'll both escape destruction! [*To* FAUST] Little fox, let's rub a salamander![16]

MEPHISTO AND FAUST [*singing twice through*]:

> *Çaça* carousing, let's not go out of our mind!
> Those who don't come along get left behind!
> *Edite, bibite, collegiales,*
> *Post multa saecula*
> *Pocula nulla!*

MEPHISTO: So we float, as long ago in our roaming days, over the last horizon into the kingdom of the Lord!

[MEPHISTO *and* FAUST *rise at the same moment, and they appear to grow bodily to enormous human figures.*]

MEPHISTO: Dear brother, lean closer to me so that you can reach me and I, you. [*Handing* FAUST *a dagger*] And strike the dagger into my heart . . . And so kill the salamander!

[FAUST, *appalled, refuses.*]

Now that I want to separate the Devil from him, he's smitten with the Devil!

FAUST [*smiling*]: On the way to Heaven's path—my senses ramble enlightened, my heart transfigured, through the time stages of all times.

[*Crowns of clouds form around* MEPHISTO'*s and* FAUST'*s brows*.]

Now Paradise is shining upon us . . .

MEPHISTO: God's true world sweeps away the illusion of worlds, like a spider's web!

[*Moaning and cursing are heard from the sinking* NAZI SOLDIERS. ADOLF HITLER *stands, armored, before the gate of Hell with his bodyguard and with* JOACHIM VON RIBBENTROP, HEINRICH HIMMLER, *and* ALFRED ROSENBERG.]

HITLER: Where is he?

RIBBENTROP AND HIMMLER: Where is Satan?

BAAL: Please be so kind as to enter the luxury pool, gentlemen, in your uniform of barbed wire.

HITLER [*to* ROSENBERG, *shivering with misgiving*]: Luxury pool? What does the stuffy fellow mean, "luxury pool," Rosenberg?

BAAL: Herr Adolf, make haste and step in! Satan has long since capitulated!

HITLER [*boasting like a megalomaniac*]: Hear that! Capitulated!

BAAL: That is, before God, Lord of the world!

[HITLER *with* RIBBENTROP, HIMMLER, *and* ROSENBERG *enter through the gate. An upwelling lava wave engulfs them, and they sink hopelessly into the lava flood*.]

BAAL: Go ahead and writhe freely, Messieurs, and enjoy your *Dîner* in the slimy lake.

MEPHISTO [*laying his arm paternally around* FAUST'*s shoulder*]: He poisoned the wine blood of the Germans.

He failed to bring the spirit of sacrifice into the battle.
He stirred the youth up to murder! He! A cowardly dissonance
in the whirling chord of humanity!
He leaves behind no ashes, not the smallest pile of rubble!
An unredeemed death for the anti-Christ and anti-Jew!
—But my own self, divided after its original creation,
Bestows a new life upon me—
And through this latest evolving
Of the I and I
I come enlightened and purified to myself!—
I advise everyone in the Audience, try this royal operation on yourself.[17] It puts everything back together clearly and purely! First let us empty our tankards to the well-being of this world! Be patient, Audience, soon comes the last line of act 5. I'm not in any hurry. Whoever laughs last, angel or devil in human form, laughs best. But you listened to me in the Audience, sir, ma'am—fill another tankard, old auntie, Madam Innkeeper!
Long live my Audience!
Down from the gate flows the past,
I am united with myself in pure melody and joy,
. . . Like distant music . . .
And between struggle and peace
My glances rise, pyramids,
And are the destinations behind all time.

[*Psyche on the fountain, with the help of a cupid, hands* BAAL *a wreath of iris and sedge for the burial of the Nazis.* BAAL *tosses it onto the Nazis in the morass.*]

BAAL: Rest easy in your black mausoleum!
FAUST: The heavens, solicitous angels,
Weave wings around our shoulders . . .
Soon we'll be in the blue meadow—
And looking back at the world we have left.
MEPHISTO: As they buried you, my heart's joy, and me.

FAUST: The two of us—silently joined in the body: I and I.

MEPHISTO: And in their original language, Old Hebrew, the clergy will go into raptures over our noble reconciled body.

FAUST: Though we are through with the earthly life!

MEPHISTO AND FAUST [*singing softly, turned toward the audience*]:

Freut euch des Lebens, da noch ein Lämpchen glüht,
Pflücket die Rose, eh sie verblüht . . .[18]

ACT 6

[*In the garden of an eye doctor in Jerusalem.*]

SPECTATOR [*who has followed* ELSE LASKER-SCHÜLER, *unnoticed, up to the gate of the tropical garden*]: Dear Poet, forgive my short question: Did you write this play entirely—by yourself?

ELSE LASKER-SCHÜLER [*imitating the thundering voice of* BAAL]: Laughable!

[*The disconcerted* SPECTATOR *hurriedly leaves.* ELSE LASKER-SCHÜLER *comes exhausted into the garden and sits down on a bench at the edge of the broad lawn.* A SCARECROW, *very picturesquely dressed, totters over and stops in front of her.*]

ELSE LASKER-SCHÜLER [*after a short pause*]: *Take a seat, sir, if you please.*

SCARECROW: One gets tired on the gravel. And also I'm hungry for English and Hebrew. In other gardens, fruits and vegetables grow.

ELSE LASKER-SCHÜLER: I still have a package of cookies—

SCARECROW: Give them to the street urchins. What I relish are turnips, lettuce, and radishes, and I'm also mad about all kinds of cresses. How can the great eye doctor's wife think that a scarecrow needs nothing to eat? And on guard day and night in harsh sun, without sunglasses—and without umbrella, when the November damps come.

ELSE LASKER-SCHÜLER: I'll gladly keep you company.

SCARECROW: Best of all, what if we went away over the Easter days?

Get away from the gossip—I'm romantically inclined, and the world, it would become an adventure for me.

ELSE LASKER-SCHÜLER: We're both poor children of Israel, in the same situation. And traipsing through the wilderness still today.

SCARECROW: Allow me to ask, where were you before, when it was still light?[19]

ELSE LASKER-SCHÜLER: I had a friendly invitation to *Switzerland* from Wilhelm Tell, before I found my way here.

SCARECROW: And Madame von Stein in Weimar hid me under her clothes stand.

ELSE LASKER-SCHÜLER: How funny!

SCARECROW: However, I immediately went for a stroll on foot with Wolfgang, my intimate friend—

ELSE LASKER-SCHÜLER: Through the eastern Divan?

SCARECROW: Through the eastern and western Divan, *entre nous, ma petite chérie*.

ELSE LASKER-SCHÜLER: You traveled with Wolfgang von Goethe?

SCARECROW: I blush at your doubt. In summer days, ah, how often he and I rambled through the Valley of the Eifel. I was very jealous if Dorothea gave my friend a kiss in the twilight on the little lake.

ELSE LASKER-SCHÜLER: Hermann's Dorothea? Oohh!

SCARECROW: Women are like that . . .

ELSE LASKER-SCHÜLER: Ohh . . .

SCARECROW: But anyway, I was boiling mad! But to make up for it he yielded his muse to me for a few days.

[SCARECROW *sings, heartbreakingly off key.*]

> *Kennst du das Land, wo die Zitronen blühn,*
> *Im grünen Laub die Goldorangen glühn?*[20]

ELSE LASKER-SCHÜLER: It was actually you who gave the song to the whole great world?

[SCARECROW *lays his hand affirmatively on the brim of his hat.*]

Looking at the genius-like curve of your chin, I willingly credit you with these dreamy verses.

[SCARECROW *puffs himself up vainly.*]

You seem well read, Monsieur Scarecrow. I have read little in my life, Monsieur Scarecrow, for I cannot stand the sound of pages turning.

SCARECROW: *Eh bien,* if I may praise myself, I'm particularly sharp on all the trashy old books. [*Pointing to the eye doctor's house and winking confidentially at* ELSE LASKER-SCHÜLER] If a patient dozes off and forgets some classic in its paper cover, snap, I hold it by the tail, the fish, and educate myself as is proper among the upper classes.

ELSE LASKER-SCHÜLER: That's why I always took my meals alone, too—so seldom have Tom, Dick, or Harry invited me, not well read, to their table.

SCARECROW: Ah, don't cry, my poor child, for a long time no one has invited the scarecrow for cinnamon liqueur and cookies, either.

If I just had my fiddle,
We would dance the minuet.

ELSE LASKER-SCHÜLER: In a gown of this eternally white garden mist . . .

SCARECROW: Then, I'm telling you, it wouldn't only be the cats screeching in rut.

ELSE LASKER-SCHÜLER [*haughtily turning away*]: Oh . . .

SCARECROW: Have no fear, honored Poet, I am, be it noted from the first, made of brooms and straw, a higher being through paint and makeup. My grayed pigtail comes from the trunk, from the Rococo of Wolfgang's times—a disagreeable asceticism—they drown me in Lethe. What do I have to forget—

ELSE LASKER-SCHÜLER: How painfully above all you move me—

SCARECROW: Yes, I—seduced you—

ELSE LASKER-SCHÜLER: Why me specifically? But I would like to know your name; tell me, how are you called?

SCARECROW: On festive occasions: Abraham! Also Isaac, from garden aspects of all angles. Also Jacob on occasion. When the ladies come often to the eye doctor's lady in her tea-salon, they call for me, the little Cohn.

ELSE LASKER-SCHÜLER [*sympathetically*]: Your cheeks, dear Abraham, bloom like the young poppy.

SCARECROW: Although the blue, turtle-blue color of my necktie was already faded in July.

ELSE LASKER-SCHÜLER: Extremely interesting, on the other hand—

[*She indicates the split in his forehead.*]

GERSHON SWET [*entering the garden unseen, hearing the last words*]: The deep scar from defying the weather. Here I find you, princely Poet, [*ironically*] and in fact with a chic *chevalier.* Are you so poor as to steal away from backstage on tiptoe after *that* applause?

SCARECROW: Do not insult me, Monsieur. Above all, do not go on insulting *madame la soeur!*

GERSHON SWET: It wasn't my intention, *parole d'honneur!*

SCARECROW: Here in the garden I am in charge and much more besides!

GERSHON SWET: It was not my intention, grand seigneur, to insult you.

SCARECROW: You should just try it, Mr. Minister! For a long time there hasn't been a sound from the entrance and exit doors.

GERSHON SWET: I'm amazed, garden prince, at your hospitable manners.

SCARECROW: How to interact with people was taught to me by my uncle Flachsmann—Privy Counselor Flachsmann, in fact.

GERSHON SWET: I beg you, enough of this!

SCARECROW: And in addition, anger doesn't become me, *excuse*, for harsh, Sir Swet, is *my duty*.

ELSE LASKER-SCHÜLER: Indeed, as a matter of fact, for ten hours, and overtime besides, he scares the sparrows away from the seed.

SCARECROW: My sleeves hurt, and the stilts in my pants legs, and I have no assistant like him above, on whom to push off the work, and no time for me to rest.

GERSHON SWET: Judging from your facility in expressing yourself, Monsieur, you have an enormous talent for journalism. I suggest, Monsieur, that you write me an essay on gardening for *Ha'aretz*—about thirty lines.

SCARECROW [*very flattered*]: It's just striking twelve on the waiting room's prehistorically out-of-tune clock.

[*The* SCARECROW *totters past his place in the middle of the garden, back through the door into the doctor's house*.]

ELSE LASKER-SCHÜLER: He staggers, poor fellow, as though in the grip of strong wine. I'm afraid he'll break his pants leg.

GERSHON SWET: He can get a new broom in Schwarz's department store.

ELSE LASKER-SCHÜLER: But you see that he is a higher being . . . even if he wasn't ever small like us.

GERSHON SWET: *All right!* And no one even misses him. When autumn comes and ruins him, the fellow will get thrown onto the trash heap.

[*Sits down at the other end of the bench, opposite* ELSE LASKER-SCHÜLER, *in order to tie his shoelace*.]

I hope your friend the scarecrow will leave us in peace for a little while now?

ELSE LASKER-SCHÜLER: And what is your desire, *dear Sir;* what led you here, Mr. Swet? All this way?

GERSHON SWET: *All right!* Your play interests me very much.

ELSE LASKER-SCHÜLER: That honors me greatly, Mr. Swet.

GERSHON SWET: Though between writing poetry and reporting—a difference as wide as the heavens, honored Poet!

[*The* SCARECROW *returns to the bench, carefully carrying a beat-up old top hat in his hands*.]

ELSE LASKER-SCHÜLER: I'm so tired—

GERSHON SWET: The reader of a newspaper, particularly a theater fan, expects the cold truth, unvarnished and objective!

ELSE LASKER-SCHÜLER: Without breath, without life, like this present time.

SCARECROW: Look, *Sir,* the doctor feels himself honored, his house consecrated, and he sends you this Boer hat from his collection of antiques.

GERSHON SWET: Ohm's top hat?

SCARECROW: It used to look marvelous on your gray parchment grandpapa. I'll lay it on our poet's blue, dove-blue, lap. Be so kind as to put it on—it will look excellent on you, the grandson, as well.

GERSHON SWET: *I thank your doctor,* Mr. *Scarecrow, with heart and hand!*

SCARECROW: I still see in my mind's eye *friend* Krüger, with his arms crossed.

GERSHON SWET: What?

SCARECROW: *Oh yes*, after the election we two strode home to the Mississippi Valley together, on both sides—the waters rush still in my ears.

GERSHON SWET: *All right*, come to the editorial office tomorrow, if you please, when I should already be there—

[*The* SCARECROW *carves a heart into a tree trunk near the bench. Short pause*.]

But now, honored Poet, do you believe the problem of this world solved in your great rhyme?

ELSE LASKER-SCHÜLER: No! As half of me already said quite plainly in the second part: To prove the truth beyond attack—I'm ready to do on a higher track.

GERSHON SWET: Never will the world problem be solved in this world: not in the circle of friends, not in the transformation I and I, not in the valley between heights, and not dancing in the arms of one's beloved!

ELSE LASKER-SCHÜLER: For it is not to be solved in this world, Mr. Swet.

GERSHON SWET: A fragment remains in wine and Lethe itself.

KING DAVID [*disembodied voice*]: A fragment remains in the golden beaker, in the most kingly.

ELSE LASKER-SCHÜLER: And what further questions do you have to ask me, Mr. Swet?

GERSHON SWET: What can I set before my readers, my very spoiled readers, over the breakfast table?

ELSE LASKER-SCHÜLER: Rhyme a rhyme, Scarecrow! Perhaps more anointed than you and I.

GERSHON SWET: That could be edited out if need be.

ELSE LASKER-SCHÜLER: And all nerves will relax.

SCARECROW [*again from the lawn*]: Don't ask so much. Isn't everything relevant in the play? Your grandpapa Ohm Krüger was a political genius, and he left his art to you, Mr. Swet. And his dignified top hat. Put it on, if you please; it will look good on you too.

[ELSE LASKER-SCHÜLER *closes her eyes*.]

GERSHON SWET: So tired?

SCARECROW: Dead tired, Sir.

GERSHON SWET: It seems to me, she's dying? . . .

SCARECROW: The right eyelid is moving softly up and down and—chirping—

KING DAVID [*disembodied voice*]: Little dove swimming in its own blood—[21]

GERSHON SWET: In death even the lukewarm world ill-humored . . .

SCARECROW: She is so little—she would go into a newly dug mole hole—

GERSHON SWET: We'll cover her with fine quaking grasses—

SCARECROW: Ah, if I could set my feet as nimbly as you—

GERSHON SWET: I'll cut a lock of her hair in memoriam—

SCARECROW: Look, and I'll cover her little hands with my *mouchoir.*

KING DAVID [*disembodied voice*]: She painted a golden arch over her dark hair, like my poor Absalom long ago—

GERSHON SWET: She is dying . . .

SCARECROW: And without clergy, rabbi, sheik, pastor—

GERSHON SWET: Dead—

POSTLUDE

ELSE LASKER-SCHÜLER [*now a heavenly angel*]:
And the moral of the Hell play's theater story:
The little devil is again carrying on tomfoolery in Heaven.
With Faust, and the Poet in her place between them,
He stepped before God even before the midday meal.
And as the dear Lord looked at the boy,
His halo smiled in his hair.
And that did not escape the notice of the little devil.
He stroked the dear Lord's careworn face
And politely offered Him in a long tube
The still undistilled atmosphere he had stolen from Him,
That brought so much unhappiness to God's world
And put seductive fairy tales into the heads of his creatures.
And then both sprang to the celestial ladder,
Played horseback riding with the great angels.
In Paradise we become little again . . .
But sometimes Father God looks around:
"Klummbumm! Klummbumm!"
When the little devil, the arch-rascal,
Buzzes and slurps a psalm
From the tube through a finely cut straw
Before the wreathing blue clouds of His Sabbath gate . . .
The play is done—
I can no more . . .

[*But a voice is heard from the Earth star nearby—asking: "Do you believe in God?" Curtain falls.*]

ELSE LASKER-SCHÜLER [*singing softly behind the curtain*]: I'm so happy, I'm so happy: God is *here!*

Translator's Notes

1. "Hell Ground" may be a creation of Lasker-Schüler's. Neither reference libraries nor the Israeli Embassy in Washington can identify her *Höllengrund* with any actual area in Jerusalem. Possibly there was such a designation in the years between 1939 and 1945 when she lived in Jerusalem.

2. This is the first line of a previously published Lasker-Schüler poem entitled *Mich Führte in die Wolke mein Geschick* (*My Destiny Has Led Me to the Clouds*).

3. This phrase is English in the original. The play is sprinkled with many foreign expressions in English, French, and Hebrew, which have been italicized here. Phrases such as "at home for the weekend," the words "myself," "business," and "lunch," were all English in the original.

4. These ten lines are the text of a previously published Lasker-Schüler poem entitled *Weltende* (*World's End*).

5. The phrase *ich liebe dich* means "I love thee."

6. The phrase *haute volée* means "pedigree, belonging to the upper classes."

7. A play on words: *verwachsen* means "to grow together, or to grow wrong, deformed, or crooked."

8. Herschel Grynspan was a seventeen-year-old Jewish boy who assassinated a Nazi official in Paris in November 1938. The incident was used by the Nazis as a pretext for their extensive *Kristallnacht* pogrom a few days later.

9. Marinus van der Lubbe was a tousle-headed young Dutch Communist with a penchant for confessing to crimes he had not committed. Handicapped by a work accident, he remained jobless and in 1933 planned to emigrate to the USSR. He got as far as Germany, where he was arrested at the Reichstag in Berlin the night of the famous Reichstag Fire, under suspicious circumstances. He is considered to have played some role in the fire but probably not to have been the main or only instigator. He was tried and beheaded by the Nazis.

10. The meaning of the phrase "our Führer, Germania's god" is ambiguous, depending on whether "our Führer" is taken to mean Hitler

or in its literal meaning of "leader," and whether the apposite "Germania's god" is understood as Hitler or Christ. Marthe Schwerdtlein understands it as Christ, while Goebbels is referring to Hitler.

11. These seven lines are the text of Goethe's famous poem *Über allen Gipfeln ist Ruh.* The "kiwitts" are added by Mephisto.

12. The line "my emperor, my emperor, in captivity" (*mein Kaiser, mein Kaiser gefangen*) is from Heine's poem *Die beiden Grenadiere* (*The Two Grenadiers.*)

13. This is a well-known old German student drinking song: "Eat, drink, comrades, / After a few centuries, no more beaker!

14. The German has *Raufen sie* ("Pluck her") as a non sequitur due to her deafness, to rhyme with *Versaufen sie* ("Drown her"). Since a literal translation does not have the desired effect here, an equivalent bit of rhyming nonsense has been used.

15. These four speeches (Faust, Mephisto, Faust, Mephisto) are an almost identical quotation from Lasker-Schüler's early poem *Chaos*, a monologue lament recast here as a dialogue between the two halves of one person. An important change from the 1902 original to the reprise in 1940 to 1941 occurs in the first lines. Where the early version has "I cannot find myself again/In this death abandonment," the lines as quoted in the play read triumphantly: "I cannot find myself again/In an eternal blessedness"—a perfect self-quote to confirm the reconciliation of I and I.

16. The German phrase *einen Salamander auf jemanden reiben* ("to rub a salamander to someone") means to toast the person ceremoniously by rubbing full drink glasses on the table. There are no explicit stage directions to do this, but it should be done as the two sing the drinking song again.

17. The phrase *königlicher Schnitt*, literally "royal cut" or "royal operation," is a play on *Kaiserschnitt* ("cesarean section").

18. *Freut euch des Lebens, da noch ein Lämpchen glüht, / Pflücket die Rose, eh sie verblüht* ("Find joy in living, as still a lantern glows, / And while it's still blooming, gather the rose"). The usual wording in the first line is *weil noch ein Lämpchen glüht*—"because" a lantern still glows. At the end of act 2, when the brutal Nazis are singing it, Lasker-

Schüler uses *wenn* ("if") instead of "because." Here, after the destruction of the Nazis, she uses *da*, with its connotations of both "because" and "while."

19. "When it was still light," that is, before the Nazi era.

20. These are the opening lines of the poem that begins Book Three of Goethe's *Wilhelm Meisters Lehrjahre:* "Knowest thou the land where the lemons grow, / In leafy green the oranges glow?"

21. *Täubchen, das in seinem eigenen Blut schwimmt* (*Little Dove Swimming in Its Own Blood*) is the title of a Lasker-Schüler poem written in response to Richard Dehmel's poem describing her with this metaphor.

BIBLIOGRAPHY

Bauschinger, Sigrid. "Ich bin Jude. Gott sei Dank." In *Im Zeichen Hiobs: Jüdische Schriftsteller und deutsche Literatur im 20. Jahrhundert*, ed. Gunter Grimm and Hans-Peter Bayerdorfer. 2nd ed. Frankfurt: Athenäum, 1986. 84–97.

———. *Else Lasker-Schüler: Ihr Werk und ihre Zeit*. Heidelberg: Stiehm, 1980.

Baldwin, Peter M. "Zionist and Non-Zionist Jews in the Last Years before the Nazi Regime." *Yearbook of the Leo Baeck Institute* 27 (1982): 87–108.

Buber, Martin. "Ost und West." *Illustrierte Monatsschrift für modernes Judentum Berlin* 1 (1901).

Dane, Gesa. "Die Dichterin als Rabbinerin." *Text & Kritik* 122 (1994): 55–64.

Giesing, Michaela. "Theater als verweigerter Raum." In *Schreibende Frauen*, ed. Hiltrud Gnüg and Renate Möhrmann. Stuttgart: Metzler, 1985. 240–59.

Gilman, Sander L., and Jack Zipes, ed. *The Yale Companion to Jewish Writing and Thought in German Culture, 1096–1996*. New Haven: Yale University Press, 1997.

Ginsberg, Ernst. Letter to Manfred Sturmann (executor of Else Lasker-Schüler archives in Jerusalem) of September 2, 1958, quoted by Werner Kraft in *Else Lasker-Schüler: Verse und Prosa aus dem Nachlass, Gesammelte Werke*, ed. Werner Kraft. 3 vols. München: Kösel Verlag, 1961.

Grimm, Reinhold. "Arthur Aronymus and His Brethren: Three Glances from Outside." In *Else Lasker-Schüler: Ansichten und Perspektiven, Views and Reviews*, ed. Ernst Schürer and Sonja Hedgepeth. Tübingen: Francke, 1999. 147–68.

Hahn, Ulla, and Hajo Jahn, ed. *In meinem Turm in den Wolken: ein Else-Lasker-Schüler-Almanach*. Wuppertal: Peter Hammer Verlag, 2002.

Hallensleben, Markus. *Avantgardismus und Kunstinszenierung*. Tübingen: Francke, 2000.

———. *Hologramme der Kunst: Avantgardismus im Werk Else Lasker-Schülers*. Dissertation. Berlin: Freie Universität Berlin, 1998.

Heizer, Donna Kay. *Jewish-German Identity in the Orientalist Literature of Else Lasker-Schüler, Friedrich Wolf and Franz Werfel*. Columbia, S.C.: Camden House, 1996.

Hessing, Jakob. "Dichterin im Vakuum." *Text & Kritik* 122 (1994): 3–17.

———. *Else Lasker-Schüler: Biographie einer deutsch-jüdischen Dichterin*. Karlsruhe: von Loeper, 1985.

Jahn, Hajo, and Hans Joachim Schädlich, ed. *Momente in Jerusalem: Welchen Inhalt birgt das Wort— Erinnern in Israel*. Gerlingen: Bleicher Verlag, 2002.

———. *7 Tage in Jerusalem: Fotografien im Dialog mit Else Lasker-Schüler*. Gerlingen: Bleicher Verlag, 2002.

———. *Fäden möchte ich um mich ziehen: Ein Else-Laskeer-Schüler-Almanach*. Wuppertal: Peter Hammer Verlag, 2000.

Jones, Calvin. "The Play's the Thing: Author, History, and Drama in Else Lasker-Schüler's *Ichundich*." In *Else Lasker-Schüler: Ansichten und Perspektiven, Views and Reviews*, ed. Ernst Schürer and Sonja Hedgepeth. Tübingen: Francke, 1999. 169–86.

———. "Representing the People: 'Darstellung' und 'Vertretung' in Else Lasker-Schüler's Drama *Die Wupper*." *The Germanic Review* 69.1 (1994): 7–13.

Klüsener, Erika. *Lasker-Schüler in Selbstzeugnissen und Bilddokumenten*. Reinbeck bei Hamburg: Rowohlt, 1980.

Kraft, Helga. *Ein Haus aus Sprache: Dramatikerinnen und das andere Theater*. Stuttgart: Metzler, 1996.

Krumbholz, Martin. "Hölle, Jahrmarkt, Garten Eden: Zum dramatischen Werk der Else Lasker-Schüler." *Text & Kritik* 122 (1994): 42–54.

Kupper, Margarete. "Nachwort" (note). *Else Lasker-Schüler: Die Wupper und andere Dramen*. München: DTV, 1986. 301–44.

Lorenz, Dagmar. "1939: Else Lasker-Schüler Becomes Permanently Exiled in Jerusalem When Swiss Authorities Deny Her Reentry to Switzerland." In *The Yale Companion to Jewish Writing and Thought in German Culture, 1096–1996*, ed. Sander L. Gilman and Jack Zipes. New Haven: Yale University Press, 1997. 563–70.

Martini, Fritz. "Epilogue" to *Die Wupper*. Stuttgart: Reclam, 1977. Reprinted in *Modernes Deutsches Drama*, ed. E. N. Mennemeier. München: Fink, 1979.

O'Brien, Mary-Elizabeth. "Masquerade of Gender in Else Lasker-Schüler's (Prose) Work." *The German Quarterly* 65.1 (1992): 1–17.

Otto, Theo. "Ein bergischer Kräher berichtet." In *Lasker-Schüler: Ein Buch zum 100. Geburtstag der Dichterin*, ed. Michael Schmid. Wuppertal: Hammer, 1969. 41–49.

Parr, Andrea. *Drama als "schreitende Lyrik": Die Dramatikerin Else Lasker-Schüler*. Frankfurt a.M.: Peter Lang, 1988.

Pazi, Margarita. "Verkünderin west-östlicher Prägung: Else Lasker-Schüler in Jerusalem." *Text & Kritik* 122 (1994): 65–74.

Rumold, Inca Molina. "*Der Malik:* Else Lasker-Schüler's Anti-War Novel." In *Women in German: Feminist Studies in German Literature and Culture*. Lincoln: University of Nebraska Press, 1999. 143–62.

———. "Class, Gender, and Sexuality in Imperial Germany: A Reading of Else Lasker-Schüler's Drama *Die Wupper*." In *Society for the Interdisciplinary Study of Social Imagery [conference proceedings]*. Pueblo: University of Southern Colorado, 1998. 113–19.

Schürer, Ernst, and Sonja Hedgepeth, ed. *Ansichten und Perspektiven, Views and Reviews*. Tübingen: Francke, 1999.

Tyson, Peter. "Else Lasker-Schüler's Drama *Die Wupper:* Between Naturalism and Expressionism." AUMLA 64 (1985): 144–53.

Yudkin, Leon. *Lasker-Schüler: A Study in German-Jewish Literature*. London: Lonsdale Press, 1991.